loyalty.com

Praise for *loyalty.com*

"Fred. Newell's thought leadership in marketing rises to the top in his book, *loyalty.com*. His latest work provides a myriad of case studies and actionable insights into building a successful business strategy using the interactive tools of CRM."

John R. Goodman, Vice President
Helzberg Diamonds, a Berkshire Hathaway Company

"In *loyalty.com*, Fred. Newell has delivered a first-rate compass to guide marketers and business strategists through the murky waters of CRM. The book provides an insightful but practical discussion of loyalty as the by-product of a meaningful dialogue between a company and its customers. More importantly, Fred. explores the critical investments in human resources, knowledge, and technology that successful businesses must make in order to develop true relationships with their customers—and he does it through the real experiences of real companies."

David W. Miller, SVP
Customer Information and Delivery Strategy, First Tennessee

"After reading *loyalty.com*, I was impressed with the breadth and depth of its CRM content. Fred peels back the CRM hype and addresses the key issues and opportunities in a straightforward, refreshing way."

Mark Poole, Business Leader
Acxiom Corporation

"This is essential reading for not only marketing students, but graduates and post-graduates. It will bring all those interested or indeed committed to customer relationship marketing into the 21st century."

David Mattingly, Founder/Chairman
Young & Rubicam, Mattingly, Australia

"Just finished reading your new book *loyalty.com*. You are truly a gifted story teller, and that's what makes the book so valuable. Story after story brings to life the tactical application of CRM strategies. Your book documents, in case after case, that technology is merely an enabler, and that imagination and creativity will be the primary constraint in implementing 1:1 relationship marketing in the internet age. I will share your stories in my training courses across Harte-Hanks."

Spencer Joyner, Ph.D., President
Harte-Hanks Software and Systems Integration

"A provocative and widely researched guide to the power of new digital technologies to transform customer relationship management."

John Deighton, Professor
Harvard Business School

"Fred. Newell has been helping retailers acquire and retain loyal customers for over 30 years, but he is not one to stick to the old, tried-and-true ways of building loyalty in today's increasingly competitive retail marketplace. In this book, Fred. recognizes the changes in technology and in customer lifestyles and translates what is often high-tech demographic jargon into a simplified, easy-to-understand, and actionable guide on how to maintain customers for life. He takes the mystique out of CRM and focuses on what companies need to do now to grow their businesses with existing customers profitably. This is a back-to-basics book with a real understanding of today's cyber world in plain English and with solid examples of how to do it—and do it right."

Ken Banks, SVP, Marketing, Branding, Advertising
PETsMART, Inc.

loyalty.com

Customer Relationship Management in the New Era of Internet Marketing

Frederick Newell

McGraw-Hill

New York   San Francisco   Washington, D.C.   Auckland   Bogotá
Caracas   Lisbon   London   Madrid   Mexico City   Milan
Montreal   New Delhi   San Juan   Singapore
Sydney   Tokyo   Toronto

Library of Congress Cataloging-in-Publication Data

Newell, Frederick
　　loyalty.com : customer relationship management in the new era of
　　Internet marketing / by Frederick Newell.
　　　　p.　　　cm.
　　Includes index.
　　ISBN 0-07-135775-0
　　1. Internet marketing.　2. Customer relations.　I. Title.
HF5415.1265 .N495　2000
658.8'4–dc21

99-058215
CIP

McGraw-Hill

A Division of The **McGraw·Hill** Companies

　 　 　 4　5　6　7　8　9　0　DOC/DOC　0　9　8　7　6　5　4　3　2　1　0

ISBN 0-07-135775-0

*The sponsoring editor for this book was Kelli Christiansen, the editing supervisor
was Janice Race, and the production supervisor was Elizabeth J. Strange. It was set
in Times Roman by Inkwell Publishing Services.*

Printed and bound by R.R. Donnelley & Sons Company.

McGraw-Hill books are available at special quantity discounts to
use as premiums and sales promotions, or for use in corporate
training programs. For more information, please write to the
Director of Special Sales, Professional Publishing, McGraw-Hill, Two
Penn Plaza, New York, NY 10121-2298. Or contact your local bookstore.

This publication is designed to provide accurate and authoritative information in regard to the subject matter covered. It is sold with the understanding that the publisher is not engaged in rendering legal, accounting, or other
professional service. If legal advice or other expert assistance is required,
the services of a competent professional person should be sought.
*—From a Declaration of Principles Jointly Adopted by a Committee of the
American Bar Association and a Committee of Publishers.*

 This book is printed on recycled, acid-free paper
containing a minimum of 50% recycled de-inked fiber.

For my many mentors—clients, colleagues, associates, industry leaders, friends and family who have all taught me valuable lessons.

Contents

Foreword

We entered the Interactive Age in 1995. That was the year that personal computers outsold TV sets for the first time. The same year, the number of e-mail messages exceeded the number of regular stamped letters. By 1998, the Web was headed inexorably toward normalization, as those hopping onto the Internet for the first time included a growing percentage of people who hadn't been to college. The year 2001 has been designated as the year one in six world citizens will be online, many of them wirelessly. In five years, we will all be spending more waking hours online than offline.

When I met Don Peppers in January 1990, we knew that communication was being miniaturized and that technology was giving us newfound powers. Over the next three years, we devoted nearly all of our attention to figuring out what that would mean for business. Our first book, *The One to One Future: Building Relationships One Customer at a Time,* appeared in 1993, before widespread use of the Web. Back then, we proposed that as the Industrial Age inevitably yielded to the Age of Information and Interactivity, strategies of successful companies would likewise have to change. Thus an enterprise would plan strategies designed to win share of customer rather than market share and to measure its success on retention, customer equity, and returns on data assets rather than just on ROI and market share. Companies would learn to measure each customer's profitability and put customer managers in charge of portfolios of customers. More and more, the enterprise would bring products to customers, not just customers to products.

The resulting 1to1 enterprise would engage in a *Learning Relationship* with individual customers that worked like this.

I know who you are. I remember you. I get you to talk to me. And then, because I know something about you my competitors don't know, I can do something for you my competitors can't do—not for any price.

This means *the customer* actually adds the value to what you can do for her and will find it easier and less costly to do more business with you than to start over somewhere else. You will help her create her own barrier to exit. You will no longer buy her loyalty—you will sell it to her.

In working with blue-chip clients worldwide, we have learned a great deal about the strategies an enterprise will follow in progressing toward 1to1. The first requirement is to *identify* customers—to tag them so that each one can be identified through any channel, across transactions and interactions over time. Once an individual customer can be seen as one complete customer across the enterprise, the enterprise can *differentiate* customers by both the different values that customers have to the firm and the unique needs that each valuable customer has from the firm. To learn enough to differentiate customers, the enterprise will *interact* with customers and keep track of these individual dialogs, learning a bit more with every interaction, at every touchpoint. Finally, the enterprise will embark upon the hardest strategy: *customization*, or treating different customers differently, often by automating the personalization process in a way that increases customer loyalty even as it almost inevitably reduces the cost of operations.

These steps are tough. Those companies that can achieve the first three—*identify*, *differentiate*, and *interact*—can claim to have achieved CRM and database marketing. The enterprises that go one step further, which learn to use feedback from each customer to *customize* for each one individually, will be engaged in active 1to1 Learning Relationships.

Six short years and three books later, now everybody wants to "do CRM." Consulting companies, software enablers, client businesses, large and small, public and private, business to consumer and business to business—all want to get under the CRM umbrella. The irony is that Customer Relationship Management is often none of those three: Often it's not about the customer; it's about the sales force. It's not about relationships; it's about data mining. And it's not about management; it's promotion marketing. Fred. Newell, in his first book, *The New Rules of Marketing* (1997), began the process of offering practical advice to companies trying to make the transition to CRM and 1to1. Here he continues, in even more depth, by offering real help that turns data into strategies, and customers into equity.

Most managers and companies have heard the wakeup call, and they believe that customer centricity is the key to success in the future. The hard part now is becoming fluent in alternative thinking, strategies, and tactics—breaking away from the responses and policies that our parents and grandparents taught us for the past 100 years. Fred. Newell, in his practical style, tells you *how* in simple, straightforward language and then punches the point with one real-world case study after another. I can already envision many readers using the case studies to make the argument for funding their 1to1 pilot programs and CRM initiatives.

The new chief relationship officers, customer portfolio managers, CRM consultants, business-oriented IT and CIO leaders—and 1to1 pioneers—are dedicated to turning customers in valuable assets. The question now is how to get CRM *done*. This book will tell you how.

Martha Rogers
September 1999

Martha Rogers, Ph.D., is cofounder of the Peppers & Rogers Group based in Stamford, Connecticut, and adjunct professor of the Fuqua School of Business at Duke University. She and Don Peppers wrote *The One to One Future* (1993), *Enterprise One to One* (1997), *The One to One Fieldbook* (with Bob Dorf, 1999), and *The One to One Manager* (1999). You can reach her Web site at www.1to1.com.

Thank You

Thank you for becoming a valued patron of the Park County Public Libraries. Please take a few minutes to review this pamphlet and keep as a reference.

Your Card

Our library cards are free to any Colorado resident with proper ID and proof of physical address. Children of any age can get one if a parent has a card and signs for child.

Your card is good at any Park County Library location.

The information we obtain from your library card application and your borrowing record at our libraries is strictly confidential.

We will issue a replacement card for $2.00.

Reciprocal Borrowing

To participate in the Colorado Library Card (CLC) Program you must be a registered patron with your local library. Present your library card to a CLC establishment; register with them, and you will be able to check material out at any participating public library, school media center, academic or special institution.

Borrowing Items

You may have a maximum of 6 items on your card at any time with a limit of 3 videos per card.

Borrowing Period:

3 weeks (most items)
2 weeks for all new fiction books
& ILL material
1 week for videos and DVDs

Renewing Items:

2 weeks (most items)
1 week for videos and DVDs

New books may only be renewed if not on reserve for another patron.

Material obtained through Interlibrary Loan cannot be renewed.

You may call during business hours or log on to our website to renew material.

Returning Items

You may return your items in the overnight drop box or at the counter during library hours.

Overdue Fines

.15 per item per day
1.00 per video per day

Lost/Damaged Items

The replacement cost plus a processing fee.

Online Catalog

You can access our Park County libraries online catalog by visiting our website at:

www.park.ipac.epixasp.com

or link onto the Park County home page at:

www.co.park.co.us

By using the catalog you can:
Search for items by title, author, keyword, etc.

Renew material within your account.

Reserve material. *Note: You should only reserve material from the library that you are registered with. If you would like to obtain material from another library in our system, please inform a librarian at your library.*

Other Colorado Libraries

Search other Colorado Library collections at Colorado Virtual Library:

www.aclin.org

Interlibrary Loans

If you can not find what you are looking for within our library system, we are able to obtain materials from other libraries throughout Colorado, and the United States. Just ask a librarian for more information.

Services

Park County Libraries offer popular reading, basic reference services, books for children and young adults, a large collection of books on tape, and videos.

The main library in Bailey has an extensive collection of local history, Colorado books, and a World War II collection.

All four libraries offer basic reference materials, non-fiction on a variety of topics, medical, craft, and fix-it-yourself books.

Additional services

- Fax machine
- Copier
- Computers with internet access
- Typewriters
- Microfiche/film machines
- Meeting rooms
- Arts and Humanities Cultural Connection

Special Services

- Children's storyhour
- Children's reading programs
- Book Clubs
- Friends of the Library
- Book sales at "Judy's Place" *(Bailey)*
- Craft sales at "Friendshop" *(Bailey)*

Park County Library Locations

Bailey Library (Main Branch)
350 Bulldogger Road
Bailey, CO 80421-0282
Tel: 303-838-5539
Fax: 303-838-2351
Hours: Monday, Tuesday, Thursday, Friday, Saturday 9 AM - 5 PM
Wednesday 11:30 AM - 7:30 PM
e-mail parklib7@hotmail.com

Fairplay Library
P.O. Box 592
Fairplay, CO 80440
Tel: 719-836-2848
Fax: 719-836-4297
Hours: Monday - Saturday
9:30 AM - 4:30 PM
e-mail fairplaylib@hotmail.com

Guffey Library
P.O. Box 33
Guffey, CO 80820
Tel: 719-689-9280
Fax: 719-689-9304
Hours: Tuesday and Thursday
12 noon - 6 PM
e-mail guffeylib@hotmail.com

Lake George Library
37900 Hwy 24
Lake George, CO 80827
Tel: 719-748-3812
Fax: 719-748-1240
Regular Hours: Monday, Tuesday, Wednesday 10 AM - 12 noon, 1 PM - 4:30 PM
Thursday 1 PM - 4:30 PM
Saturday 10 AM - 2 PM
Summer Hours: Monday - Thursday and Saturday 10 AM - 2 PM
e-mail kplutt@worldnet.att.net

E-MAIL A FRIEND...

RESERVE A MEETING ROOM..

STORYTELL...

READ....

CRAFT SALES..

RELAX..

STORY HOUR....

BOOK CLUB..

Volunteer...

BE A FRIEND....

Summer reading...

Fundraising events..

RESEARCH...

HANG OUT..

BOOK SALES...

Check out a video....

@ your library

Preface

loyalty.com is not for a limited audience of techies or database managers or Web masters. It is filled with hands-on explanations of sophisticated, state-of-the-art customer analysis and relationship-building techniques and new tools of the Web. It is written for the tens of thousands of business people who are looking for the definitive overview of Customer Relationship Management (CRM). It is indispensable for marketers who are learning that customer loyalty can't be bought and who are looking for new solutions and profitable ways to use the tools of the Net economy in combination with the tried and true. It is the perfect solution for business people at all levels in all industries who want to develop customer loyalty.

In the two years since my first book, *The New Rules of Marketing*, was published, companies in every country of the world have invested millions of dollars to deploy customer data warehouses to capture customer information to become database marketers.

When marketers first began to understand the customer leveraging capacity of the accumulating customer information, they rushed into all kinds of costly bribery schemes under the guise of "loyalty programs." Most believed that their points and discount programs would build loyalty, yet customer satisfaction rates remained at an all time low.

In our consulting practice we have seen, firsthand, the confusion that exists between trying to buy customer loyalty with points and discounts versus earning customer loyalty by providing value in ways that are meaningful to the individual customer in her or his terms. We have learned that you can't *buy* customer loyalty.

The building of customer relationships must go beyond our earlier database marketing efforts, beyond the concept of 1to1 marketing, and far beyond today's loyalty program rewards that are not building customer loyalty as many had hoped they would. The challenge for executives in any company who are concerned with keeping customers coming back is not points and discounts. It is Customer Relationship Management.

CRM is now moving to the center of corporate strategy as a process of learning to understand the values that are important to individual customers and using that knowledge to deliver benefits the customer really wants and making it easier for the customer to do business with the company.

To get full benefit from *loyalty.com,* it is not necessary for you to have read *The New Rules of Marketing.* The first book was about the process of database marketing that was *company-centric,* that is, targeting customers to sell them more at less cost. *loyalty.com,* by contrast, is a study of *customer-centric* marketing that will teach you to concentrate on *customer* benefits and values rather than what your company wants to sell and thereby to strengthen the relationship between your customer and your company.

What makes this book unique and especially timely is the blending of the strengths of CRM with the new marketing tools appearing in these early turbulent days of the Internet era. The Internet will be part of any new marketing solution and will build a new culture not unlike the revolution that shopping malls created in the 1970s and 1980s that redefined not only how consumers shopped but how they spent their time.

This book defines CRM and teaches how you can use the CRM process to add value to the customer relationship in the *customer's* terms to maximize the value of the relationship to the customer for your customer's benefit and your company's profit. It explains why CRM is much more than an outgrowth of direct marketing, why the Internet is such a vital tool, and why these new challenges call for new and different skill sets. It delivers practical, workable guidelines and strategies for the creation of successful CRM projects on and off the Internet and provides action steps for those wanting to sharpen their CRM skills. With case histories from manufacturing, packaged goods, retailing, banking—even media—this book brings the exciting principles of CRM to everyone whose success depends on selling to customers: consumers, business to business, any kind of customer.

The profit rewards of creating close connections with customers can be substantial, but they will not be gained by skimming over the fundamentals of relationship building. The real winners have learned Customer Relationship Management cannot be just another campaign. It must be a continuing process—a dedicated, enterprise-wide effort driven from the top and embraced by everyone at every level of the company.

Acknowledgments

Thanks must go first to the many fine people at the companies with whom I work throughout the year. I learn from every visit.

Then to the many folks who made special contributions. Paul Leblang for again reading early drafts and heading me in the right direction, and my editor at McGraw-Hill, Kelli Christiansen, for persuading me that the Internet had to be an important part of any study of Customer Relationship Marketing.

For the foreword I went to the one professional certain to agree with the premise of this book—you can't buy customer loyalty. My sincere thanks to Martha Rogers for accepting the challenge.

I am grateful to Garner Bornstein, of Generation Net, for helping me learn the ways of the Web, Julia Adamson of @Once, for teaching me about strange things like streaming media and the wonders of e-mail, and to my other e-mail guide Regina Brady of Acxiom Meh & Speh/Direct Media.

Equal thanks to Todd Alexander of Kreber Graphics and James Morris-Lee of the Morris-Lee Group for helping me through the technicalities of digital printing.

Thanks, as always, to my associate, coach, copy editor, and severest critic, Helen Blanchard, and my assistant, Dottie McLean, for the many hours they spent helping me to get things right. And to my wife, Harriette, for putting up with it all with patience and loving care.

Fred. Newell

Also by Frederick Newell

The New Rules of Marketing: How to Use One-to-One Relationship Marketing to Be the Leader in Your Industry

loyalty.com

PART ONE

CUSTOMER RELATIONSHIP MANAGEMENT: LAYING THE FOUNDATION

Companies of every kind have rushed to offer customers all kinds of bribes and discounts under the guise of loyalty programs. As one consumer has said, "It's overkill," referring to the number of advances she fields from companies wanting to initiate or improve their relationship with her. "I must get 10 mailings every day," she said, "and each one is as meaningless as the rest."

The winners in this melee are learning that the way in which they express their caring for their customers must be meaningful to the individual customer—consumer or business—and must be communicated on the customer's terms. The invaluable lesson winners are learning is that customer care must involve more than discounts and point program rewards.

Since my book *The New Rules of Marketing* was published in 1997, the marketing world has changed again. The world is moving even more in a 1to1 direction. The winners have learned that the real challenge is to build and manage customer relationships in ways that will modify customer behavior over time and strengthen the bond between customers and the company. It's not about cards but about building relationships and maximizing the value of the relationships to the customers and to the company for the customers' benefit and the company's profits.

The next new rules must go beyond our earlier customer database marketing efforts and far beyond today's loyalty program rewards that are not building customer loyalty as many had hoped they would. As marketers learn that customer loyalty can't be bought, they are looking for new solutions. The winners are finding new ways to develop customer relationships, and they're using the latest technology to manage them.

The building of customer relationships in this new culture will call for a broad shift from database marketing to true *Customer Relationship Management*—a process of modifying customer behavior over time and learning from every interaction, customizing customer treatment, and strengthening the bond between the customer and the company. This is the principle of important 1to1 marketing.

All 1to1 marketing is Customer Relationship Marketing (CRM) but lots of companies trying to implement CRM don't yet understand the basic 1to1 principles—that is, to add value to the customer relationship *in the customer's terms* to maximize the value of the relationship to the customer for the customer's benefit and the company's profit.

Martha Rogers says this best in her foreword. Companies that can accomplish this "will be engaged in active 1to1 Learning Relationships."

The main purpose of this book is to help companies understand how and why building 1to1 relationships will lead to successful business growth by increasing not just sales but more profitable sales.

Part One will build the foundation and analyze the process of Customer Relationship Management as well as the necessary measurements of its success.

Part Two will explore effective tools, many of them new, for managing customer relationships without points and discounts.

Part Three will get into the fun of what some winners in a variety of fields are doing to manage their customer relationships in real time in the digital 2000s.

Part Four will look at why customers want the service, not just the stuff. It will also review strategy and execution and show how dialog can help sell solutions, not just products. Finally, it will examine the important issue of privacy and then take a last look at the matter of loyalty and what really delivers profit for the CRM marketer.

CHAPTER

Carolyn's Lament

Why do so many companies think they can buy her loyalty?

Carolyn Johnson is shopping for a new wallet to go in her handbag, and she's not happy about having to do so.

Carolyn is a marketer's dream customer—a 38-year-old fashion industry executive, married with two children, two dogs, a cat, two computers, and a six-figure household income. Her job requires substantial business travel. She communicates with business associates and friends by e-mail, and she's a Net surfer.

Every consumer marketer wants to learn how to capture more business from customers like Carolyn. Marketers are reaching out to find every way possible to solve the problem of keeping Carolyn as a loyal buyer. Have too many started with loyalty card programs?

This is not a book solely about loyalty cards, but as loyalty schemes have spread quickly across industries as companies use them to try to *buy* loyalty, it is important to look at the actual influence on customers. The card issuers think they have solved their problem, but they haven't helped Carolyn.

Carolyn's problem: She has *lots* of loyalty cards—too many, in fact. Her three bank credit cards, two supermarket loyalty cards, six hotel loyalty cards, eight airline loyalty cards, two rent-a-car loyalty cards, two department store loyalty cards, plus loyalty cards from her long-distance phone service provider, her drugstore, her gasoline company, her newspaper company, and her two favorite specialty stores simply won't fit in any wallet she has been able to find. She is not a happy camper. What have we done wrong?

Our first question is, have any of these loyalty card programs made Carolyn a "loyal" customer? We asked Carolyn.

I never think about these cards as loyalty cards. Of course, I like the discounts. I like some of the perks, but the truth is I feel as though I have to carry some of these cards to keep from being ripped off. If I don't have my card with me when I shop in the drugstore or super-market, I pay higher prices. I feel as though I was better off before the card programs when I could save on the supermarket's adver-tised specials without having to go to the trouble of carrying their card.

Most of the discount cards are a hassle. The programs that make me keep track of points are an even bigger pain. No, I can't say any of these schemes make me loyal to the card issuer—well, maybe some. I like the things that make my life easier or save me time. I like my "Executive Platinum" privileges on American Airlines that let me board early while there is still room in the over-head bins for my roll-aboard, and, of course, I like the upgrades to first class. I like having my car ready with the trunk open and the heater running at "Avis Preferred," and I appreciate the time I can save with the separate check-in for "Diamond Honors" members at Hilton Hotels. I will go out of my way to stay with these folks, so I guess you can call that loyalty.

But discounts and points won't cut it. Discounts are no big deal. It seems as though the department stores are 40 percent off every day. Why do I need a 25 percent off coupon? I often wonder why so many of these companies think they can buy my loyalty. Why can't they understand what I really want from them?

And now, because of all these stupid programs that make me do the work, I have to waste my valuable time trying to find a wallet that will hold 29 cards!

Is our friend Carolyn a typical customer? She really exists. We've just changed her name to protect her privacy. Perhaps she's not the average customer, but she helps us focus a laser beam on a serious challenge for marketers. The proliferation of loyalty initiatives is not limited to card-based programs but marketers' new drive to develop customer loyalty is reshaping the business landscape, rewriting the rules of competition, and changing the nature of customer relationships.

The average U.S. consumer in a loyalty marketing program participates in 3.2 programs. Sixty percent of U.S. supermarkets now have loyalty programs, yet household panel data show that even heavy shoppers give their preferred supermarket chain only half of all their grocery spending. One-half of all U.S. households now belong to a loyalty program. In Chicago, Charlotte, Los Angeles, Buffalo, and New York, over 70 percent of households shop with some retailer's loyalty card. All of these programs are capturing valuable knowledge about their customers. Many programs are driving sales. Few are building loyalty.

If marketers really want to build customer loyalty, how can they use the knowledge they are gaining about Carolyn's interests to deliver benefits she wants, to make her feel better about having to buy that new wallet, or, better yet, to build a real relationship that doesn't require her to even carry the card? As one expert has said, "Most loyalty program failures occur because a marketing organization cannot answer a fundamental question: They don't know how the customer benefits from it."[1]

CRM executed properly in true 1to1 fashion is a big change from the traditional database marketing that focused on targeted promotion.

From the start, database marketing was company-centric: The whole purpose of targeting customer segments was to help the company sell more stuff for less cost. CRM, in contrast, is customer-centric. While its objective is still to add profit to the company's bottom line, it accomplishes that goal by concentrating on *customer* benefits and values rather than what the *company* wants to sell, thereby strengthening the *relationship* between the customer and the company. CRM is not an overnight cure but rather a long-term profit builder.

Mark Rieger, vice president of marketing and sales, MarketVision, Inc., calls CRM "a customer-focused strategy that drives profitable growth by giving customer value." He stresses that customer value must be the key measurement to establish a cycle of continuous learning to achieve success.

The New Rules of Marketing detailed the swift growth of database marketing and covered the evolution of the tools and strategies that give the marketer the ability to gather enormous amounts of information about the customer and turn that information into knowledge. While it touched on 1to1 marketing, it focused on database marketing and how marketers could use customer knowledge to target special offers for more effective response. *The New Rules of Marketing* is still an important book because the new rules detailed in that book still apply and are, in fact, necessary stepping stones to CRM, but those rules are just the first steps in this change to customer-centric marketing.

This book is more than an update of the new rules and much more than a study of card marketing or Web marketing. Here we move on to the important evolution from database marketing to 1to1 CRM. We also address the Internet—what it will mean to marketers in every field and how businesses can use it to create and implement the best and most effective CRM strategies.

The selling environment is undergoing enormous change. The stakes are high. Success may not lie in discounts and points programs and it is certainly not sell, sell, sell on the Web. Carolyn raised the critical question: "Can companies really buy customer loyalty?" There is a lot to learn on our way to answering her.

2

The Ears of the Hippopotamus

There is more to Customer Relationship Management than technology.

There is a lot more to Customer Relationship Management than we can see sticking up out of the river of current publicity. Article after article in the trade press continues to point out how companies are now realizing that the key to long-term sustainable revenues and profits is identifying, acquiring, and retaining profitable customers to get a bigger return from marketing investments.

Reports of companies spending millions to use customer data warehouses to capture customer information, personalize communications, and improve marketing and sales effectiveness are everywhere: "Banks: Big Money in Data Warehouses,"[1] "Loyalty marketing, long the redheaded stepchild of the direct mail industry, may finally come into its share of the family fortune."[2] etc., etc., etc.

The reports are accurate. The world market for database solutions expenditures is forecast to grow at an average annual rate of 51 percent over the period 1997 through 2002 to more than $113 billion,[3] but that's just the tip of the iceberg, or, as they say in Swahili, the ears of the hippopotamus.

The customer database is still an important ingredient in an effective marketing strategy. The next new rules will not work without this important customer information and customer understanding, but there's more to it than just identifying, acquiring, and retaining profitable customers and capturing information about and personalizing communications with customers. These tools are neither the base of the iceberg nor the 4-ton body of the hippopotamus.

The core mission for marketers is now CRM, and that requires a lot more than the kind of customer contact we have known as direct marketing. It requires more than the product selling we are currently seeing on the Internet, and it demands new tools for customer communication.

We will examine Internet opportunities, but we'll be examining opportunities to use the Web to build relationships rather than for cheaper, faster, better sell, sell, sell. Case histories, examples, and strategies will show the strength of CRM when it is developed as a coherent outpouring of marketing communications *and actions* in real time—a giant leap from earlier database and direct marketing.

Today many direct marketing agencies are jumping on the CRM bandwagon, offering their expertise in direct marketing as credentials for CRM customer contact strategies. It is important to understand that CRM is much more than an outgrowth of direct marketing. Instead, CRM calls for skill sets new and different from the old direct marketing paradigm. It calls for an understanding of the new economic order of the Web, which sometimes does not even involve direct mail or other advertising media.

Direct marketing is defined by the Direct Marketing Association (DMA) as "an interactive system of marketing which uses one or more media to affect a measurable response at any location with this activity stored on a marketing database." This expresses the action of a specific measurable response, usually a purchase. Saying it another way, *direct marketing* refers to transaction-driven applications of the customer database. In every case the purpose of the communication is to solicit an immediate response or sale.

On the other hand, CRM is an attempt to modify customer behavior over time and strengthen the bond between the customer and the company. CRM as a true 1to1 process takes us from the traditional objective of new customer acquisition at any cost to customer retention, from share of market to share of wallet, and from developing short-term transactions to developing customer lifetime value. Once again, the purpose of CRM is maximizing the value of the relationship to the customer for the customer's benefit and the company's profits.

Carlson Marketing Group defines *CRM* as "a business strategy which pro-actively builds a bias or preference for an organization with its individual employees, channels and customers resulting in increased retention and increased performance." This is an excellent definition and one the industry would do well to adopt.

The key to CRM is identifying what creates value for the customer and then delivering it. While individual customers have different views of value, there are many common value concepts. In the real world a firm must satisfy the common value concepts for each customer group and communicate and deliver them to each of the customer groups.

The key CRM tasks then are the following:

1. Identifying those consumer values that are pertinent to a particular business
2. Understanding the relative importance of those values to each customer segment
3. Determining if delivery of those values will affect the bottom line in a positive manner

4. Communicating and delivering the appropriate values to each customer segment in ways *the customer* wants to receive the information

5. Measuring results and proving return on investment

Not all value concepts will motivate a change in behavior or reinforce loyalty, and not all values are worth delivering or are practical to deliver. An affluent customer may buy tools at Sears but not clothing. To stock the clothing assortment that this customer wants might change the character of Sears and adversely affect the Sears image with a large group of existing customers.

CRM is a perfect tool to help retailers stock merchandise assortments they know their customers will want. One way Blockbuster Entertainment maintains its global leadership in home-video entertainment is by using CRM knowledge of customers to make sure that customers go home with the titles they come for when they visit a Blockbuster store. They utilize a set of predictive modeling applications called *Center Stage*, developed by Blockbuster's strategic systems team and software developer Ceres Integrated Solutions.

In the home-video rental business 14 to 20 percent of customers walk out of stores dissatisfied because they are not able to get the video they want. *Center Stage* gives Blockbuster an unprecedented ability to have the right titles available for the right customers. Customer data modeling defines appropriate comparison titles and matches them to customer segment rental history to predict specific customer demand for a new release. *Center Stage* has been so successful that Blockbuster now guarantees the availability of key new titles in most markets, a sure way to build customer loyalty.

As an important part of their CRM program, Bloomingdale's uses aggressive cluster analysis of customer segments. Using *InfoBase* demographic and lifestyle data from Acxiom Corporation, they optimize inventory allocations for specific customer groups, which show their customers that they understand what they want.

Blockbuster and Bloomingdale's represent simple examples of how small CRM actions can accomplish a lot more than points and discounts can accomplish in affecting customer behavior. On a more complex scale, CRM requires a clear understanding of what actions are needed to affect the behavior of different customer groups. CRM deals with segmentation based on what different groups value and what will make them loyal. It is important to reinforce the loyalty through customer-identified value for the items the customer buys from you and to determine if it is profitable to develop loyalty and value concepts for the things the customer does not now buy from you.

Marketing's contribution to business success lies in its analyzing future opportunities to meet well-defined consumer needs with products and services that deliver the sought-after benefits better than the competition offers. This means that marketing must always be trying to find out what consumers are doing (behavior) and thinking (feelings) and what external things (environment) are affecting their buying decisions. Companies can then use this information to alter the mix of those factors to produce a desired buying behavior.

It is important to remember that in order to attract and/or keep customers, you are asking them to do something different from what they would be doing in the absence of your CRM program or you are asking them to keep on doing the same things despite someone else's efforts to change their behavior.

All of this requires sophisticated studies of customers, sophisticated market research, and the will of management to invest in the knowledge gained. The required research has always been the least-used element of this challenge. The cost of traditional market research is so high that it sometimes exceeded the value of the information gained. Furthermore, traditionally market research has been a very time-consuming process. However, the Web has changed all that. We have seen studies completed in four or five days on the Internet that would have taken two months or more using clipboards and telephones and pencils. It is certainly safe to say the research element will begin to play a stronger role in today's CRM.

Finally, to use all of this knowledge to maximize value to the customer, each contact or communication must be positive (and, if possible, exceptional) from the customer's viewpoint.

This is not always complicated stuff. Sometimes it's as simple as not cluttering up customers' lives and taking their time for things you should know have no interest for them. Refining our communications to reflect individual merchandise interests is the simplest way to maximize the value of our contacts, for the customer's benefit.

The key phrase in all this is "making each contact or communication positive from the customer's viewpoint." That's very different from trying to solicit an immediate sale or response, and, therefore, very different from direct marketing.

One cable TV company we spoke with relates a good example. They make their customer contacts positive, sending weekly newsletters with personalized television guides and a bag of popcorn. They ask customers what types of TV programs they like to watch and react appropriately to the information. They reward customers for sharing information by sending them small premiums like tickets to telecasts and TV channel and program mugs. The CRM program also involves a member-get-a-member plan, which has brought in enough new members to pay for the full CRM program, and the program has reduced churn by three times—all because they have learned to make their customer communications positive from the customers' point of view.

The process of CRM is, indeed, a process of finding ways to add value to the customer relationship *in the customer's terms*. It's not just what companies say in their communications; it's what they do to maintain an ongoing relationship, to show they care. If you buy a Porsche in Germany, the company will offer you a free Park & Wash benefit. Whenever you have to fly, you just drive your Porsche to the airport and leave it at the Avis car rental lot. The folks at Avis will keep your car safe while you are away, and then wash it and clean it inside and out and have it ready and waiting for your return.

At the 1998 Direct Marketing Day Conference in New York, Stephen Butscher of Simon, Kucher & Partners, the German consulting firm, used the Porsche example to make the case that it takes more than discounts and free memberships to build loyalty. "Offering discounts," he said, "merely strips dollars from your bottom line, and anything you give away free is likely to be perceived as worthless."[4] The Porsche owner's peace of mind regarding his car's safety while traveling, his appreciation of the bright, clean car ready on his return, and his sizable savings on airport parking fees become a constant reminder that the folks at the Porsche factory really do care. These things differentiate this carmaker from its competition and add value to the company-owner relationship.

In the modern marketplace the customer continues to gain in power, which means we must know and understand her or him and provide personalized value.

The original database marketing was a first step. It relied heavily on direct mail without a true understanding of the customer. Through these earlier efforts we learned to show some special customers we understood them. Now the customer wants more. To quote the *Harvard Business Review*, "Relationships between companies and customers are troubled at best. Customer satisfaction rates are at an all time low. Some of the very things we are doing to build relationships with customers are often the things that are destroying those relationships. Too often we are skimming over the fundamentals of relationship building in our rush to cash in on the potential rewards of creating close connections with our customers."[5]

The bar has been raised. "Customers don't want to be treated equally. They want to be treated individually." That's a quote from a slide I saw at my first Peppers & Rogers presentation years ago. They were right then, and the message is as valuable today as it was then.

Customers want to have immediacy and remembered customization more than they want to collect points.

N2K Music Boulevard, the online music retailer, knows this. They spent $34 million to acquire 560,000 customers. The customers have told N2K what they want to hear about and how frequently they want to be contacted. The company sends announcements of new releases but only those they know will be of interest. Because customers have given N2K their birth dates, the company is able to send appropriate gift suggestions. Hypothetically they could say, "You told us your son was born on January 12, 1985. That means his 14th birthday is coming up. A gift we are sure he will like is Everclear's new release, *So Much for the Afterglow* with the hit song 'Father of Mine.'" Meaningful communications like this are appreciated, and they do build customer loyalty.

We have now learned that whatever the marketer develops to express customer caring must be meaningful to the individual customer in her or his terms, and the expression must involve more than discounts and rewards and free stuff, and must be more than faster, better, cheaper on the Internet. Recognition comes first, then rewards.

In the nineties marketers began to develop their customer information files, and they rushed to all kinds of customer bribes under the guise of loyalty programs. While marketers hoped these points programs, rebate schemes, and other rewards would build customer loyalty, the original purpose of most programs was to capture customer data.

That was particularly true in the retail field. If the retailer could persuade customers to carry a "club" card and show it or swipe it on every purchase occasion, it was easy for point-of-sale technology to capture transaction data and add that to customer records in the database. Still many believed the club rewards would build loyalty.

But that has not happened. Despite all of the loyalty program efforts, customers are still switching stores at a great rate. The Food

Marketing Institute, which asked customers if they had switched their most-used self-service store during the past year,[6] found that Switzerland had the smallest percentage of customers switching stores (7 percent), followed by Germany (10 percent) and Spain (11 percent). This compared with 24 percent in the United Kingdom and 26 percent in France.

Interestingly, low-switching Switzerland had the lowest participation in loyalty schemes (15 percent), as opposed to the high-switching United Kingdom which had the highest number of customers participating in loyalty programs—83 percent of customers.

The study also revealed that 52 percent of UK customers admit to participating in two or three loyalty programs, and another 40 percent do not consider such schemes "worthwhile." Even though most loyalty card programs are discounted, 30 to 50 percent of customers in existing programs are not participating.

Across the board 65 percent of companies with loyalty programs offer discounts, and a whopping 86 percent of business-to-business marketers do as well,[7] but studies are showing us that's not enough.

In the 1997 *Retail Advertising and Marketing Association, International Research Project on Loyalty Programs*, conducted by Marshall Marketing and Communications, Inc., only 33 percent of consumers said that they are recognized and made to feel special for participating in their loyalty program. Interestingly enough, it was the highest-income consumers ($75,000+) who rated "being recognized and made to feel special" an important element for a loyalty program. In the same study 12.7 percent of those not participating in a customer loyalty or frequent shopper program said the programs take too much time, the discounts are not worth it, most programs are too confusing, and the rewards aren't worth the hassle. Finally, 35.5 percent of customers queried said they purchase the same as before the frequent shopper program started, and 87.5 percent said they would shop at this store or purchase from this company even if they weren't in their program.

The proliferation of loyalty programs, points, and discounts has now made these programs normal, and they are no longer special. Any discount or point program can be duplicated quickly by any competitor. The company with the deepest pockets always wins the game.

And it is becoming a deep-pocket game. As retailers are learning that the loyalty card and its discounts are not keeping customers from switching stores, they are adding new attractions. Rather than getting to the heart of the loyalty question, they are throwing more money at the problem. In my local paper on the first Sunday of 1999, two supermarkets opened the money battle with full-page ads. From Vons: "This year we'll pay you to shop at Vons. $1,000,000 Grocery Giveaway." And from Ralphs: "Two million reasons to use this card every day. Shop with your Ralphs card in 1999 to win $2,000,000." Where will the deep-pocket battle end?

There is an alternative: CRM can offer benefits that are harder to duplicate and that may appear to the customer as unique and personal because they are based on previous dialog with the company.

A few retailers have managed to keep their loyalty programs special in their customers' minds. The Neiman Marcus In Circle program launched in 1984, Saks Fifth Avenue's Saks First program started in 1992, as well as Dayton Hudson's Regards program and Bloomingdale's' Premier Gold both developed in 1993, involve some bonus offers, but the great strength of these programs has always been the element of special customer communication and recognition. It is true that a customer spending $1 million at Neiman's gets to host a Texas Gala for 100 guests or enjoy 10 hours of air service aboard a private, luxurious Lear jet, but Billy Payton, vice president for customer programs at Neiman's, says, "We're talking with our customers constantly to try to make them feel special and to recognize them with special services."

One marketer who really understands the role of CRM in building customer loyalty is Ken Banks, senior vice president of marketing at PETsMART. When Ken arrived at PETsMART, there was no loyalty program. We talked with him about his plans.

"My number one priority in joining PETsMART," he said, "is to build a brand position for the stores, and by the nature of building a brand position you really have to talk about loyalty, because a brand feeling for a customer is not only getting someone coming into the store but the feeling they have toward you.

"To do that you have to build a loyalty program of some sort. You can't possibly have a good strong customer base just based on customers coming in, buying something and leaving. You have to generate a feeling about the store and have an emotional attachment.

"The pet supply business is a $76 billion business. We have a $2 billion share. The potential is enormous. How will we build a loyalty program to earn a bigger slice of the $76 billion pie?

"We could talk about a points program but my feeling on that is that trying to build loyalty by giving people frequent flier miles or something like that gets into the problem most marketers have of being 'me too.' People are getting tired of carrying another card or another little thing on their key ring to swipe when they come into the store to get a discount they might not have gotten otherwise. They're tired of accumulating points they may or may not ever use. You have to find something more to build loyalty.

"The key to that, I believe, is personalized programs that give customers things they really value. Our programs will be specifically designed to show we understand our customers and care about them and their pets. If we can help them from the first day they get that puppy, we will keep them for life. We want customers to change from thinking of us as a big-box retailer to a center where they can always find what they want and have some fun doing it. After all, having pets is fun.

"We don't expect this to take off like a rocket. We know CRM and building loyalty is a long-term process, but it is the only answer. I always say, what do you do after the 365th one-day sale? That's what customer relationship management is all about."

Those marketers who are still trying to earn a strong customer following on the basis of an impersonal points or discount or bribery loyalty program just don't get it. As Carolyn says, "I wonder why so many companies think they can buy my loyalty?" The hurdle that must be jumped to convince the customer you care has been raised. You can't buy customer loyalty.

It is now time to graduate to the advanced classes and advanced communication tools like the Internet and new digital tools where we can take our early learning and create the kind of true customer care that will be perceived as positive and even exceptional from the customer's viewpoint.

Firms need to treat the CRM issue as a 1to1 business process, not a marketing program. Companies that can show real caring will be the winners, and we'll have better business and perhaps even a better world.

CRM—whether by mail, by phone, by e-mail, or the Net—has many requirements, but in spite of the perceived enormity of the effort, it should be easy to sell to any management because it is not about demographic profiles, psychographic analysis, or behavioral models. It's about something all marketing executives understand: increasing the bottom-line contribution of your customers by tailoring your marketing efforts to manage the value relationship. It should be easy to sell, but is it? If you do sell it within your company, who will be affected, and what organizational changes may be required to assure success? We'll begin to see the answers in the next chapter.

3

The Leap of Faith

Organizational changes for successful CRM

"Are you bold enough to walk into a management meeting and ask for a half million dollars to build something few of the people present have ever heard of and for which there may appear to be no hard financial return for two years or more?"[1]

A publication named *Case-in-POINT*, published by Acxiom Corporation, is one of the most valuable I receive. I devour each issue cover to cover. Editors Janet Smith and Richard Cross, together with the other members of their skilled editorial team, consistently deliver well-documented case studies always full of database marketing wisdom. More than that, the *Case-in-POINT* group often files special reports examining specific challenges of interest to database marketers. In 1996 they reported that seasoned practitioners and newcomers alike had asked the editors for more information on how to gain and keep management support for customer database efforts. They surveyed the available literature, talked to the gurus, and went straight to practitioners who were working with databases. Then they issued the excellent report that starts off with the quotation at the start of this chapter.

Selling the concept of database marketing to management is no longer a big issue. An overwhelming majority of consumer and business-to-business marketers have now accepted the fact that a customer database is a requirement for any successful business. Thus, we have reached the point predicted a few years ago by Professor Robert Blattberg of Northwestern University. Having a customer database is no longer a competitive advantage. Not having a customer database is now a competitive disadvantage. Now we face the new challenge of moving beyond our earlier database marketing and direct marketing efforts to develop true Customer Relationship Management programs that will strengthen the bond between the customer and the company and maximize the value of the relationship to the customer for the customer's benefit and the company's profits. That requires the same leap of faith the *Case-in-POINT* editors addressed with that opening quote.

Top management may be unfamiliar with the CRM concept or may consider the rewards too long-range. An accurate *return on investment* (ROI) for the CRM program is difficult to calculate due to the variety of intangible variables that can affect the results. Some of the costs and many of the benefits will not be known until the program has run a significant course, the organization has changed to take full advantage of the added customer knowledge, and the long-term impact on both market position and customer value have had time to become evident.

The old report on selling databases to management makes the point that even a good-faith leap can be a mixed blessing if management doesn't understand the fundamental changes the customer database can cause organizationally. "Sometimes database champions find it easier than expected to get initial support," the report continues, "only to get the rug pulled out from under them the first time there is a glitch in the development or a downturn in the company's overall business."

Most important, the CRM program will require a senior-level champion. Literally everyone I talked to in the research for this book said getting buy-in from the top was the most critical issue. One said, "It amazes me the amount of support that came when folks realized this was important to the chairman, CEO."

Beyond that, CRM requires as much ownership as possible throughout the organization and a pro-active process of frequent communication—sharing information throughout the enterprise—about every success achieved *and* every goal missed. Even a missed goal is an opportunity to learn.

The key word here is "enterprise." To succeed at CRM, the company must get everyone on board, and they must teach all the players to see CRM as a benefit to them and to their customers. As part of the enterprise development, the company must make the CRM objective part of the brand. Because establishing the company's store, product, or service as a brand is essential to success, it is important to understand that CRM and the CRM dialog become tools to help you understand the power of your brand and the image it creates in the customer's mind.

The height of these hurdles is raised in the selling of CRM to management. A company's dedication to CRM as a way of doing business will require fundamental changes within the organization. Understanding the value of CRM requires a significant shift in mindset—learning to value qualitative rather than just quantitative benefits. Managers new to CRM must understand that tapping its real power requires a new way of doing business. As the *Case-in-POINT* report says about our earlier shift to database marketing, the old ways of defining success by share of market, brand awareness, or total sales must give way to such new, odd-sounding measurements as "share of customer," "lifetime value," and "return on data assets." The very nature of the company's business mission may ultimately change as new customer knowledge reveals truths about the marketplace that may not have been evident before. And, finally, there is certain to be some resistance from some within the company who have a vested interest in maintaining the status quo and who will try to discredit the program the first time there is a glitch in the development or a downturn in the company's business. With all of these hurdles, it can be a serious challenge to gain and keep management support for a dedicated CRM effort.

We're not talking about changes only in marketing strategy. Intensive CRM efforts require changes throughout the company.

Viking Office Products believes in CRM and implements it with a devotion to personalized, over-the-edge service that has helped it become a $1.3 billion global player in a crowded, price-conscious marketplace. Over 60 percent of the firm's sales originate overseas. To assure that its over-the-edge CRM extends to every market, Viking has established a local branch staffed with local people in every country of operation. As a result, they are able to customize each customer's catalog with local consumable office supply items that they know the customer purchases with a certain frequency. Each country's branch office maintains its own physical database, and an in-house analytical staff performs country-specific segmentation analyses to individualize the CRM process. These moves required major operational changes for Viking, but Viking's 70 percent plus retention rate and their proven ability to compete on value instead of price would suggest the changes were worthwhile.[2]

Great Plains Software of Fargo, North Dakota, which provides *Windows NT*–based financial management solutions to mid-sized companies, has made organizational changes to reinforce its CRM goals. They have set up steering committees within the company to apply CRM best practices to partners, customers, and employees, and they have created a "knowledge manager" position to develop the requirements from a customer knowledge standpoint for all the firm's interactive systems and to coordinate the efforts of IT, operations, and marketing.[3]

We're beginning to see that all areas of the company will be affected by a shift to CRM and that certainly includes sales personnel and customer service representatives. Thomas Haas of Hunter

Business Direct says, "Maximizing customer relationship management process productivity is the top-level goal. Field roles, and for that matter all selling roles, should be subordinated to this goal."[4]

It is the selling team who can help confirm that those you have selected as your best customers truly are your best customers, and they can often spot some potentially best customers you have missed. They are the ones who can be the most help in discovering what it really is that your customers value about a relationship with your company. It will be important to arm these front-line teammates with information about the products their customers want or need, to provide them with the information that allows them to speak to customers as if they know them—relating to the experiences the customers have had in their interactions with your company and understanding what they like or don't like about your products or services—and perhaps to teach your front-line personnel some new CRM skills.

Susan Harvey, vice president of marketing at Bloomingdale's, says, "As point-of-sale (POS) register system technology continues to advance, we will get even better at anticipating customers' needs and enriching the dialog between sales associates and customers." She understands that marketing and sales must feed each other in order to sustain and grow profitable customer relationships.

What other areas of the business will face change? Some you might never guess. One Seklemian/Newell client learned through its CRM program that customers perceived their delivery and repair people to be an extension of the sales force and expected them to have the same level of knowledge and customer service skills as the sales staff. After all, sometimes this is the only company representative the customer sees in person. To make its CRM efforts work, this company had to institute a substantial training program to teach the delivery and repair staff new skills.

Researchers will be among the first to face change. Douglas Pruden, senior vice president, Marketing Metrics, Inc., makes the case that customer satisfaction measurement in most American corporations has been the province of the research department. After all, since they have the experience in writing the questionnaires and managing the data, they have been allowed to set the agenda. But traditional research demands anonymous answers with a focus on means and averages. That's all fine for opinion polls and new-product evaluation, but that won't cut it for CRM. CRM must focus on the individual customer and manage interactions with specific individual customers.[5]

Once a researcher identifies the sponsoring company and tells the customers that he wants their opinion about the company's products and services, then from the customer point of view, it is no longer research. You are now engaged in a dialog with your customers.

From the customer point of view, everything from the paper stock to the salutation to the layout of the questionnaire communicates how little or how much you know about them and how much you value them as customers. If your Web site is crude or slow, your customer experience will suffer. If a package is personally addressed to them on the outer envelope but has a letter that begins, "Dear Valued Customer" and proceeds to ask which of your products the customer buys, how long he or she has been purchasing them, and in general suggests that the company and the customer have never, ever communicated in the past—that sends a terribly wrong message.[6]

CRM companies are beginning to move from product managers to customer managers. Hickory Farms customers can purchase products at grocery stores and other retail outlets throughout the country. But, with more than six food catalogs, Hickory Farms realizes the importance of better understanding most valuable customers, and those who purchase directly from them are each assigned a "personal sales rep." These representatives interact with their customers no less than twice a month, and they are rewarded strictly on retaining customers in their group and increasing the share of business that each customer gives to Hickory Farms.[7]

Buyers and merchandisers will have to change to an understanding of mass customization of product offerings—not just what do we have in inventory but what does the customer want.

Telemarketers will have to learn new dialog skills and new Web-enabled technology. Their supervisors will have to change performance measurement from the speed of the call to the quality of the call.

The creative team will have to learn the art of 1to1 communications and variable data printing—very different from the words and phrases of mass-marketing selling. Of all the changes required for CRM, we have found this to be one of the more difficult for some companies.

Another change will involve media choice. CRM requires the kind of integrated marketing that can achieve precise, synchronized, and highly accountable and measurable deployment of media and field sales channels. Integrated marketing takes a customer-driven view and implements this through the precision use and integration of:

Publicity and public relations

Advertising

Direct mail

Telemarketing—inbound and outbound

The Internet and e-mail

Field sales channels

RadioShack has one of the strongest CRM programs we studied. As a result, they take a customer-driven view of media choices. David Edmondson, executive vice president and COO, told me, "With our huge amount of data stored on an individual household basis, our analysts can look at our penetration of a media marketing region and see how many people in that area match the demographic profiles of our customers. That guides our decisions about how much to invest in which media in that market."

Those responsible for channel selling will have to be experts at protecting partner relationships as you begin to talk directly to your customers' customers. One of the most difficult challenges in business-to-business marketing is taking ownership of the end user through forging relationships with a channel partner, whether they are an independent sales rep, distributor, value-added reseller (VAR), dealer, or other reseller. Because your channel partners may feel threatened, you need to educate them and sponsor a shared understanding of the customer and the customer's needs.

Even more than marketing and operations, the technical experts—the information services (IS) team—will face change. Managing the database system will require new technical skills from those responsible for the building, management, and access of the datamart or data warehouse. While producing a direct-mail file from a multi-million name customer file is a batch process dependent only on processing power, CRM's need for customer information requires speed and precision rather than horsepower. CRM executives want their customer information fresh and relevant, and they want it now.

The difference is that CRM uses the marketing information to guide operational decisions. Real-time interaction is required to coordinate all interactions with a customer. Therefore, the IS team will have to find new ways to manage data and new tools for hierarchical image management to facilitate the sharing process across systems.

Finally, top management will need to invest time in learning about the company's data and the ways they are used for CRM "just as they would if they were building a new facility, staffing a new division, or rolling out a new product," as someone said recently. As management seeks to monitor progress, the old ways of measuring success will change while executives learn to value qualitative benefits like customer retention, share of customer, customer lifetime value, brand loyalty, and greater insight into market needs. The *Case-in-POINT* report said it best: "This will require new, long-term strategic vision because the knowledge obtained from the customer data is cumulative. It is only by using and building upon your data [your CRM program] for a period of time that you accumulate the knowledge of how to use it most effectively."[8]

Moreover, top management will need to learn the right questions to ask and the new measurements to follow. And these measurements need to be just as important in the company as the other quantitative analyses that have been used in the past, because they may be even *more* important.

Mike Miller, when he was vice president of relationship marketing for Sears, explained this to me in the clearest terms. In describing his experience learning to leverage customer information for the nation's second-largest retailer, he said, "We were very good at managing SKUs and merchandise categories. We were very good at managing stores. We were weak at managing customer segments. We had to learn to manage the *customer* P&L as we did the other business elements. In the end it is customer acquisition, customer mix, customer loyalty development and retention that will drive the share price."

The new measurements must gauge more than just customer satisfaction because, in the end, it is the loyal, high-quality customer that will be the key to the company's profitability, not just your cost or technology position or your inventory turnover.

The first question that must be asked is, what does the *customer* value about the relationship? The best way to find that answer is to ask the customer.

4

CHAPTER

The Four Things Your Customers Want to Tell You

Start by learning what it is your customers really want.

Most companies think a "satisfied customer" will be a loyal customer. That may have been true at one time, but it's not now. The traditional measurement of satisfaction is no longer good enough. Today customers demand more than simple satisfaction in return for their loyalty. Value, however it is defined by the customer, is the primary driver of customer retention. The more customers value what you do, the more loyal they will be.

This confirms the fact that a most important ingredient for any Customer Relationship Management effort must be learning what it really is that customers, segments of customers, and individual customers value about a relationship with your company. Making that discovery requires some form of value analysis that begins where most customer satisfaction studies end, delivering more than just answers to questions—knowledge, not just numbers. The critical issue is to learn what added values different segments of customers want.

There are specialists in the business of value analysis. One of the best I know is Message Factors, Inc., a 31-year-old company based in Memphis, Tennessee, with value analysis experience in both consumer and business-to-business marketing. Their trademark product is Value Analysis. In a recent report they discuss the four recurring themes they have discovered in conducting more than 400 of their customer Value Analysis studies over the past 10 years. The "four things your customers want to tell you" are the key components of Message Factors' Value Analysis:

1. "I expect you to have mastered the *basics* of what you are in business to do. If you haven't, I will switch to a different source. Even if you have, that alone is not enough to keep me loyal."

2. "I expect you to go beyond the basics and provide me with that which I *value*. If you do, you will have a *loyal* customer. If not, my business is 'up for grabs.'"

3. "Some things you do *irritate* me, but they are not important enough to drive me away. Besides, your competitors do the same things."

4. "Some things you do, I *don't care* anything about."

These four themes suggest sound standards for development of the values to be set forth in a solid CRM effort. They are worth a further exploration.

1. *The basics are the cost of entry and a first priority.*   The kind of basics that represent cost of entry include such things as location or having the right quality and assortments of merchandise. Customer surveys have shown that the great Nordstrom reputation for "service" is based more on merchandise quality and assortments than on actual sales associate service. The basics

would certainly also include the ease with which customers can get information and, today, that includes an easy-to-navigate Web site and customer-friendly telecommunications capabilities. There are many consumers who hate businesses' automated phones where it is impossible to get to a real live person or the call requires listening to 10 minutes of dull music or, worse yet, company commercials. All of these are time costs to a customer. If there are weaknesses in the basics, it won't matter how much value is added, and it may be a wasted investment to try to do the basics too well.

2. *Value is what companies should be communicating to customers—not basics.*   Here is where it becomes important to talk to customers and conduct research to find out which added values are most important to them. In the 1980s it was customer research that told Hertz their customers didn't like having to keep coming to the counter at the airport and wait in line to sign rental forms. Hertz learned customers wanted the rental process speeded up and streamlined. From that early research the Hertz #1 Club Gold was launched in the United States in April 1989. Now, in 600 locations worldwide Hertz Gold members arrive at the Hertz lot to see their name and car location in lights and their car waiting in a weather protected #1 Club Gold rental area with the trunk open, the motor running, and the heater or air-conditioner already at work. Hertz has done such a good job of understanding what values their #1 Club Gold customers want that these customers now represent 40 percent of total rental business and are Hertz's most loyal customers.

3. *While the* irritations *aren't enough to drive away customers and they are not as important as basics, they can still offer opportunities for innovation that can add value.*   Message Factors uses the example of Federal Express. FedEx overcame an irritation by "absolutely positively guaranteeing" overnight delivery by a fixed time the next day. They learned from research that shippers were concerned when sending a package through the U.S. Postal Service because they never knew when it would arrive.

Another example of building relationships by overcoming irritations comes from Hartness International, a company that makes case-packing machines which prepare bottles for shipping on assembly lines. Talking to customers enabled the company to capture their "need set." Through their research, Hartness learned that when a Hartness case-packer faltered, their customers' entire production process would grind to a halt. Hartness responded to the challenge, recognized the customers' needs, spent the money, and corrected the problem by developing their Video Response System, a wireless camera product that can transmit detailed images from anywhere on a customer's plant floor back to Hartness service technicians. Now, when machines malfunction on site, the customer's techs can fix 80 percent of the glitches on the spot guided by Hartness advice. Using customer research, the company has established a working dialog with their customers and has locked in loyalty simply by making it easier for the customer to depend on its products.

The video system has even become its own business, attracting new customers such as Hewlett-Packard and Chrysler and moving Hartness beyond its core product to enhanced services.

Publix Supermarkets in Florida overcame an irritation for young mothers who had to shop all over the store for baby needs. In response, Publix set up one complete aisle as a "Baby Store" with diapers, Infant Tylenol, and baby food all in one convenient place.

The American Airlines pilot sick-out that cancelled thousands of flights over the President's Day weekend in 1999 was certainly an irritation to me and to thousands of other American flyers. However, because I am an Executive Platinum member and one of American's best customers, I received a nice letter from Michael Gunn, American's senior VP, marketing, apologizing and saying he had added 2000 Award miles to my record to help make up for any inconvenience the sick-out had caused me.

4. *The unimportant issues are exactly that—either customers aren't aware of the issues or they don't care about them.* Hotel

guests don't care if their room is cleaned at 9:00, 10:00, or 11:00 A.M. as long as it's cleaned. Consumers rarely care as much about a product's packaging as most marketers think they do.

One Message Factors client learned that their award-winning newsletter was unimportant to customers. When they asked why, they learned the newsletter was being included in the customers' billing statement. After removing the invoice, many customers discarded the envelope without realizing there was a newsletter in it. Many customers did not know the company had a newsletter because of the way it was being distributed.

In responding to these four things, your customers want to tell you it is important to remember that people spend their time and money first on what they need and second on what they value. Customers are seeking more and more value for their time and their money, and the value must be specific to their needs and wants. The only way you can learn what specific added values different segments of customers want is by allocating an important piece of the CRM budget to research.

Ray Khavanin, manager of database analysis, Blockbuster Entertainment, and Greg Osenga, senior vice president, Cadmus Direct Marketing, call this important research "observing the unobservable—the next level of CRM." They suggest that CRM takes many marketers outside their traditional walls of brand comfort, but doing so is necessary to expand their thinking and to understand the role of CRM in the concept of the brand.

Behavior measures today's sale. Research is the only real measure of attitude. Attitude precedes behavior. Attitude is tomorrow's behavior. Attitude produces consistent behavior. As Ray Khavanin and Greg Osenga say, "Research provides a window to the unobservable."

Harley Davidson is certainly one of the best at bridging youth and aging baby-boomers looking to recapture their youth. Harleys sell so well that customers are willing to wait as long as a year to buy a new model. Harley reinforces that customer loyalty by giving owners a free one-year membership in the Harley Owners Group (HOG). When HOG members are due to renew their $40 annual membership, they are mailed humorous reminder cards, club member magazines, and easy-to-use renewal kits. The campaign has produced a 75 percent renewal rate among the 400,000 HOG members.

Land Rover knows how to provide solutions that make life easier and provide escape from and/or rewards for the stresses of life. Sandra Gudat, president of Customer Communication Group, a company that produces magazines for many CRM programs, tells me *Land Rover's Journal* customer magazine doesn't try to hide behind the guise of a four-wheel-drive magazine for just anybody. To its owner, a Land Rover is more than simply a vehicle. It is a story. Where it's been. Where it could go. What kind of adventure it could encounter. One issue provided everything from vehicle specifications for the most popular models to an accessories order form to a travelogue feature on the outer reaches of Mongolia and a profile of the U.S. equestrian team. "All this," Sandra says, "further builds on the Land Rover experience and cements brand loyalty—leaving readers anticipating the next issue's arrival like mail from heaven."

Listening to customers as they tune in to your Web site or your call center is another important piece of the customer research that will help you learn the kind of information different customer segments will value.

And never underestimate the power of information. Information is more important than product, and it is an important ingredient of any CRM program. President Reagan once called information the "oxygen of the modern age." If information is the heart of modern commerce, knowledge is the soul of CRM.

When Sony surveyed their customers to learn what the 11 million owners of Sony's PlayStation valued in a Sony relationship, they learned that these 12- to 34-year-old customers typically spent two hours or more daily "playing" and often owned more than one system. While they were eager to be the first to try new game releases, they weren't interested in joining a club. However, they did value a dialog with Sony and also with other gamers for which they communicated online. For true CRM, the creative trick was to use this research-gained information to develop a vehicle to enable a dialog that would not be seen as a corporate sales effort. The result was *Sony PlayStation Underground*, a quarterly CD magazine, featuring software demos, game tips, interviews, behind-the-scenes looks, and lots of information. The magazine is formatted on a disk playable only on PlayStation units.

Subscribers also get access to a member-only section of the PlayStation Web site offering game codes and chat rooms. "Anything that makes the PlayStation relationship stronger," says Peter Dille, Sony's senior director for product marketing, "will sell more product." Now that Sony has found what their customers really value, they are not hesitant to communicate. In a 12-month period *PlayStation Underground* members receive some 47 mailings from Sony, 9 from third-party software developers, and 5 from PlayStation distributors. One result: PlayStation owners average more than six $39 to $49 software purchases a year for each hardware unit compared with the industry norm of three to four.[1]

What does this confirm? In the end, it still comes back to the need for serious research and value analysis to build the knowledge about *your* customers that will direct you to the creation of the specific added values that different segments of your customer base really want. And it is important to remember that time changes all things, and what your customers want is no exception. As business environments and customer groups change, research must be refreshed.

Bringing in specialists like Message Factors is one good way to attack this challenge. Another is called *discrete choice modeling*. There is also *Conjoint analysis*, a sophisticated tool for uncovering the realistic importance of product and service features.

Recent developments in discrete choice analysis have moved the process from aggregate discrete choice models that assumed all respondents had the same preferences to the new disaggregate discrete choice model, which provides a separate choice model for each respondent. The disaggregate model captures differences in customers' choice behavior in a discrete choice exercise and therefore allows the researcher to identify segments of customers with different types of choice behavior.

It doesn't have to be that complicated. Some of your research can be as simple as customer surveys online. In Chapter 12 we'll show how some companies are using online customer surveys with outstanding results.

No matter how you perform the research and the value analysis, they are still the most important ingredients for any CRM effort—learning what it really is that your customers and segments of customers and individual customers value about a relationship with your company. And it is important to remember to ask what else your customers would value if you offered it.

Talking to customers, studying their actions, and trying to learn what they really want and why they act the way they do is a sound plan, but how can you possibly find the time and the manpower to talk to all your customers? Maybe you shouldn't. There are some shortcuts you can take.

5

If Nominated I Will Not Run; If Elected I Will Not Serve

You can't build a profitable relationship with every one of your customers.

Let's face it. Not every one of your customers wants to have a relationship with your company. In every business we have studied, there are customers whose purchase decisions are influenced only by price. These customers will leave you in a heartbeat for a lower price on another shelf or across the street. Just as consistently we have found customers in every business who care enough about quality and value and service and time saved and recognition to rank price low on their priority scale. In some cases, they are even willing to pay a bit more to avoid the hassle of shopping around.

Arthur Hughes, executive vice president of the Database Marketing Institute and author of *Strategic Database Marketing*, gives a great explanation of this:

As Paul Wang, Professor at Northwestern University points out, there are, in general, two types of customers: transaction buyers and relationship buyers.

A transaction buyer is someone who is interested only in price. These buyers have no loyalty. You can keep your warehouse open on a Saturday afternoon to meet some special need that they have. The following Tuesday when they have another requirement, they will bid it out. They will leave you for a penny's difference in price. They have all the catalogs and know all the competitor's prices. They spend hours on the Internet researching before they buy. They can afford to wait. They take pride in getting the best deal.

The other type of buyers are relationship buyers. These are people who are looking for a supplier that they can trust. They are seeking friendly companies with reliable products—people who recognize them, remember them, do favors for them, who build a relationship with them. Once they have found such a supplier, they tend to give them all their business. They know they could save a buck here or there by shopping around, but they find the process wastes too much of their time and emotional energy. Relationship buyers, if properly cultivated, will stay with you for a lifetime.

Transaction buyers give you very little profit. Since they only buy discounted items, the margin on their sales is much lower than the margin on relationship buyers' sales. In fact, you may find that your relationship buyers are subsidizing the sales to your transaction buyers."[1]

So, you're not going to manage customer relationships with every customer. Some, like President Coolidge, don't want to participate. The important questions are which ones and how many—two different questions.

Obviously you will want to invest your CRM efforts where they will bring the most profitable return. That means starting with the customers who are and who potentially can be your most profitable. This, of course, is the strength of loyalty programs like Neiman's, Saks', Dayton Hudson's, and Bloomingdale's. It is also the core concept for Hallmark's Gold Crown Card program and much of RadioShack's CRM efforts, as we will see.

Finding these most profitable candidates is really a two-step process. First, of course, comes the process of separating Paul Wang's transaction buyers from the field so that you don't spin your wheels and waste money trying to build relationships with folks who are interested only in price and will never have any degree of loyalty. The best breed of database marketing software systems currently available makes it possible to track customers by their individual gross margin contribution or the average discount percent of their cumulative purchases. For those whose customer files cannot be queried for profit by customer, some system of flagging lower-profit transactions is required. Flags should be set to identify deal purchases, coupon purchases, or other discounted transactions. In some businesses there are time periods when all transactions are off-price sales. Customers who purchase only in these time frames are easy to identify as transaction buyers.

One Seklemian/Newell client company has a customer file of 18 million names. When we separated out the transaction buyers who had purchased only with discounts or coupons or deals, we were down to just over 4 million. This ratio is not as unusual as it might seem.

Having separated out the barracuda, it is possible now to look at the rest of the school as a separate universe of potential relationship buyers and begin to determine the targets with the most profit potential for your CRM efforts. The universe of profitable relationship buyers will break into three rather distinct segments:

1. Those who are far and away the most profitable

2. Those who are delivering good profit and suggest the capability of becoming top-profit customers

3. Those who, while profitable, are only marginally so

For this we get back to one of the most basic of all the basic database marketing tools, the monetary decile analysis. The *monetary decile analysis* segments the customers in the universe into tenths showing the total profit dollars each decile contributed in the time period specified and the percent of the total universe of business that decile represents. This is the analysis that verifies Pareto's law, which says that 80 percent of a business's revenue derives from 20 percent of its customers. In all businesses we have ever studied, somewhere between 30 and 50 percent of the company's total sales come from the top 10 percent of customers. In most businesses 60 percent of the customer base accounts for at least 90 percent of sales and an even greater percent of the profit.

A further refinement of this customer profitability analysis is the purchase decile analysis. Instead of segmenting the *customers* into tenths to show the profit each decile contributed, the *purchase decile analysis* separates the *total sales and profits* into tenths to show how many customers account for each 10 percent of company profit. Most managers are blown away when they first see this analysis. It always shows that just a bit less or a bit more than 1 percent of all customers account for 10 percent of company sales with an even smaller segment contributing 10 percent of total profit! Thus for a company with 150,000 potential relationship customers, fewer than 1500 represent 10 percent of company profit—not a bad group to start with to manage relationships.

With these analyses we have now identified the three distinct segments of profitable relationship buyers, as follows.

1. *Those customers who represent 10 percent of the company's business and are far and away the most profitable should be the first to be targeted for CRM.* The purpose of the CRM efforts aimed at this top group will be retention. You are probably getting most of their business in your category already. Even the best Customer Relationship Management may not make these customers more profitable, but it will help to assure that none of these valuable customers are lost to the competition.

2. *The balance of the customers in the top 40 or 50 percent as ranked by sales and profit.* It will be just as important to target this middle group of buyers who are delivering good profit but may

be capable of moving up to the top-profit level. Customers in this group are probably giving some of their business to your competitors. CRM activities for these customers should be aimed directly at increasing your share of their business. A detailed ROI analysis at Allsports, a 240-store sporting goods chain in the United Kingdom, revealed that targeting second-best customers could encourage them to spend in line with best customers, substantially increasing in-store traffic and boosting the bottom line. The CRM marketing strategy developed for this middle group of buyers more than paid for the company's significant investment in database software within the first year.

RadioShack concentrates on this group of customers to move them from the company's basic "anchor" businesses—parts and accessories—up to what they call "opportunity" businesses like wireless phones and hand-held technology products.

3. *The third group of customers represent those who, while profitable, are only marginally so.*   While it is possible that some in this group would move up the sales ladder as a result of extra caring and communications, it will probably not be worth the effort and expense to try to manage significant relationships with this group of marginally profitable customers. Typically this group will represent almost half of the customer file, so this simple, basic analysis has greatly reduced the size of the challenge of implementing CRM.

Some management types will have trouble with the thought of leaving transaction and low-profit customers out of the CRM loop, but this is the real purpose of knowledge-based marketing—to avoid wasting marketing investments on lower-performing segments of the customer file. Winner companies concentrate on winner customers.

To help convince folks who don't see this light, you can use FedEx as an example. When FedEx calculated a profitability metric for each of its clients, they literally closed some accounts, dropping customers who, combined, shipped 150,000 packages a day.[2] They had the courage and good sense to move marketing and operating expenses that had been supporting low- or no-profit customers to drive more business from high-profit customers.

With the CRM target analyses completed, a next step is to rank these CRM targets by recency and frequency in order to devise different strategies for the hot-list buyers who are giving you solid business every week or every month and those who, though profitable when they buy, have not made purchases in some time. Further refinements to this selection process can come from serious data mining. More about data mining in Chapter 15.

The next question is, how many of these profitable customers can you afford to cultivate? Based on your incremental profit objectives, how much time, money, and resources can be allocated to the CRM project, and how far will those resources stretch? If your company happens to be located in Bermuda, the question is answered quickly since there are only about 24,000 households in the entire country. One very successful company Seklemian/Newell works with there has just 13,000 customers. By the time we separated out the transaction buyers and completed the profit decile analyses, we ended up with very manageable groups of top-profit relationship customers for retention and middle-profit relationship customers for trade up. With just 750 customers in the first group and about 3700 in the second, we could afford some serious 1to1 CRM activities.

Not all CRM opportunities are Bermudian in scope. The customer file at Toyota records more than 10 million owners representing about 80 percent of the Toyotas on the road today. The file at Kraft exceeds 25 million names. The more than 7000 RadioShack stores track the customer behavior of 119 million customers, 89 million households. Can companies this size execute Customer Relationship Management? Absolutely. Can they afford to talk to individual customers in magical 1to1 fashion? Yes, and some are doing just that.

Pontiac-GMC now publishes customized magazines three times a year personalized for individual customers based on owner lifestyle profiles. Each issue opens with a letter from the customer's dealership and is personalized from cover design, to coupons redeemable at that customer's dealership, to articles based on customer lifestyle selections. Business reply cards are included to create dialog by allowing the customers to update profiles, acquire product information, and comment or ask questions. There are 22 million possible versions of the magazines.

The magazine has achieved survey response rates of 18 percent, and this dialog "teaches" the magazine to become "smarter" over time. Pontiac-GMC has gathered detailed lifestyle data from 250,000 customers, and the program generates 50 to 100 cards and letters from customers each day. The company collects only that information customers wish to submit and then uses that data to change the way it treats each customer.[3]

But, do you have to talk to individual customers 1to1 to execute CRM? Certainly not. A basic of CRM is adapting products and services and offers to meet specific customer needs and wants. Customers—consumer and business to business—now expect that technology will allow companies to adapt to them and their specific needs, but "specific" does not necessarily mean "unique." The two are not synonymous. *Unique* means the only one of its kind, not like anything else of its kind. *Specific*, on the other hand, simply means clearly distinguished, stated, or understood.

Just as we segmented the customer file to separate transaction customers from relationship customers and high-profit customers from underperforming customers, we can now split the file into subsegments. Grouping customers with clearly distinguished and understood needs and wants will enable us to offer the kind of recognition and special treatment that will be meaningful in their terms.

A recent study by Deloitte & Touche, commissioned by the Direct Marketing Association, explained how recognition and special treatment can affect customer behavior. Speaking about loyalty programs, the study said:

> Members earn and save points based on their purchases and spend the points on free trips and prizes. But we soon began to realize from watching membership behavior in the programs that there was more going on than just millions of people winning free stuff. We saw customers jump at the chance to be recognized as special and to get special treatment. We saw customers respond positively toward programs and program sponsors and, most important, we saw and heard customers transform their attitudes as they made the subtle shift from customers to "members." Customers sound off, complain and demand; members discuss, advise, collaborate and advocate."[4]

So what have we learned about the process of implementing a CRM program? Not every one of your customers wants to have a relationship with your company, and there are many who will never develop any degree of loyalty. It is simply not worth the time and effort to try to manage relationships with these folks. Don't waste the money. Take the time to find the customers who have given some indication that they are looking for more than price—a company they can trust, a friendly company with reliable products, people who recognize them, remember them, and do special things for them. These will be your winners who will deliver the biggest return on your CRM investment.

Use the CRM program to help move away from price incentive offers using recognition, service, helpfulness, and nice surprises to build relationships that will mean more to your customers than price.

The CRM program at Safeway uses laser-personalized monthly mailings to 1.2 million best customers, versioned with personalized offers to add value for these special customers without discounting to the casual shopper. Funding for this CRM effort came from the elimination of one page of price specials in their weekly newspaper insert.

Finally, invest your CRM resources where they will bring the most profitable return by retaining your best customers and increasing your share of business from middle-range customers who can become best. All of this means your customer selection process must involve a lot more than the "model scores" learned in the old direct marketing school. Your service elements, helpfulness, and nice surprises must be relative to specific customer interests. Use all possible 1to1 strategies where they can be effectively and affordably applied, but be just as quick to adapt to the specific interests of customer segments as part of the process.

Set incremental profit goals and objectives for your CRM efforts by customer and by customer segment before you spend any money—even before you present your plan to senior management. Finally, a most important issue: have a plan and the necessary tools in hand to keep score and measure success. Just like all the other pieces of CRM, the measurement process involves many elements.

6

The Real Profit Players Are Not the Home Run Kings

It's not enough to go to the plate— you have to make hits.

Mark McGwire and Sammy Sosa know something about keeping score and measuring success. We all stayed glued to the tube in September 1998 and cheered when Mark McGwire broke the Roger Maris record, and the stadium usher returned the ball to him, and the usually mean-spirited IRS relented and said the usher did not, after all, have to pay $150,000 in gift taxes. Record crowds came to the final games of the Cardinals and Cubs hoping to see the winner of the duel, and they weren't disappointed as Mark McGwire hit a record 69 and 70 on the last day.

But the real profit players are not the home run kings. They're guys like Larry Walker who led both leagues that year with a .363 average and, yes, Sammy Sosa, not for his 66 home runs but for his 158 runs batted in—fourth best in National League history. The count of home runs is not the way to measure the success of

Customer Relationship Management. The important count is measured in singles and doubles and runs batted in or in the victories CRM achieved in one-run games.

We'll talk more in Chapter 9 about long-term measurement, but the important point here is that an effective CRM plan must include strategic tools to measure the slow, incremental gains that are adding value to the customer relationship and growing profit for the company—tools that can measure by the inch, not just by the yard. Remember what we said at the start: CRM is not an overnight cure, but a long-term profit builder.

What can be measured? It is important to decide up front just what will constitute hits—singles, extra base hits, or runs batted in. You will have to plan how you will construct your box score and what kind of flashing-light scoreboard you will build to report results, not just to top management but to your whole company.

Mike Miller who told us how Sears manages the customer P&L also reported at a recent conference that the company has created detailed box-score measurements to monitor the value of individual customers and customer segments in their 101.1 million customer database. They have established 1500 measurable attributes, both promotional and behavioral. They speak of their CRM program as one of "Leveraging Customer Information" (LCI) and they describe it as "investment based" as opposed to "expense based."

Believing that you get only what you measure, the Sears CRM team uses proprietary scorecards to measure the performance of specific behavioral segments of the file against the average Sears customer. To be sure they are talking to each customer in her or his terms, they have developed 125 separate programs based on life stage—from young singles and young couples to empty-nesters—and life events like weddings, new babies, and families moving to new residences.

Your definition of success must be broad enough to include more than runs scored. On the positive side it must give credit for hits and even walks. On the down side it must communicate the bad news of errors and men left on base.

Specific measurements and specific definitions of success will vary by industry, but some elements of the process will be common to all businesses. The age-old measurement tools of recency, frequency, and monetary will come into play. A strong CRM effort certainly should reduce the time between purchases, thus increasing recency and frequency, and, above all, it should increase the value of customers as measured in purchase and profit dollars.

The measurement of change in cross-selling effectiveness will be another strong evaluator of CRM success. It should follow that customers who have developed the strongest relationship with a company should welcome the broadest selection of that company's products or services. Improved cross-sell can be a gold mine of untapped sales and profit.

I have been told that Sony has made the point that the U.S. audio business would double if just 1 out of 10 video buyers would buy audio. People spend $40 billion a year to buy or rent video, DSS, and cable but only about $3 billion a year to listen to the programs.

I have seen many companies where more than 50 percent of their customers purchase in only one of their many product categories. This, of course, brings us to one of my favorite measurements—share of wallet. If a purchaser has bought a computer and a printer at Office Depot but is buying paper or toner or ink cartridges elsewhere, Office Depot is missing a share of that customer's wallet. In a very specific case, Blockbuster's share of customer videotape rental is only 42 percent, a huge opportunity.

Perhaps the most powerful profit producer that will record in your return-on-investment box score is customer retention. My good friend David L. Schneider, executive vice president of consulting at RTMS, Inc., has this to say about customer retention in the retail field: "At the close of business, no sensible retailer would leave the store's front doors unlocked—allowing strangers to wander through the aisles to pilfer valuable merchandise. But many retailers are doing essentially the same thing by allowing their competitors to steal one of their most valuable assets—their customers. Because of the growing realization of the long-term impact of a customer's lifetime value, more and more companies are beginning to view their customers as valuable assets, in the same manner as inventory, personnel, and positive name recognition."

Southwest Airlines knows how valuable it is to retain every customer. Their break-even customers per flight is 74.5, which means that only when customer 75 comes on board does a flight become profitable. Their studies show that only 5 customers per flight account for their total annual profit. Losing the business of just 1 of each of these 5 customers would mean a 20 percent decline in profit for that flight.[1]

Customers, particularly best customers, are a company's most valuable asset. The top 20 percent of a typical bank's customers generate 140 percent to 150 percent of its overall income. Yes, you read that correctly: 150 percent. That extra 50 percent gets eaten up by the bottom 20 percent of customers whose activities drain that much from the bank's profit. The retention of most profitable customers can be increased with CRM, and the increase can be measured.

The CRM program at Charlotte, North Carolina–based First Union Corp targets its most profitable customers to receive courtesy calls from branch or customer service executives thanking them for their business and asking if they have any concerns or needs. The program has increased retention of the bank's most valuable customers by 25 percent!

When planning for increased customer retention, it is important to remember that customer retention comes not just from the way you treat customers but from recruiting the right customers in the first place—the same selection process we discussed in Chapter 5. Lexus targets former Mercedes and Cadillac owners who are attracted to service, reliability, and long-term value, whereas Infinity seeks younger people who drive BMWs and Jaguars and are more interested in fashion and high performance. The result:

The Lexus repurchase rate was 63 percent two years in a row, while Infinity rates were stuck at 42 percent. Lexus got loyal customers by seeking loyalists in the first place.[2]

Your ROI box score should record more than the changes in net numbers of customers retained. Each business or household or customer record should be watched for changes in behavior and therefore value to the company. Retention analysis should track changes in customers' dollar value and frequency of interaction. It is obvious that reduced frequency can be an early warning sign of trouble in the database, but there's more to it than that. Carla E. McEachern, senior consultant at Nykamp Consulting Group in Chicago, made the point at a 1998 NCDM conference that in the case of some cellular telephone companies, *increased* activity— which quickly uses up an allocation of free minutes—rather than decreased activity may be an indication that a customer has made a switch to a competitor's plan, as can lower terms on successive renewals or declining cross-sales. It gets complicated.

Now that you have begun to clarify your definition of the kind of base hits you will measure, there remains one question to be answered for any truly accurate measure of the return on your CRM investment. How many of these singles, extra base hits, and runs batted in would have been accomplished without all the CRM efforts?

The start of this discussion of ROI measurement made the point that an effective CRM plan must include strategic tools to measure the slow, incremental gains that are adding value to the customer relationship and growing profit for the company—measuring by the inch not just by the yard. The key word in that admonition is *incremental*. It is never enough to measure just the changes in behavior of the customer group involved in your CRM program. These changes must be judged and evaluated against some consistent benchmark. The trick is to be able to show whether or not these behavioral changes might, in fact, have occurred without the CRM efforts—that they are truly an *incremental* result of your CRM efforts. That requires a control.

Perhaps the best example of the importance of the control in experimentation was used by Martin Baier in his excellent book *Elements of Direct Marketing.*[3] He used the example of the mathematician Blaise Pascal, who hypothesized in 1648 that atmospheric pressure declined with increasing altitude. Pascal first took a barometric reading in his village. An hour later, after he had climbed to the top of a 3000-foot mountain, he took another measurement, and his second observation did, indeed, show significantly lower atmospheric pressure. What Pascal did not know, however, was whether the atmospheric pressure had become lower at the bottom as well as at the top of the mountain during the hour that it took him to climb to the higher elevation.

Pascal wisely changed his experiment design. He calibrated two barometers to each other and read them simultaneously before he began his trek up the mountain with one of them. At the precise time he read the barometer in his hand at the top of the mountain, another villager read the control barometer at the bottom of the mountain. His subsequent comparison, with control, showed that although both barometers had lower readings at the end of the hour it took him to climb the mountain, the barometer he carried with him to the top had a significantly lower reading than the one left in the village.

For our purposes it will not be as simple as finding another villager to stand at the bottom of the mountain. A sound control for our measurement of ROI must be a carefully controlled sample of the exact customer segments that will be part of the CRM program. Measuring the changes in recency, frequency, monetary, cross-sell accomplishments, and retention within the CRM customer group and comparing those changes with the changes, if any, in the behavior of the control group will give the only true reading of the two barometers—the only true measurement of the *incremental* return on investment.

As a final thought about setting ROI goals for your CRM efforts, let's return to our baseball analogy of going after hits and batting averages rather than home runs. Remember the thoughts of Kevin Costner when he was teaching his protégé, played by Tim Robbins, in the movie *Bull Durham*. He explained that the only difference between a ball player batting .250 and .300 is 25 hits in a season. Since the season lasts about 25 weeks, he said, "That means if you get just one extra flare a week, just one, you get a gork, you get a ground ball, you get a ground ball with eyes, you get a dying quail—just one more dying quail a week—and you're in Yankee Stadium." Singles are more important than home runs.

Now with your box-score system constructed and your flashing-light scoreboard built to keep score and measure success, how many games or how many seasons of games will you have to play before you will know the final score?

7

Keeping the Relationship Alive

A profitable customer relationship is not a one-night stand. Do you know where your profit zone is?

An executive of one company told me recently, "Yes, we have a strong customer relationship marketing program. We track transactions, and we have appended third-party data to the customer file. Our targeting for last month's 25 percent off promotion enabled us to mail 20 percent less pieces and still have a sales increase over last year."

That company may or may not have a real customer relationship *marketing* program, but they don't have anything approaching a Customer Relationship *Management* program. A profitable customer relationship is not a one-night stand. Relationships are not built with 25 percent off promotions. The purpose of CRM is to build customer loyalty. Laura Rifkin, vice president of Harte-Hanks Market Research, commenting on the Harte-Hanks National Study of Customer Loyalty, says, "If you buy that a loyalty strategy is the right thing for your company, some of the things that will create short-term revenue will not be part of a loyalty strategy." That certainly includes 25 percent off promotions.

Occasional home runs will not be the measure of success, and CRM is not about building *overnight* relationships. Scoring the return on investment for the CRM program will require long-term measurements to track the 25 weeks of the season that can take players to Yankee Stadium, and it will require measuring new elements of business success as well—more than the old market share measurements we learned in business school in the 1960s and 1970s.

In their important book, *The Profit Zone: How Strategic Business Design Will Lead You to Tomorrow's Profits*, Adrian Slywotzky and David Morrison say that market share is no longer the guaranteed profit producer. They site companies like General Motors, IBM, American Airlines, and Sears to make the point that huge market share does not always assure high profit. The premise of their book is that what matters more than market share is "the design" of the business. What they mean is that a business must be set up in such a way that management understands where the company's real profits are coming from and continually refines and expands those profit strengths.

The authors ask, "Do you know where your company's profit zone is? Do you know how to find it? Do you know how to get there once you do find it?" They suggest that the best companies have started with the customer and worked back from there. The book talks a lot about the points made in our last chapter: The secret is not just getting a lot of customers; it is identifying the right ones and, as these authors say, "jettisoning the high-maintenance, high-cost customers who are creating a drain on profitability."[1]

This suggests that the design of the business we need for measuring the return on investment for the CRM program must start with knowing where the company's profit zone is and learning how to get there once we find it. As Slywotzky and Morris suggest, that starts with the customer.

The business of measuring customer behavior to determine ROI is not very complicated. In simplest terms, we want to measure the change in behavior of two groups of customers: heavy purchasers and midrange purchasers.

We want to be sure we retain the heavy purchasers. We can't measure that by checking to see which of the 25 percent off promotions prompt them to buy. We need to start with a benchmark that shows the share of heavy purchasers we are currently keeping as loyal customers and measure improvement from there. It may be that improved retention of heavy purchasers is the most profitable result of CRM. When you deal with best customers, a 1 percent change in retention or attrition is a big-time return on investment.

It is impossible to overstress the value of keeping customers. If you accept the fact that the rate of customer attrition for most companies is around 50 percent the first year and about 20 percent of the balance every year after, you see that of 100 customers today only 32 will still be with you three years from now. Do the math for your company. Assume CRM can keep just a small percentage of the 68 percent of your customer base that is defecting. Multiply that number by your customers' annual average spending. The result may surprise you.

So the measurement of customer retention will be the first of our tools to score the return on CRM investment. Obviously this will require measurement over time, not just overnight. Arthur Hughes says, "Database marketing [CRM] requires a minimum of three years to show real payoff in terms of increased customer loyalty, reduced attrition and increased sales."[2]

Midrange purchasers represent a different challenge. We want to move them up the loyalty ladder. With the right program strategy, we can move them up, but only one rung at a time, so again, that too will take time to measure.

What we are talking about here is finding ways to get a greater share of wallet from these customers. One of the tools that will accomplish this is increased cross-sell. I can't understand why more companies are not concentrating on this. U.S. companies spend millions of dollars a year collecting information on customers through database marketing. Yet, according to a study conducted by Northwestern University, a good percentage of these companies don't take advantage of the data they collect.

Little more than half (59 percent) of those surveyed customize the information gathered to cross-sell other products or services. And not enough companies are going beyond transactional data to measure attitudinal data. Don Schultz, a professor at Northwestern Medill School of Journalism, says, "Attitudinal data—including consumers' feelings, awareness and recognition of brands—often have taken a back seat. You cannot understand return on customer investment unless you understand why they're doing what they're doing."[3]

This brings us back to some of the loyalty programs as they exist today. Are they really building customer loyalty that can be measured?

In the Harte-Hanks survey, when customers were asked how well they felt they were served by the hotel industry, almost 10 percent ranked it "excellent," a rating more or less in the middle of all industries surveyed. But when respondents were asked how loyal they felt to the hotel they used most often, fewer than 5 percent said they were "very loyal" to their preferred chain and that it would take a lot for them to switch. This despite the fact that almost all major hotel chains have some form of loyalty program.

When matching customer perception of rewards programs to customer loyalty, this same study found mixed signals. While 71 percent of respondents agreed either strongly or somewhat strongly that these programs are a nice way for a company to say thank you for business, 72 percent felt the rewards weren't really rewards but a means to get them to buy more.

Sixty-nine percent actually believed rewards programs probably cause them to pay higher prices for products from the companies that have them. Almost half the respondents said they preferred rewards in the form of special services rather than discounts or prizes. But 40 percent indicated that they thought rewards were a waste of time, and only 37 percent agreed that they are seriously motivated by the programs.

Remember, CRM is attempting to change customers' behavior and that takes time. Winners measure the changes in customer behavior as recorded in the recency, frequency, monetary, and cross-purchase indices, but the true measurement of ROI must include in the profitability analysis retention rate, referral rate, marketing expenses, and the effect on behavior of the relationship management activities. The only measurement that will capture all of these elements is the lifetime value measurement. Lifetime value has been defined as "the amount by which a person's, household's or business' revenues over time exceed, by an acceptable amount, the company's cost of attracting, selling and servicing that customer."[4]

The lifetime value measurement historically has been used to establish the true ROI of customer acquisition endeavors. Since a company may spend more to acquire a new customer than the amount of that customer's first purchase, it has always been important to be able to calculate the ultimate value of the customer acquired. Only recently have marketers begun to use the lifetime value calculation for ongoing marketing activities. The measure is perfect for calculating ROI for CRM programs because everything aimed at strengthening the customer relationship has the objective of increasing the customer's profitability over time. For those who want more details, the most complete and professional explanation of lifetime value and the important lifetime value calculation formula will be found in two books by Arthur Middleton Hughes: *Strategic Database Marketing* and *The Complete Database Marketer*, both published by McGraw-Hill.

Profitable customer relationships are not built on a one-night stand. CRM is not about creating overnight relationships. Mark Voboril of the broadband utility MediaOne, recently merged with AT&T, says, "You've got just two to four years to deliver to senior management a return on most database marketing investments. Goals need to be specific, attainable, relevant and timebound."[5]

CRM requires, as Slywotzky and Morrison described, a new design of your business to find your company's profit zone and the most direct route to get there when you find it. The authors urge companies to think of designing the new business model as an investment, because that's what it is. They make the point that too many companies spend as much as $1 billion a year on R&D for product and nothing on business design research to learn where their profits are coming from. "And yet," they say, "that kind of research and rethinking and redefining could determine whether a company survives into the twenty-first century."

Because the return on investment for CRM must be measured over time, the design of the CRM business model forces a company to think about what they will have to be good at tomorrow. That raises many questions beyond CRM as we look at the changing customer in the next chapter.

8

CHAPTER

"Eveolution" and Other Surprises Ahead

Demographics and business decisions

In September 1998, 200 senior marketing executives representing industries as diverse as automobiles and dishwashers met in Chicago at the Polk Summit to discuss the latest trends in consumer marketing and how the customer mix is changing. Talking about consumer behaviors and the reasons for them, many in the summit's audience disagreed on what makes today's consumers tick, but they all agreed that the customer mix is changing and what marketers will have to be good at tomorrow. Two fast-moving changes stood out.

First, all agreed that women as a group are changing the landscape more than ever. Radical changes in women's education and income over the past 20 years have created a powerful decision maker or influencer in the females of our households.[1]

Faith Popcorn, who is the founder and chairperson of BrainReserve, a New York–based marketing consulting firm that tracks cultural and consumer trends and who is a favorite forecaster among Fortune 500 companies, is way ahead of these marketers. She calls this trend, "Eveolution," the subject of her next book.

She believes that women are truly going to change the marketplace: "Women currently buy or have veto power over about 80 percent of what we purchase. Women are starting new businesses at twice the rate of men. They are becoming the new supervisors in many businesses, but they don't appear on the radar screen yet. Female-owned companies produce $3.2 trillion worth of goods a year."[2] And, the share of female PC users in the population nearly doubled from 1996 to 1998, growing from 19 to 37 percent, while time spent on a PC for online personal applications grew 60 percent.

Is Faith Popcorn right? Think about this as a small example. Three women are now responsible for a quarter of General Motors' sales of 4.6 million vehicles: Karen Francis, 36, became the new boss at the Oldsmobile division in early 1999, the youngest person ever to head the division, Cynthia Trudell, 45, runs GM's Saturn Corp; and Lynn Myers, 56, heads Pontiac-GMC. These three are not just figureheads. Each has profit-and-loss responsibility for her brand, from conception to design and marketing.

Karen Francis says, "I can walk into a room and look at something differently—whether it's because I'm a woman or I have consumer products experience or three years ago I was driving a BMW.[3]

In July 1999 Carleton "Carly" Fiorina became CEO of Hewlett-Packard, with 123,000 employees and $46 billion in revenue, by far the largest company ever to be run by a woman. On her first full day on the job, she told reporters, "Gender bias is a luxury companies can no longer afford. Everyone has figured that out."[4]

Executives at the summit suggested that marketers have not yet embraced this reality. They said, "Many marketers are addressing this vocal group of the population superficially, and must change in order to satisfy the demands of the new female. Women are sophisticated and vocal, and marketers who don't significantly recognize that will miss this group with huge buying power."

Faith Popcorn's "Eves" are far from a niche market. They represent 51.2 percent of the U.S. population and influence or buy more than two-thirds of the $3 trillion spent in the United States. America Online now has more female members (52 percent) than males. Women now represent 45 percent of the 9.2 million online book buyers, 38 percent of the 7.2 million CD/video buyers, 24 percent of the 5.4 million buyers of computer hardware, and 53 percent of the 4.5 million online buyers of clothing. It will be critical for the Customer Relationship Management marketer to understand these important differences in such a powerful segment of the buying public.

Forty-two percent of the Super Bowl 1999 television audience was female, and they were not amused by Victoria's Secret's attempt at media convergence capitalizing on the male thrill of seeing Tyra in a thong. As one writer said, "Since women account for 90 percent of Victoria's Secret sales, what will happen to the longer-term growth of the brand if it continues to attract men by making women feel uncomfortable? That was the feeling in a lot of living rooms that Sunday. Kind of how a Viagra commercial feels to a guy."[5]

Women respond to emotional truth, to real-life experience. And women have very high expectations for themselves.

Faith Popcorn seems to understand these women better than the executives assembled in Chicago. She doesn't use words like *sophisticated* and *vocal*. She gets closer to the real mark when she says, "The way women think is different from men, and it is starting to inform a lot of our business decisions. We are saying there will be new rules for Eveolution, one of which will be marketing to a woman's peripheral vision. It does matter that she can find what she wants on your shelf. But it also matters what kind of corporation you are, what kind of parking lot you have, what kind of benefits you give employees, what kind of 800 numbers you have, how late you stay open. In other words, market beyond the obvious destination of *buy my product*."[6]

UK supermarket chain Tesco understands this need for good citizenship. They are so committed to tackling environmental concerns that they recycle 100 percent of secondary packing such as cardboard and plastic, thereby eliminating 70,000 tons of card from landfills and recycling 10,000 tons of shrink-wrap annually.

Beyond its recycling, Tesco has adopted a strategy for vehicle selection based on reduced emissions. The strategies of monitoring fuel selection and using regenerating traps on all vehicles in the Tesco fleet have cut particle emissions and put the company's vehicles well ahead of current EU guidelines on the required ceiling for emissions.[7]

Some associates, reading early drafts of this chapter, suggested these thoughts about marketing differently to the new woman consumer are not new. Grocery stores and most retailers, they said, have already learned to sell to women. I think they missed Faith Popcorn's points that the power growth of women in business will even affect business-to-business marketing and will require that companies market to women's peripheral vision.

One who understands Eveolution is Geraldine Laybourne who is starting Oxygen Media, a multimedia company aimed primarily at women that pursues the ever-elusive goal of convergence—combining the entertainment power of television with the interactivity and specificity of the Internet. She says, "Five years from now we'd like to be in 50 million homes with a cable network and to be part of women's daily lives online." With the backing of superplayers like Morgan Stanley, Walt Disney Company, America Online, Inc., and Oprah Winfrey, she stands a good chance of creating a narrowcasting giant that will reach women who, as she says, "want to take charge of their lives and have money to spend."[8]

Demonstrating real understanding of the new woman customer will require a lot more than having what she wants on your shelves. We are good at understanding rational wants. Eveolution will require a much deeper understanding of the emotional drives of this not-so-new customer.

Faith Popcorn brings us right back to the very soul of CRM. CRM requires a lot more than the kind of customer contact we have known in the past and is a giant leap from earlier database marketing. It is as much emotional as it is rational. It's not just what companies say in their communications; it's what they do to maintain an ongoing relationship, to show they really care. Eveolution will change the answers to questions like what does the customer value about the relationship? What are some of the core benefits that have value to the customer? What is it the customer values about these? What is the value provided to the customer that differentiates your company from the competition? As we said earlier, and as Faith Popcorn confirms, all of this is very different from trying to solicit an immediate sale—and vastly different from merely sending coupons or offering discounts or giving points for frequent buying.

When Faith Popcorn talks about women wanting to know how late you stay open, she gets into the arena of shopping convenience that is important to many time-starved women. One new CRM marketing tool that uses new technology to enable companies to add real convenience to a company's relationship with time-starved customers is "Village Square," a wireless service from Intelligent Information, Inc., that notifies people about upcoming personal events of which they have asked to be reminded.

When a user signs up for the Village Square service through her wireless telephone carrier, she goes to the carrier's Web page and creates a personalized calendar of events that are important to her, like birthdays, business meetings, and anniversaries. The user then decides how far in advance she wants to be reminded of each event. At the chosen date, either the person's telephone or pager will ring or buzz letting her know she has a message. A text message will then appear with a reminder of the occasion.

1-800-Flowers was one of the first firms to sign up for Village Square. At the end of their message, a promotional suggestion appears reminding the user that it would be a good idea to order flowers for the occasion. The user can then press a button on the phone and be connected directly to a 1-800-Flowers representative. Chris McCann, senior vice president at 1-800-Flowers, says, "Since the user has decided they want this message, it is easy for us to deliver very targeted and personalized material directly to them in the anytime-anywhere world of wireless communication." McCann estimates that by the middle of 1999 there will be close to half a million people using the service.[9] It's not hard to believe that some busy women will value this kind of very personal service much more than they will care about a few more frequent buyer points.

Another company, National Westminster Bank in London, has developed a service called "Zenda" that they are offering free to help them build relationships with bank customers. Zenda will be customized to each customer, reminding her of key dates such as birthdays and anniversaries, and it will also include customized news including weather reports, traffic and travel information, as well as legal and health services, all personalized so the customer gets only the information she wants. A spokesman says the bank is leveraging its expertise in data management to build customer relationships."[10]

The second point of agreement at the Polk Summit was the radical change in the age mix of the consuming public. The fact that every 7 seconds a baby-boomer is turning 50 will mean that products will no longer live or die by the 25 to 44 market.

A Roper Starch Worldwide study confirms this, pointing out that the 50+ segment, now 68.2 million Americans, will grow by 47.2 million to reach 115.4 million, 35 percent of the population, by 2020, with life expectancy up to 79, nearly a decade longer than it was in 1970. At the same time, all age categories less than 34 years are projected to decline, with the exception of 20 to 24 which will increase only 1 percent.

Today's 50+ boomer age group's behavior is just not the same as that of the "silent generation," which preceded them and includes their parents. Generational cohorts are influenced by the totality of their life experience. The boomers' parents—today's older group—were born between 1925 and 1942 and are a generation that endured war and depression. They are conformist and traditional. They were influenced by the depression, wars, and the traditional family values of the *Leave It to Beaver* 1950s.

In contrast, the boomers, born between 1943 and the early 1960s, are the heirs of the World War II triumphs and were born into a sea of optimism. They have always been free spirits—flower children, advocates of free sex, draft resisters, yuppie singles, and, more recently, the leaders in the ecological, educational, and health care crusades. They also have a weak instinct for social discipline.

They love travel, which was not as readily available to the silent generation. They love cars—from the BMW to the Beetle to trucks and off-road vehicles—but not their father's Oldsmobile. They loved being yuppie singles and marrying late (the preceding generation was the earliest marrying generation in our history).

What all this means is that as the boomers age past their early fifties, they will still want the good life, an active life, and new experiences. In addition, they are living longer and healthier. Of all those who have ever achieved the age of 85, half are alive today.

As boomers enter their fifties, they will enter a diversity of life stages and will be looking for values quite different from the 50-year-olds of the past. While older, boomers will still want the good life, a marked contrast to their current, more conservative elders of the silent generation.

Some French direct marketers are leading the way in the discovery of this robust 50+ market. The over-50 generation accounts for 35 percent of the French population today and is expected to reach 53 percent in 2020. Their purchasing power of 800 billion francs (U.S. $133.3 billion) is 25 percent higher than those under 50. They control 43 percent of French disposable income, a figure expected to pass 50 percent in 2005.

One French consultant says niche catalogs and special sections in general catalogs are exploding because this audience has time to read, wants to know the benefits of products they buy, and understands that quality tends to cost more, making them willing to pay more for products they buy—15 percent more for beauty creams and 6 percent more for textiles, for example.[11]

Bill Burkart, executive vice president at Age Wave *IMPACT*, is a specialist helping companies market to boomers and older adults. He describes six myths that hobble marketers trying to learn what 50+ customers will value about a relationship and what core values will be of special importance to these customers.[12]

> *Myth 1: Today's mature adults are similar to their parents.* Not so. Americans between 55 and 65 grew up with Elvis Presley, Rock Hudson, Doris Day, and Paul Newman. Using the same music, images, and language to sell your products and services to different generations is doomed to failure.

> *Myth 2: The mature audience is homogenous.* Again, not so. We become less, rather than more, alike as we age, and we become increasingly confident and independent. Life stages are important. Whether your customer is retiring or returning to the workplace, is recently widowed or divorced, is concerned about health issues or is buying or selling a home will all help define the core benefits that will have value to the individual.

> *Myth 3: Mature adults are brand loyal.* Research shows that as many as 30 percent of insurance customers switch companies every year. Sixty-eight percent of older adults are willing to switch brands—more than any other generation. Mature adults are usually amenable to new products and services that they can use immediately.

> *Myth 4: Mature adults have consistent and predictable behaviors.* Not true, says Burkart. In fact, they often experience a personal renaissance in their mid-life stages. Age is less relevant to their behavior than ever before. All

this means changing needs and life stages are windows of opportunity for marketers who are willing to use CRM to learn what values provided to the 50+ customer would differentiate their company from the competition.

Myth 5:   Mature adults are inflexible and resistant to change.   In fact, mature consumers are just as likely to try new things as any other age group. At no time in their lives have they been less restrained. They act more on information than impulse—a fact that supports our belief in the importance of providing as much relevant information as possible as part of a CRM program.

Myth 6:   Marketing models that have worked in the past will work in the future.   Mature adults have been overmarketed and oversold. They've become increasingly resistant to overused appeals. They want a company, product, and service they can trust. Nothing undermines that sense of trust faster than the feeling that you're being "sold."

This brings us back to Paul Wang's definition of *relationship buyers*—that is, people who are looking for a supplier that they can trust, friendly companies with reliable products, people who recognize them, do favors for them, and build a relationship with them. And for the important Eveolution customer and the 50+, it reinforces the point that successful CRM activities must make each contact or communication positive from the customer's point of view. As Faith Popcorn says, that goes way "beyond the obvious destination of *buy my product*."

QUICK TIPS FROM PART ONE

CHAPTER 1: Carolyn's Lament

- Most loyalty program failures occur because a marketing organization does not know how the customer benefits from it.
- Customer Relationship Management is not traditional database marketing.
- CRM concentrates on what the *customer* values, not on what you want to sell.
- CRM is not an overnight cure but rather a long-term profit builder.

CHAPTER 2: The Ears of the Hippopotamus

- Remember the definition of CRM from Carlson Marketing: "A business strategy which pro-actively builds a bias or preference for an organization with its individual employees, channels and customers resulting in increased retention and increased performance."

- The key issues are:
  - Identifying consumer values that are pertinent to your business
  - Understanding the relative importance of these values to each customer segment
  - Determining if these values will affect the bottom line in a positive manner
  - Communicating and delivering the appropriate values to each customer segment
  - Measuring results and proving return on investment
- CRM is not "direct marketing." It requires new and different skill sets.
- The Internet is an important CRM tool.
- The real purpose of CRM is to manage (and change or reinforce) customer behavior.
- Every customer contact or communication must be positive *from the customer's viewpoint.*
- Most loyalty programs are no longer special. Any discount or points program can be duplicated quickly by any competitor. The company with the deepest pockets always wins.
- Customers don't want to be treated equally. They want to be treated individually.
- CRM must give the customer more than points and discounts.

CHAPTER 3: The Leap of Faith

- A dedication to CRM as a way of doing business will require fundamental changes within your organization.
- The CRM program will require a senior-level champion.
- CRM success requires enterprise-wide communication resulting in all of the players seeing CRM as a benefit to them and to their customers.

- The CRM objective must become part of the brand.

- All areas of the company will be affected by a shift to CRM.

- The process of developing customer knowledge is cumulative.

- New measurements will be required in order to measure success. The traditional measure of satisfaction is no longer good enough.

CHAPTER 4: The Four Things Your Customers Want to Tell You

- You must learn what customers and segments of customers value about a relationship with your company.

- Basics are the cost of entry. Get them right, but don't count on them to build loyalty.

- Constantly communicate value in individual customer terms.

- Add value by getting rid of irritations.

- Ignore the unimportant.

- You must observe the unobservable, and that requires research.

- CRM is about finding ways to make your customers' lives easier.

CHAPTER 5: If Nominated I Will Not Run; If Elected I Will Not Serve

- You can't make CRM work for every customer, and you shouldn't try.

- The real purpose of knowledge-based marketing is to move marketing investments to influence best and potentially best customers.

- Fewer than 1 percent of your customers deliver almost 10 percent of your sales, and an even smaller share contribute 10 percent of your total profit.
- Customer retention starts with recruiting the right customers in the first place.
- Winner companies concentrate on winner customers.

CHAPTER 6: The Real Profit Players Are Not the Home Run Kings

- Customers, particularly best customers, are your most valuable asset.
- The true measurement of return on CRM investment is customer lifetime value.
- The only results that count are incremental gains.
- Singles are more important than home runs.

CHAPTER 7: Keeping the Relationship Alive

- Huge market share does not always assure high profit.
- The secret is not getting a lot of customers. It's getting the *right* customers and keeping them.
- The return on investment for CRM starts with knowing where your profit zone is.
- CRM can take three years or more before the big payoff.
- You must learn what you will have to be good at tomorrow to serve the changing customer mix.
- The marketing model that has worked in the past will not work in the future.
- The only true measure of CRM success is customer lifetime value.

CHAPTER 8: "Eveolution" and Other Surprises Ahead

- Women are changing the marketing landscape, and the way they think is different from men.

- We must market to a woman's peripheral vision.

- The belief that the mature audience is homogenous, consistent, and predictable is a myth.

- It's not just what you say in your communications; it's what you do to maintain an ongoing relationship, to show you care.

- You can't buy customer loyalty.

PART TWO

TODAY'S TOOLS FOR CRM: TECHNOLOGY AND THE INTERNET AND MORE

Like any other marketing strategy, CRM requires special tools. Part Two looks at some of the old database marketing tools and how some companies are using them for CRM and then looks at the new tools the "builder" needs to build the CRM "house."

We'll examine the many new communication tools from the Internet and e-mail to the Web-enabled call centers to digital printing, and more. The process of data mining for CRM will be explained. We'll take a look ahead to dream about some tools yet to be invented, and finally we'll summarize the importance of capturing the right mix of all the new technology to exploit CRM to build loyalty in the digital 00s.

9

New Tools Require New Skills

If all you have is a hammer, everything looks like a nail.

Many of today's senior advertising and marketing executives grew up in the business when the only efficient tool in the toolbox was the mass-media hammer. Direct-mail (DM) advertising was considered definitely second class. This was especially true in the minds of advertising agency types who couldn't see DM and other personal contact tools adding much glamour to their personal portfolios. The television reel of commercials was the magic wand for pitching new accounts or scouting for a new job. Historically, advertisers and agencies always took the position that any form of direct marketing was "below the line" and general advertising, above the line. There was always something dark and demeaning about "direct."

This devotion to mass media helps to explain the misdirection that often occurs with the introduction of Customer Relationship Management in some companies. Winners have learned that new tools require new skills. To develop the new skills it is important, first, to understand the new tools.

The master tool, of course, is the customer database. The database is the central repository for all of the information pertaining to the relationship of a business and its customers. It keeps track of all contacts by the customer including the customer's purchase transactions, calls, comments, returns, service calls, even complaints, as well as all company-initiated contacts including promotional offers, letters, calls, and personal visits. Moreover, the database includes all other available information about each customer including such things as age, income, presence of children, home ownership, pets, hobbies, and sports interests. On the business side, the database includes company size by employees and revenue *standard industry codes* (SICs) that define business types plus extensive data such as buying behavior by individual and by site.

When we talk about building relationships with customers, it is important to remember that good relationships are built on trust. If your customer file cannot give you enough information about your customer to assure the fact that the information you will provide through your CRM efforts is of real value, you will not build that trust—hence the importance of the database, the master tool.

To build the customer database, we have to capture the information from the customer. Capturing customer information is the foundation of a CRM program. The capturing process is not always easy and must be accomplished with great customer care and understanding.

For a discussion of the capture process, I went to an expert. As senior implementation analyst for STS Systems United Kingdom, Tanya Bowen has helped companies large and small develop effective customer information capture strategies. She started by reminding me that, in addition to the questions of what to capture and what technology to use, there are two critical issues to address when developing a data capture strategy: ensuring employee acceptance and implementation and explaining data capture to the customer.

Tanya believes data capture can spell the success or failure of any Customer Relationship Management program: "It either improves customer relationships or destroys them." To improve customer relationships and not harm them, she gives us this advice:

> A CRM program must be communicated properly, and not as an intrusive data capture effort. The most personal way to communicate a customer-focused strategy is through the company representatives who meet the customer face to face. And you must ensure that these representatives are as convinced of your company's dedication to excellent customer service as you want your customer to be.
>
> CRM training is a critical step, and refresher courses are essential to your program if technology is involved, if the program changes, if temporary staff are hired, or whenever there is staff turnover. In all cases the following recommendations apply: Overall company and individual representative capture rates should be measured and reported, incentives should be considered, and data capture rates should be addressed during salary reviews and included in individual job descriptions. As well, one person at the head office should be responsible for resolving all CRM issues.
>
> Convincing all company representatives that data capture is important can be challenging. However, once everyone is convinced, customers are more easily recruited. It is important to be honest and informative with customers and with your company representatives about how customer information will be used. This is not only desirable; in many lands it is the law. This means that all company representatives should be aware of data protection issues and that CRM literature should include customer rights and how information will be used.
>
> Explaining how the information will better serve the customer is paramount to the success of a CRM program. Asking for personal or business information can be a delicate situation. Counter this by placing emphasis on the program's benefits for the customer. Company representatives must be sufficiently well informed with up-to-date information to be able to explain quickly how the pro-

gram benefits the customer, how it works, and why the company is introducing this initiative.

Remember, data capture is just the start. Program benefits should be reinforced beyond the sign-up phase to build the customer relationship. Each subsequent communication should reiterate program objectives and thank the customer.

Finally, remember the process of capturing customer information serves only one objective: the creation of a good CRM program that encourages existing customers to keep coming back and give you the biggest share of their spending to your category. The integrity of the data becomes a critical issue.

Most data, whether coming from old or new systems, are not fit for use in an analytical database. Seventy to 80 percent of the cost of operating a data warehouse is in extracting and transforming operational data for decision-making use.

All of this business intelligence must be acquired, stored, and accessed in some form often referred to as a *data warehouse*. The development of the data warehouse requires a data model—the tool needed to bring the data complexities under control. Like an architect's blueprint, the *data model* defines the structure of the warehouse. It defines the written plan for the database project, lays out a road map for how information will be organized and deployed, and defines how the data will be restructured in order to load them into an analytical database.

You will hear the terms *data warehouse* and *datamart* often used interchangeably. There is a difference, and it is covered in some detail in my book *The New Rules of Marketing*. To simplify it for our purposes here, a data warehouse is established by a process of assembling disparate data from all over the company, transforming it to a consistent state for business decision making, and empowering users by providing them with access to this information from multiple applications. The true data warehouse is an operational tool serving all areas of the business. Because it serves all functions within the company, it is often referred to as the *enterprise data warehouse*.

A datamart, on the other hand, is simply a subset of the data warehouse. A marketing datamart is specifically designed to create a "view" of customers to meet the detailed needs of the marketing function. The enterprise data warehouse is fine for data acquisition and storage but often cumbersome in providing easy access to the customer information. Since it is the access functionality and reporting capabilities that empower the marketer, winners need a tool that will provide quick answers to the marketing end users as simply and inexpensively as possible. The marketing datamart, usually with a desktop query tool right at the hands of the marketing team, fulfills that requirement.

Today "right at the hands of the marketing team" means just that—the query tool is on a PC or even a laptop. The day of the mainframe trying to act like an efficient query tool is past. With the geometric advancement in PC technology, coupled with greater data processing capacity at lower cost, a laptop with 5-gig hard drive can store a database in excess of 10 million names, addresses, data, and indexes. Related applications can now be performed on a laptop such as address standardization and zip-coding with a processing rate in excess of 2 million records per hour. This performance exceeds the rate that can be achieved on many mainframes. Soon palm-sized computers will be able to store hundreds of millions of names and addresses with hundreds to thousands of specific data attributes. Response time for complex queries will take less time than it takes to read this sentence.[1]

So now we have a query tool on the marketer's desktop, and soon a palm-sized computer that will do the job, but what will we want to ask of the customer file? What are some of the traditional tools that will still be important for CRM?

Some of the most critical tools are the same ones we used way back in the old days of direct marketing: *recency, frequency, and monetary* (RFM); cross-sell; and demographic and lifestyle append and modeling. These are simple indices, but they are still powerful tools. Most were developed years ago by some of the best direct marketing pros. We just use them a bit differently for CRM:

Recency: When the customer last purchased something from your company (a big measure of retention)

Frequency: The number of purchases the customer made from your company within a time frame specified by your company

Monetary: The amount the customer spent on purchases from your company, again within the time frame specified by your company

Demographic and lifestyle append: Other information your company has about the customer other than purchase transactions—data enhancements obtained from surveying actual customers, from marketing partners with whom your company shares data, or from external compilers—including the customer's age, income, number and ages of children, interests, and hobbies

Modeling: The weight of the stored variables in predicting the customer's profitability

Don Hinman is a group leader responsible for assembling Acxiom Corporation's consumer and business data, including the *InfoBase* file, one of the largest and most complete compilations of individual customer demographic and lifestyle data in existence. He makes the case for promotional use of appended data by showing that modeling behavioral information with transaction information can increase response in the top customer decile 4 times better than average and in the top four deciles, 2.5 times better, an incremental improvement over models using transaction data alone.

He suggests three scenarios for promotional use of behavioral data: *customer acquisition* where the appended data can be used to create in-the-mail savings and better response, *customer retention* where the data can be used to identify individuals at risk of attrition, and *share of wallet* where the data can be used to help companies up-sell specific customers for added profit.[2]

The uses of customer demographic and lifestyle data are a bit different for CRM. Here we use the behavioral knowledge to gain a better understanding of what a customer will value about a relationship with our company, which of our core products or services or benefits will have the most value, and why these benefits are important to the individual.

An example of the use of some of these traditional tools for CRM can be found in the Sears Best Customer program. When Sears first decided to recognize its best customers and try to improve the management of the customer relationship process, they looked for ways to select the most profitable target segments and chose three of the most basic tools. To qualify for Best Customer status customers had to have spent more than $1000 annually (monetary), had to have shopped in at least four merchandise categories (cross-sell), and had to have come into the store more than six times a year (frequency).

To start the CRM program, Sears sent each of these special customers a small 3M strip to attach to their charge cards. The message on the strip was "Sears Best Customer." Then Sears offered these folks things like priority repair service and priority installation on some equipment, special zero percent finance offers, free specialty catalogs, private sales events, and money-saving certificates.

They originally targeted this group for four mailings a year. However, the success of the program soon led to monthly mailings. Al Malony, who developed the original Best Customer program for Sears, says, "The more you communicate in the right manner, consistently and meaningfully, the better the program works." But what does communication in the "right manner, consistently, and meaningfully" really mean? There are differences of opinion.

One well-known CRM advisor has been quoted as saying that Sears needs to do more than offer these soft benefits to lock in best customers and drive share of customer among these superbest customers who can spend well above the $1000-a-year qualifying level. What he is saying, of course, is that Sears must offer discounts or other financial incentives to make the program work. This consultant still doesn't understand true CRM. The customer wants more than discounts. Discounts don't build loyalty. Customer loyalty is something you can't buy.

Al Malony shared with me some of the research Sears developed to validate the program. Customers told Sears that the benefit they valued most—beyond the zero financing offers and the notices of special sales and the discount certificates—was the personal recognition. They loved it when a sales associate noticed the Best Customer sticker on their charge card and called over the store manager to meet this "VIP." All of this is part of something we will cover in depth in a later chapter, that is, the importance of dialog with the customer.

Because Sears considers the maintenance of ongoing dialog so critical to its mission of customer retention, it has incorporated customer-satisfaction scores in its performance measures. Customer performance measures are now weighted as heavily as traditional financial measures in determining senior executives' compensation packages. Additionally, customer-satisfaction scores are being used in the field as a basis for pay at both the manager and sales associate level. Improved customer satisfaction is being used as a justification for variable incentive pay for hourly associates in close to 50 locations.[3]

In July 1999 Sears introduced a new Premier credit card for customers who had spent $600 or more in the preceding 12 months on their Sears credit card, a program that involved about 11 million accounts out of a total of 60 million. The new card offers priority for in-home service calls, special preview shopping days before key sales, and what Sears describes as "exclusive discounts." They believe the distinctive blue and gold Premier card will differentiate Sears' best customers to a greater degree. The objective here may not have as much to do with CRM as it does with the need for credit card income. In the second quarter of 1999, Sears' retail store operating income dropped 13.1 percent with two-thirds of profits coming from its card program.

RFM and cross-selling still work for CRM as they have always worked for direct marketing, but they are still only tools. We will use them more for the measurement of ROI than for promotion segmentation.

Long-term sales and profit growth should be the goal of all CRM activities. The old mass-media mentality too often looks at the fast nickel. CRM begins with the search for the slow dime.

As we alluded to earlier, if you compare the construction of a CRM program to the building of a house, these tools all help develop the blueprints that will guide the builder.

10
CHAPTER

The CRM Blueprint

Now that we have the working
drawings, how do we build
the house?

The database tool helped us develop the working drawings that give
us the construction details. The important customer data—recency,
frequency, monetary, demographic, and lifestyle append—are all
there on the blueprints. Now we have to build the house or, in our
case, the customer relationship. What does the builder need?

Many builders starting out to construct the Customer
Relationship Management program rush to focus on the technology they will develop to warehouse and query the data. The technology is important, but more and better technology does not necessarily help to build a better house or lead to increased value and
ROI for CRM.

David Cameron is the director of product integration for new
and emerging markets at Harte-Hanks Data Technologies. In that
role he is an expert and has a vested interest in the technology of
database marketing. Nonetheless, he is the first to counsel for shift-

ing the emphasis away from a technology-centric view, which unnecessarily narrows the initial framework for evaluating options and making intelligent business decisions. He says:

> To begin, you must focus on where the real value is in database marketing [CRM]. The real value is not in the data. Actually, large quantities of data can remove value from database marketing by making the exercise confusing and complex. To be valuable, data must be turned into marketing [customer] information. It must be transformed from operational bits and bytes into the information marketers need in segmentation, promotion, and analysis. A data warehouse is just that—a large repository of data. In and of itself, this large collection of data provides only potential value and is useless.[1]

This brings us back to our discussion of the "data warehouse" versus the "datamart." The data warehouse is an operational tool serving all areas of the business, but, as David says, in and of itself it is useless for the marketer and useless for the CRM program construct. The datamart begins to provide the view of customers that turns the data into useful marketing information.

So where does the real value come from? David reminds us, "Value is your customer's value to your organization and your organization's value to the customer. The real value lies in how these pieces are put together and lies beyond the tools themselves and instead in how these tools are used to create applications."

Applications is the keyword. Operational data warehouses do not always support customer-focused applications due to their organization around accounts and sales. Building a data warehouse does not provide applications, only a potential foundation for applications.

The creation of applications requires people, and the applications we need for productive CRM require specific types of people. When I asked Arthur Hughes about this, he said, "Go back and read my book again [*Strategic Data Base Marketing*]. I cover that on page 15." I did. He was right on target and was kind enough to let me share his exact words:

Database marketing [CRM] involves two very different types of professionals:

Constructors: People who know about computers and software; who understand merge/purge, postal presort, segmentation, data enhancement, coding, modeling and profiling. These people are fascinated with personal computers, cross-tabs, relational databases, and data management. You really can't do database marketing unless somebody understands these things.

Creators: People who understand the motivation of customers and how to use a database to build relationships with them, leading to increased loyalty and repeat sales. These people are fascinated with the strategy and tactics of database marketing; learning about customer lifetime value; recency, frequency, monetary (RFM) analysis; affinity tables; and attrition analysis. They come up with the great ideas that create profits. You really can't be successful at database marketing unless you have at least one very capable creator who has authority and a long-term budget.

Both of these professional types must understand the data needed for successful database marketing and the objectives of the program.

Over the years I have seen many companies make the decision to invest in CRM without making the investment in people. In too many cases they have spent their money to acquire the best possible software only to hand it off to untrained assistants in the advertising department. Without the professional "constructors," and "creators" their CRM projects never got off the ground.

What we are beginning to see emerge is a new breed of technology executives some are calling *business technologists*—technology staffers with both business and technology skills, able to communicate with nontechnologists and thoroughly versed in the businesses in which they work.

David Foote, a recognized management consultant, predicts that "7 to 10 years from now there will be no information technology organization as we know it today." Instead of units composed of technologists, there will be teams led by MBA types who stand at the juncture of business and information technology (IT).[2]

Perhaps the lack of this special talent is the reason so many companies spending millions of dollars a year collecting information on customers are not taking advantage of the data they collect, as reported in the Northwestern University study we discussed in Chapter 7.

I suspect Don Schultz might have had this in mind when he pointed out that even where research and data collected tell a company about the likes and dislikes of a particular customer, a good percentage of companies don't take advantage of the data they collect because "analysts and technologists have driven the business decisions."

Therefore, to turn the blueprint into a real house, the builder needs the professionals Arthur Hughes describes—professionals who understand your customer's value to your company and your company's value to your customer. But Hughes reminds us of three other things that will be critical to the builder's success: authority, long-term budget, and objectives.

It always starts with authority. I have seen many potentially successful CRM professionals—both constructors and creators— fail for lack of authority that comes from a real corporate commitment to the project. I have also seen outstanding success produced by companies where the corporate commitment was so overpowering that authority never came into question—one of the very best of which is Boots the Chemists, the 1300-store pharmacy chain in the United Kingdom, a true CRM winner.

The Boots story is so outstanding, it deserves a full telling, which you can read in Chapter 24. For our purposes here I will tell this one part of the story.

After hearing the details of Boots' outstanding success with CRM, I said to Crawford Davidson, head of Advantage Card for Boots, "To have accomplished so much, to be this far ahead of

almost all others I have seen in truly managing customer relationships, you must have had some serious commitment, support, and
authority from senior management. How important is that?"

His quick answer, "Totally!"

To underscore the top management commitment to his CRM
efforts, he apologized for cutting our meeting a bit short, explaining that the chairman of this 3 billion pounds sterling company
was *coming to his office* that very afternoon for his *regular review*
of the program.

Without any question the number 1 reason for the overwhelming success of this program is the authority that comes from
this company-wide dedication and commitment. The second reason
for Boots' success is their long-term budget view. It took a leap of
faith for Boots' management to commit $30 million to a program
that they knew would take time to return a profit on the investment.
Go back and reread Chapter 7.

Finally, it all comes down to establishing the important objectives before any money is allocated—before any investment is made.

The team at Boots established very specific objectives and
thoroughly tested the program before they spent 2 pence on a
launch. But we'll save those details for Chapter 24 and wrap up this
review of the role of the builder with this thought: When you think
about the builder's needs, remember that technology is important,
but more and better technology does not necessarily lead to
increased value and ROI for CRM. It all depends on people, authority, long-term budgets to stay the course, and objectives. With those
basics assured, what else does the builder need? Proper tools to
communicate effectively with customers. These, as we have said, go
far beyond the mass-media hammer, and some are still new to us.

11

But What Is It Good For?

The World Wide Web as a tool for CRM marketers

One of the new, and some say most powerful, communication tools that calls for priority recognition is the Internet. George Wiedemann, chairman of the Direct Marketing Association Board, calls it the single most important development for marketers since the U.S. Postal Service. One writer has called it the "ultimate take-out menu and the ultimate focus group." CRM marketers understand its power.

In 1943 Thomas Watson, then chairman of IBM, said, "I think there is a world market for maybe five computers."

In 1968 an engineer at the Advanced Computing Systems Division of IBM looked at the first computer chip and said, "But what is it good for?"

In 1977 Ken Olson, president, chairman, and founder of Digital Equipment Corp., said, "There is no reason anyone would want a computer in their home."

Now, to quote *Time* magazine, "Two years ago, conventional wisdom still derided the World Wide Web as an amusing toy with no practical application. No more. With striking speed the business that Yahoo! has been pioneering has grown into nothing less than a new economic order, a Net Economy!"[1]

The Internet is a place where companies can send customers targeted online communications, either as a Web page in HTML form, streaming media, or personalized e-mail. Customers can have their own personal Web site with channels they choose. The Internet is the most powerful medium of the early twenty-first century. The power will be realized when companies learn to link knowledge with content.

1-800 Flowers founder and president, Jim McCann, says, "The Internet is going to make everybody a relationship marketer, or at least those that survive and prosper."[2]

The Internet has developed with more speed than any previous communication technology. It took 35 years for radio to reach 50 million listeners and television 13 years to reach that number. It has taken the Internet only 4 years. Now seven people gain Internet access every second, and e-mail messages now outnumber regular mail by nearly 10 to 1.

Forty-one percent of U.S. households own a PC, and online use is surging.[3] And think about the prediction that 75 percent of all teens and 47 percent of children ages 2 to 12 are expected to be online by 2002. Most of the world's workforce now uses electronic mail every day. Coming next is the introduction of the sub $1000 PC and the Palm Pilot that will connect to the Internet and will put online access within reach of a new generation and income level of consumers.

In 1993 there were 3 million people on the Internet. In 1999 that number reached 200 million people worldwide. For the year 2002 the prediction is 477 million. Internet users now account for roughly 8 percent of annual U.S. electricity consumption, and it is predicted that in 20 years Internet use could soak up as much as 50 percent of the nation's power.[4]

The Gartner Group predicted that by the year 2000 online consumer sales will reach $20 billion, an increase of 233 percent over 1998's estimated $6.1 billion. Business-to-business sales will grow even faster, from 1998's $15.6 million to $175 million by 2000.

These predictions may prove to be conservative. Online purchasing increased by 34 percent just from April to August 1998. Sixty-three percent of Internet-using survey respondents had made a purchase in the preceding 90 days, up from 47 percent in April. Another 80 percent said they had shopped online in the preceding month.[5] On Saturday, October 17, 1998, Home Shopping Network recorded its largest day in the company's history, $24.1 million, an increase of 50 percent over the company's previous sales record. Sales included more than 13,000 Intel Pentium II 350-megahertz PCs and 12,000 sets of satin pajamas.

December 7 through 13, 1998, marked the biggest shopping week ever for the Web, $494 million. At the start of 1999, 84 percent of catalogers were online with 56 percent conducting real-time electronic sales.

A Jupiter Communications study in September 1999 predicted that top Internet sites would face a barrage of 60,000 transactions a day in November and December, double that of the 1998 holiday season.[6]

The greatest irony to me is Lehman's Non-Electric Catalog (www.lehman.com), the quaintly designed site that serves the Amish population's unique technology needs. The Y2K fear among technophiles and others that all electricity will fail at the millennium has produced such a demand for Lehman's wood stoves, lanterns, and cast-iron cook stoves that they now have an unusual shipping backlog.[7]

Wall Street decided 1998 was the year the Internet came of age. The stock market value of America Online soared to $40 billion, up from less than $10 billion the prior year, and became bigger than Hewlett-Packard, Oracle, Xerox, or Boeing. The stock of Amazon.com was worth more than the $22 billion value of all U.S. book sales in 1998. On December 28, 1998, the Internet as an investment tool of choice led Charles Schwab & Co., the nation's largest discount broker, to surpass Wall Street giant Merrill Lynch & Co. in market value. Later in 1999 we saw many of these stock values come down as these e-commerce firms continued to lose money, but the interest in these companies continues.

An average day sees 1.5 million pages added to the World Wide Web. In mid-1998 it was estimated that there were 20 million content areas, defined as top-level pages of sites, individual home pages, and subsections of corporate Web sites.[8] There is no question we are in the early turbulent days of a transformation of marketing and commerce.

Through all of this rapacious growth, there are some who suspect e-commerce is being oversold. Stephen Roach, chief global economist at Morgan Stanley Dean Witter, says, "It's growing rapidly but I question if it'll ever be big." He notes that e-commerce is no more than 1 percent of the U.S. $8.5 trillion economy; in fact, consumer online sales now account for only 0.2 percent of total retail.[9]

So with 150 million people on the Internet and online sales only 0.2 percent of total retail, what *is* it good for? It's nice that the complex, proprietary database systems that control the world's airline reservations systems are available online and free, but do you really want to do your own travel planning?

We're learning that the Web has enormous power to drive sales in traditional channels. Almost half of consumers with Internet access do research online, then buy products by fax or telephone. Sixty-four percent research products or services and later buy them through traditional channels. Stephanie Shern, vice chair, industry services, Ernst & Young, says, "The Internet is a shopping tool that fills the role of the knowledgeable salesperson consumers need but usually can't find. The Internet appears to be accelerating purchase decisions. The ability to shop, research, and view potential purchases on the Web is a potent weapon in the hands of shoppers."[10]

Steve Case, chairman of America Online, says, "It's not about technology but about what it does for people."[11]

What *is* it good for? What can it do for people, and how are winners making use of the Internet to develop a strong customer base, manage customer relationships, and grow sales? Not by using it for faster, cheaper, better sell, sell, sell. The Internet gives people a tool that allows them to identify themselves to businesses they want to do business with. It is the most powerful means of communication ever developed.

Case in point: Jesse Ventura, the new governor of Minnesota. All political candidates have Web sites today, but most fill them with a Xeroxed copy of national committee talking points. Ventura talked straight on the Net and issued a challenge to the nonvoters and the younger audience. His campaign established a statewide network of supporters through e-mail, Internet news groups, bulletin boards, and chat rooms. One expert called the Internet "the nervous system of Ventura's campaign." One result was an explosion in the number of young people voting. He asked for voter turnout and he got it—61 percent, the highest in the nation, which saw a turnout of only 37 percent for that election.

If e-mail, news groups, bulletin boards, and chat rooms can promote a governor to election, think what the Internet can do to foster the important dialog between companies and their customers that is a strength of Customer Relationship Management.

Patricia Seybold, CEO, The Patricia Seybold Group, worldwide strategic e-business technology consulting and information services firm and author of *Customers.com: How to Create a Profitable Business Strategy for the Internet and Beyond* says in her book:

> All of the electronic business technologies mentioned in this book—
> the Web, integrated voice response (IVR) systems, kiosks, e-mail,
> hand-held digital appliances, cell phones, and "smart" call centers—

are customer-facing technologies. They're new electronic channels through which customers can now interact with your firm. One of the wonderful advantages of thinking about your business freshly with these new technology assists in mind is that it requires you to do something you should have done long ago: Redesign your company from the customer's point of view.[12]

Once you begin to experiment with a customer-facing Web site, you'll discover that customers will tell you exactly what they want and need with great precision. And you'll probably learn, to your dismay, that in order to really streamline tasks from the customer's point of view, you'll have to do major rework on your existing enterprise systems and business processes. Once customers begin interacting with you via the Web, your company is left standing naked in front of its customers. Every wrinkle shows; every blemish spoils the customer's ability to help herself to information and transactions.[13]

The competitive imperative of making it easy for customers to do business with you 24 hours a day across a variety of channels of interaction will cause you to streamline most of your behind-the-scenes operations.[14]

Cisco Systems, the multi-billion-dollar leader in networking products for the Internet, is one winner that understands customer-facing infrastructure and making it easier for customers to do business with you. The Cisco Connection Online (CCO) is a 24-hour customer service and technical support resource developed by Cisco with the primary focus of deepening relationships with existing customers.

Outsiders can't browse the site, even to buy. Online browsers must be existing customers, and they are able to check order status, get pricing or product information, review contracts, register for seminars, and download software upgrades. Cisco even e-mails information about software bugs to CCO customers within 24 hours of their discovery.

In May 1998 National Semiconductor launched 50 private Web sites to address the particular needs and priorities of its most important clients by providing customized messages on features and proprietary information that will enhance customer relationships. At the time of the announcement, the company said it hoped to have as many as 200 private sites up and running by the end of the year.

Managing customer relations on the Web means caring enough about the customer to react in real time. For some companies that has become a problem as their e-mail traffic has grown.

The fact is that e-mail is now the single most frequently used capability of the Internet. Twenty-six years ago, the first e-mail was sent via ARPANet, the Internet's precursor. Now e-mail serves as a company's lifeline to its customers, and it is the first service customers want from their Internet service provider.

Yet a study by Jupiter Communications says many Web sites fail at customer service. The report, focusing on 125 top-ranked sites, found that 42 percent either took longer than five days to reply to customers' e-mail queries, never replied, or were not accessible by e-mail. A Jupiter spokesperson commented, "Companies that delay responses to user questions instantly lose a significant degree of credibility and user loyalty, and not responding perpetuates the consumer notion that using the Web site is not a reliable method of doing business with that company."[15]

Omaha Steaks understands this. Stephanie Healy, who oversees the company's Web site and online storefronts, says, "Our electronic media philosophy is to take customer service and customer responsiveness to new heights. Online inquiries are handled with service equal to or faster than other channels. Our Web site and e-mail base provide an almost instant communications channel and allow us to build relationships and offer news and information to our electronic shoppers."[16]

Ernst & Young sums up its special report with this confirma-
tion of the importance of the Web:

> Technology has long possessed the ability to change the world. The
> Internet is set to unleash the most powerful transformation yet.
>
> Why? Because it gives business the ability to have a dialog
> with individuals. The Net helps us understand their wants and needs.
> It minimizes the sacrifices consumers have to make to buy products
> and services. The Web offers consumers what they want, the way
> they want it, in a way that is unique to each person.[17]

Using the Internet to establish a dialog with individuals is
what it is all about. *Dialog* means a lot more than just talking to the
customer based on the knowledge in a database. The customer is
now beginning to say, "Stop relying on information about me and
start paying attention to information from me." Customers will give
you information about themselves in exchange for specific services
rendered, but don't ask until you have built a trusted relationship,
and never ask for the same information more than once. The important thing is that once customers have invested their time in giving
you their profile information, it is unlikely they will go to a competitor to start all over again.

The Peppers & Rogers Group, in their comprehensive report
"The State of One to One Online (Volume 1.0)," which profiled the
best 1to1 Web sites, speaks about gathering this kind of information
and developing this kind of loyalty:

> The top Web sites leverage the low cost of interacting with cus-
> tomers online to gather and store information on individual cus-
> tomers' tastes and preferences. The sites then use this information to
> make recommendations to a customer based on what other like-
> minded customers would want.
>
> One way to accomplish this is through a technique known as
> collaborative filtering, in which a site combines the preferences and
> interactions of similar users. A site compares your preferences with
> those of other customers in its database and then makes recommen-
> dations to you. The more it knows about a given customer, the more

useful its recommendations can be. Collaborative filtering can provide a powerful incentive for customers to be loyal, and it can help your firm increase the number and size of transactions a customer does with your firm.[18]

Customer relationships are what it is all about. You probably know that Dell is a winner, selling $6 million in computers and peripherals every day on the Web, but Dell is doing a lot more than selling. Michael Dell says, "You actually get to have a relationship with the customer. And that creates valuable information."[19]

Eddie Bauer redesigned its data warehouse for Customer Relationship Management in 1998 to bring into the customer information loop the important information coming in to its Web site. In the past the company could not recognize its customers across its retail, catalog, and Web site operations because the transaction information was housed in separate silos. Now, however, the new integrated customer information warehouse tracks customer behavior across all channels to allow Eddie Bauer to reflect customer preferences in its communications.

Merrill Lynch & Company now provides its financial professionals with a common Web-based enterprise desktop system, adding new services. Retail customers can call a broker for investment advice, and both customer and broker can view the same screens from their Web browsers as they work together—another case of a winner's embracing the Web to show that it can deliver even more value to its customers.

Even though we have this powerful new tool with which we can develop lasting relationships, companies are still rushing in to create those old points-based loyalty programs. Netcentives of San Francisco has created ClickRewards, which offers members points redeemable for frequent flyer miles, car and room rentals, and merchandise when they make purchases at Barnesandnoble.com, Skymall, and 1-800 Flowers. They claim to be giving away a million miles a day at member sites. San Francisco–based Intellipost, now part owned by Experian, asserts it has 500,000 members in private label retention programs where it rewards consumers for reading and responding to e-mail ads.

The secret of the Internet for Customer Relationship Management is not about opening an online store or trying to use the Web to sell cheaper, better, faster or about finding new ways to give points or discounts. It *is* about using this technology that has the power to change the world to build mutually profitable relationships and strengthen the bond between a business and its customers. That will require some fresh thinking.

Eugene Marlow, associate professor of business journalism at Baruch College, puts it this way:

> To advertise and market on the Net is not a matter of merely transplanting approaches that have worked in the traditional media. The inherent characteristics of the Internet do not provide a welcome mat for marketing and advertising strategies of the past. The Internet is not about mass marketing; it is heading solidly in the direction of one-to-one direct marketing. It is not about selling a can of soup, a lipstick, or a pair of pants through entertainment on radio or television; it is about providing *information that has unique value* about a can of soup, a lipstick, and a pair of pants.[20]

My friend Ray Jutkins, who has been evaluating Web sites for over two years, has learned some key marketing points for providing information on the Web. He says, "Forget all those bells and whistles on your pages; if you want to communicate something, make your pages download as quickly as possible. Too many Web sites get cute rather than offer straightforward navigational information. People want a road map, not a treasure hunt. Copy is not short or long. It is either interesting or not interesting to the reader. Content is king."[21]

DM News calls the information-rich Web sites "the next generation," citing tobacconist Nat Sherman. The new Sherman site employs a software package called *Constant Contact*, and its features are aimed at keeping customers coming back. Among the features are a gift reminder service, order-status-change alerts, a reorder reminder for regular cigar customers, and a service that remembers past orders to make reordering easier. The company sends online customers who regularly order a certain type of cigar an e-mail reminder with an embedded link to a Web page with an order form already filled out. Customers are also e-mailed specials based on personal preferences.[22]

Nat Sherman is making it difficult for customers to switch to another supplier because they would have to start from scratch to teach the new resource all the things they have already taught Nat Sherman because Nat Sherman is paying attention to information from them.

RS Components, a British industrial catalog and mail-order firm, understands how to create lasting customer relationships by providing information that has unique value. Their Web site remembers individual customers and provides a personal interface to more than 100,000 products. They found customers tended to focus on items in the catalog that were familiar—items they purchased regularly—sometimes not realizing that the catalog included items they purchased from other providers. With the personalized Web site, customer profiles are dynamically updated to reflect the input of new information, new purchases, or even the customer's behavior during a given session, which enables RS to display offers that are of greatest relevance to the individual customer.[23]

Jeff Bezos, the 34-year-old founder of Amazon.com, Inc., believes the Internet store of the future should be able to guess what he wants to buy before he knows himself. He wants to make Amazon.com that smart and that personal. "We can do that online," he says. "We can make it your store, tailor-made for *you*. If we have 4.5 million customers, we shouldn't have one store; we should have 4.5 million stores. The Internet can bring the personal touch back to commerce, only this time on a mass scale."[24]

When you sign on, if you have previously bought from Amazon, you will see a message at the top of the screen they call "Personal Recommendations." This is a real-time search of other customers' most recent purchases. I'm told it is changed every day for the entire customer file. Amazon has learned mass customization. With 64 percent of Amazon's sales in the third quarter of 1998 having come from repeat customers, it seems Jeff Bezos delivered as promised, and it is important to remember it took Bill Gates more than 10 years of work to make his first billion. Jeff Bezos has become worth over $5 billion in less than 4.

Providing information that has a unique value to customers based on information from them is a centerpiece of CRM, and it works especially well on the Web where customers are starting to expect this sort of follow-through. As Forrester Research notes, "Today, many companies are trying to generate revenues on the Internet, but they are not fulfilling the Internet self-service imperative. These offerings tend to cluster around one of the three elements of transactive content—transactions, interactivity, or content—instead of synthesizing them to create a rich experience."

One other Web expert summed this up: "We all understand that the Web is a two-way or multiway medium, but marketers rarely treat it as such. Rather than merely using it as an advertising medium, marketers need to use it as a feedback loop for delivering personal experience and trust to their customers—not mass-media messages."

The ultimate feedback loop is the online community. David Bohnett, founder and chairman of the online winner http://www.geocities.com, makes the point that online communities have been around longer than people realize, dating back almost to the time of the *Titanic*, when transatlantic telegraph operators exchanged messages about weather conditions, shipboard gossip, and how much to charge for a ship-to-shore message.

"Today," he says, "the wired and sophisticated consumer uses the Internet to chat with like-minded consumers about travel tips or air fare comparisons, but the key elements that make up online communities were no different in the time of the *Titanic* than they are today."[25]

GeoCities is now one of the five busiest sites on the Web, with more than 3.5 million active members and more than 19.5 million visitors a month, and Bohnett gives us the reasons: "Our members tell us that you stop being a nameless person in front of a monitor when you reach out and make connections with others in an online community. The online world becomes the much-talked-about global village."[26]

He lists four components of successful online communities:

1. A common interest where each group has gathered together in cyberspace to compare notes on a shared interest, hobby, or passion.

2. A member benefit, either economic or social.

3. Active participation showing that the group is functioning as a community. In the most successful communities, members take responsibility for the health and well-being of the community, making it viable through participation.

4. An economic infrastructure that sustains the growth and viability of the organization and some form of leadership and government to help the community develop.[27]

Feedback, interaction, and communication—the strengths of online communities—are the same strengths winners seek in developing online CRM.

The secret of CRM is to listen and learn, not tell and sell. CRM is about empowering and delighting and letting the customers feel as though their interaction with us is within their own control. Don't think about the Web visit. Think about the *visitor*—what the customer wants from you, what will make it easier for her to do business with you.

The Web gives consumers every opportunity to search out the lowest price for almost anything. If all you are going to do on the Internet is sell, sell, sell, you will always have to beat the lowest price out there. But Don Peppers suggests the Web also offers a wonderful opportunity: "Building one-to-one relationships to make it easier for your customers to do business with you and stay loyal might not be a license to charge whatever you want, but the deeper your relationship with a particular customer, the more margin protection you'll have with that customer."[28]

Garner Bornstein, president, generation.net, a Montreal specialist in Internet development, helps make our case:

> Don't think transactions; think relationships.
>
> Don't think ROI; think R&D.
>
> Don't think broadcasting; think narrowcasting.
>
> Think of the Internet as a salesperson in every home.

Garner sums up the message of this book: The building of customer relationships in this new electronic culture will call for a broad shift from database marketing to true CRM, a process of serving the customer in the customer's terms. That will mean using technology as a customer-facing infrastructure to make it easier for your customers to do business with you and to modify customer behavior over time by strengthening the bond between the customer and the company.

That will mean more than cheaper, better, faster, sell, sell, sell. It will mean finding new ways to simplify the Web dialog with customers.

12

CHAPTER

You've Got Mail

Using e-mail to integrate all aspects of customer communication

Customer Relationship Management depends heavily on direct mail for customer communication. How does that traditional form translate to the Web? I have heard it said that e-mail is direct mail on steroids. There are no minimums. You can turn it on or off quickly, and you can arrange for a message to be delivered on a particular day, even at a special time. By any standard, e-mail is a great opportunity for the CRM marketer.

Don Rappaport, CEO, American List Counsel, has said, "I generally have no idea what the next big thing is. When it comes to e-mail, however, all bets are off. This is a medium that delivers the goods. It also can be remarkably productive—not only in prospecting for new customers but in strengthening the relationships you already have with your existing customers. And we've only just begun to scratch the surface in terms of the marketing opportunities it represents."[1]

At its May 1999 luncheon, the Direct Marketing Club of New York heard some of the reasons e-mail marketing is working. Sarah Stambler, author of *Beyond Spam: E-Mail Marketing That Works* and president of TechProse, a company that designs and implements electronic marketing campaigns, said, "The enthusiasm for e-mail exists because it has a very high response rate, lower costs, it can be manipulated (sometimes within hours), and it has faster results." She added, "e-mail is the killer app on the Net and will soon be the killer marketing channel."

How big is big? In 1998 the number of e-mail accounts jumped 63 percent to 326 million worldwide. The average wired American sends or receives 26.4 e-mails a day. According to Forrester Research, more than 3 billion pieces of (opt-in) commercial e-mail messages were sent in 1997, and the number of pieces sent will grow to 250 billion by 2002. Compare that to 107 billion pieces of first-class mail delivered in 1998 at a cost of billions of dollars. In an informal survey of 30 mailers in 1998, half were already taking money from their postal budget for personalized e-mail. Eighty-three percent of respondents in a PriceWaterhouseCoopers study said e-mail is their primary reason for using the Internet.[2]

e-mail has changed how we communicate, whom we communicate with, and what we communicate about. It has forced business executives to learn to type and grandmothers to sign on to the Internet.

The more research we did on the use of e-mail for CRM, the more we realized that online Customer Relationship Management is a huge trial bubble at this time. We learned that 1998 was a year of testing and experimentation and that e-mail has, in the words of one columnist, gone from being a questionable practice to an accepted marketing medium, accepted not just by marketers but by the consumer as well. Consumer attitudes have changed dramatically, with e-mail becoming a welcomed addition to their electronic mailboxes because it provides them with benefits. That makes e-mail a natural tool for CRM.

In a recent study, 86 percent of respondents claimed to have sent e-mails to companies, almost a third sent 50 or more e-mails to companies in 1998, and 61 percent said they will probably send companies more e-mails in 1999.

To learn the true dimension of the e-mail opportunity for CRM, we went to an old friend who really understands customer management. Julia Adamsen built the original customer database for Pizza Hut, went on to develop an enterprise-wide consumer database for Pepsi, and then moved to develop the cutting-edge CRM program for Key Corp., a CRM leader in the banking industry.

I talked to her when she was vice president of marketing, for @ONCE, inc. @ONCE was founded in February 1998 as an outsource specialist for direct marketing and has become a leader in helping marketers develop and strengthen customer relations with online customer communication. Julia said, holding two fingers a few inches apart, "When we started into this, we thought the opportunity was this big." Spreading her arms wide she added, "When we really understood the potential and recognized the consumer dynamics, we realized it was this big."

She shared the results of a survey @ONCE conducted to gain insight into the e-mailing habits of e-mail users and to determine the appeal of various services, which could be offered by companies via e-mail. Here is some of what they learned:

Online consumers are seeking primarily personal, timely, and accurate communications.

Of the variety of services the responders were asked about, "being recognized as a preferred customer" is the service in which most respondents claimed to be interested (89 percent).

The majority of respondents (84 percent) claimed to be interested in a service that would provide customized e-mails, and many (76 percent) would like the e-mails to include new product information and availability. More than a third said they would like to receive customized e-mails on a weekly basis.

Some of the services respondents desired are especially interesting for CRM activities:

- Be recognized as a preferred customer
- Get concierge-level service online
- Move from e-mail interaction to voice interaction if the respondent needs help
- Be contacted by the company by phone immediately
- e-mail one company and have them change the respondent's address with the utility company, phone company, magazine companies, and bank
- Have a company service where online search experts help the respondent find information
- Receive a universal lifetime phone number and e-mail address
- Have online chats with company experts

With that dimension of customer enthusiasm, it is hard to imagine a more perfect medium for customer dialog. 1to1 communications are at last a practical reality. Julia Adamsen called this "customer intimacy on a mass scale." That intimacy can be accomplished, but the nature of e-mail is complex. Good content must include elements from all other forms of traditional communication channels—emotional, informative, interrogative, expressive, dynamic, multithreaded. Even with these demands the @ONCE folks have shown they can develop auto-response e-mails that provide what they call that "you've-been-heard" feeling. A service they call "email@once" is a comprehensive database and campaign management system that delivers appropriate trigger-based responses to online customers. Another called "priority@once" recognizes targeted customer segments, allowing the marketer to send special targeted messages to high-priority customers. These are the kinds of tools that will make e-mail powerful for the CRM marketer.

Julia reinforced all of our thoughts, as we elaborated in Chapter 3, about the necessity for every function within the company to be involved by reminding us that e-mail factors into the whole of the business system—brand-customer impact, quality-service levels, content-messages, marketing-revenues, and operations. Simultaneously, it integrates all aspects of the customer history and communication thread to customer tracking, measurement, and analysis systems.

e-mail provides four broad categories of value: information delivery, monetary-transaction value, right-of-access–privilege value (with personalized, dynamic pages), and service value (better service through knowledge).

The online value chain, Julia pointed out, requires a deep commitment of time, people, and follow-through: knowledgeable staff to answer e-mail, software to improve productivity, integration into the existing environment, intuitive responses and reporting, online marketing programs, online dialog services, and integration of many e-commerce applications.

@ONCE understands that intuitive e-mail communications can improve customer retention, increase sales, and fortify brand, but they caution those new to the medium to keep the communications simple at the start. They showed us some of the neat bells and whistles that can come later—things we had never heard of—like *streaming audio* and *streaming video* offered by RealNetworks. We learned that streaming is used to solve the time problem—that awful silence while you wait for a long attachment to download. With streaming, you can listen to the audio or view the video as it downloads. However, they advised us to worry first about making our e-mail personal, relevant, and always fresh from the customer's perspective. Worry about the super bells and whistles later.

e-mail brings one other magical marketing advantage: The incremental cost of contact online is near zero. Cost justification simplifies. With expensive terrestrial mail, we have learned to mail to only the top deciles of the customer file, realizing that while we would get some response from the lower deciles, they would rarely pay back the mailing cost. With incremental contact costs near zero, we can pick up the extra responses and still maintain the ROI. As one wag said, Pareto's 80:20 rule changes: to 95:40.

One of the most popular uses of e-mail today is surveys. They are quick. Typically an e-mail campaign generates 80 percent of its response in 36 hours. They are inexpensive and productive, and they are dynamic. Each answer can prompt a new and different question, putting the respondent into a new stream. As an example of their powerful productivity, Julia gave us this example.

Nintendo wanted to obtain an understanding of their Web customers so that they could deliver more relevant content. Because of the age of its audience, Nintendo proactively wanted parental approval before communicating with its 13-year-old and under user base. Nintendo players were e-mailed segmented messages based on their technology, screening players 13 years and under prior to survey participation. Once parental consent was given via e-mail, @ONCE then completed the survey with these players.

In under three weeks, @ONCE launched the Nintendo survey, captured data, built a dynamic e-marketing database, and managed the parental consent requisition process. Nintendo had a survey response rate of over 40 percent and built a knowledge database from which targeted CRM communications are now created.

Since I have opted in to the Purina ONE (pet food) e-mail site, I have received all kinds of news and information that help me keep my pet a bit healthier and happier. I value that. Because I have given Neiman Marcus permission to send me e-mail, I hear from them regularly with fashion tips, fun things like "Butterfly Games," and even a private evening of savings announced only to their e-mail opt-in customers. Purina and Neiman's are both CRM winners.

e-mail can get action. Harvard Business School Publishing uses its 90,000-name e-mail house list built through its e-mail newsletter to sell subscriptions to *Harvard Business Review* with an offer using QuickReply, a technology developed by E-Dialog, an e-mail communications firm. QuickReply enables customers to accept a subscription offer simply by replying to the e-mail message without going to the Web.

In a split test against fax and postal mail, QuickReply generated a 5000 percent ROI and a response rate four times that of fax and six times that of terrestrial mail.[3]

One of the biggest winners we found using e-mail for CRM is Bloomingdale's. Barbara Geiben, who as Bloomingdale's Internet strategy manager, told us the retailer had three objectives for its e-mail communication to customers:

1. Support existing stores by providing news and information to customers

2. Expand the "Bloomingdale's experience"—exposing more people to what customers tell them they do best at their world-famous 59th Street flagship store

3. Increase the frequency and quality of customer interactions

Features of the online communications include "New at Bloomingdale's," "First at Bloomingdale's," and "Only at Bloomingdale's." An "At Your Service" section allows customers to create personal profiles and express category interests: "Only tell me about these things," "e-mail me if you find this for me," or "Create a wish list for me." In a section called "Personal Dressing Room," the Bloomingdale's Web site reflects each customer's profile and interests and sends an e-mail to say that only those items that match are waiting in the customer's personal dressing room for inspection at the customer's convenience.

Another section, called "In Store," offers a home page for each Bloomingdale's store showing news of events, store hours, services, and directions to the store. Barbara Geiben called these "updated yellow pages." She added, "We don't want to just announce special events online; we want to *have* special events online. For example, the flagship store showed all of its famous 59th Street and Lexington Avenue holiday windows online in 1998, including a live Santa posing with customers both in the window and online."

A final section of the Bloomingdale's communication package is "About Us," giving updated store news with press releases, news about store involvement in community activities, and even career opportunities. The store has been taking job applications on the Web almost since its 1996 launch.

There are some caveats:

The biggest hurdle is finding enough e-mail addresses in your database to produce the critical mass required for success. Most companies have only a portion of their database coded with e-mail addresses, and of those coded, as many as 30 percent are returned as undeliverable because of keypunch errors. Now e-mail address data-append services are available that can take a standard mailing address and add the individual e-mail address, further increasing the e-mail marketing potential.

Sending e-mail in mass quantities can be troublesome if thousands of immediate replies overwhelm and overload your services. Experts advise time-releasing large quantities to assure a good customer experience.

Too many companies still come up short in the service department. Some winners are solving the problem by investing in expensive customer support e-mail management systems. Others are easing the pressure by building chat rooms where customers can get one-on-one help in real time from support staff.

AOL has created a customer service army of 6000 employees and contract workers who handle technical questions and inquiries. Companies large and small are turning to the outsource solution. Doug Hickey, CEO of Critical Path, a two-year-old e-mail service provider, says, "Companies aren't pulling out fiber to build their own networks and have their people handle a phone system. Why would you build a huge infrastructure to accomplish an e-mail function with limited personnel and knowledge?" The Gartner Group predicts 65 percent of midsized businesses will outsource some or all of their mailboxes by 2001.[4]

And outsourcing is not just for the giants. One young real estate agent has hired a live operator who answers homebuyers' questions from a text-based chat window that pops up on her site. The outsource service costs her $2.50 to $4 per session, and she says, "It's worth it. Real estate agents who don't do this will lose business."[5]

Be aware that how you handle your company's e-mail is a front-line reflection of your company. Your company won't be taken seriously if your people send e-mail with grammatical errors and typos.

We got our final bit of e-mail advice from Regina Brady, leader of interactive services at Acxiom Meh & Speh/Direct Media. She advises: "Don't think mass marketing. Think relevant marketing."

e-mail communications are relatively easy to design and launch. Mailings can be developed on the spur of the moment and in response to minute-by-minute changes in market conditions. As a consequence, marketers can now focus on proactive, targeted initiatives that were virtually impossible in the past.

Marketers are masters of marketing to large groups of people. Until recently, it was cost prohibitive to think of marketing to small groups or to one person at a time. But e-mail frees us from those preconceived notions. Marketers can think outside the box and think about micromarketing.

By integrating the message with a CRM strategy, any marketer can acquire and archive key marketing information about each and every message recipient. The marketer will learn which customers were most motivated by discounts, rebates, and special offers; which were most interested in hearing about the latest merchandise; and which customers did not respond at all to the message and probably need a different approach.

Although e-mail is a new and different medium, it plays by the old rules. The proven principles for direct marketing are also the keys to successful e-mail communications. Mailing the right message to the right list with the right creative approach is still of paramount importance. So too is efficient testing and the thorough analysis of results. In practical terms, therefore, successful e-mail marketing is founded on Web savvy plus direct marketing savvy.

Finally, Regina Brady advises, keep initial mailings short and to the point. Remember, recipients are reading these messages on their computer monitors. Be prepared to measure and capture results. Analyze the performance of each call to action in a mailing to determine what works and what doesn't, and archive that knowledge for future use.

And, echoing Julia Adamsen, Brady says, "Keep it simple. While it may look like 'plain vanilla' today, you should deliver text mail messages with embedded hot links because, right now, only about 30 percent of all e-mail recipients can read HTML mail."

Peppers & Rogers explain this process of embedding in an article they wrote about a firm that uses the process to learn more about customers. The firm sends e-mail containing a unique URL and PIN code for each recipient. The viewer responds by hitting the hyperlink, which opens a Web page with a personalized greeting. In addition to delivering the firm's message, the Web page asks a few survey questions designed to serve as the basis for the beginning of a relationship.[6]

If you are not reading Peppers & Rogers online newsletter, *INSIDE 1to1*, you should. I look forward to it every week as I open my e-mail. You can order your free subscription at http://www.1to1.com/articles/subscribe.html or by e-mailing subscribe@1to1.com.

We are living in exciting times. Internet usage is growing three to five times faster than the personal computer industry did in its early years, and that industry blasted into the stratosphere. Don't be afraid of it. Embrace it. As Julia Adamsen says, "It will be enormous, but it will really be enormous for the consumer."

13 CHAPTER

Should Telemarketing Be a Four-Letter Word?

Call centers and telemarketing

Telemarketing is growing. Telephone marketing expenditures in the United States grew from $40.8 billion in 1992 to $58.1 billion in 1997. The value of telephone marketing–driven sales grew from $293 billion to $424.5 billion and is projected to reach $666.3 billion by 2002. Telephone marketing employment has grown from just over 6 million people in 1992 to exceed 8 million in 1998, projected to almost 11 million people by 2002.

Is this good news or bad news?

Most people, thinking of those unwanted evening direct marketing calls, would probably call it bad news. I have a standard answer for those dinner hour calls. Before I listen to the sales pitch, I ask for the caller's home phone number. When I'm asked why I want that, I say I want to call *her* at home to interrupt her dinner. Even respecting the telemarketing process, I can't abide the invasion of privacy into my private time.

Should telemarketing be a four-letter word?

On the one hand, one might think so. Intrusive telemarketing is so pervasive that it has spawned a new business. For $3.95 a month, Ameritech will provide a service called "Privacy Manager." The system, known in telecommunications circles as *anonymous call rejection* (ACR), allows the phone line user to program the telephone switch to intercept unwanted calls rather than route them to the phone in normal fashion. The service will even play a recorded message informing the caller that telemarketing calls are not accepted and ask that the customer's name be added to the telemarketer's do-not-call list—a legally binding request.

Privacy Manager was introduced in Chicago and Detroit in September 1998, then progressively rolled out in all of Ameritech's five states—Illinois, Wisconsin, Michigan, Ohio, and Indiana. A company spokesperson said early tests of the Privacy Manager showed it to be the company's most popular service in more than a decade.

Five months after Ameritech's successful launch of Privacy Manager, US West introduced a similar product, No Solicitation, for the customers it serves in 11 western states.

However, not everyone wants anonymous call rejection. Telephone marketing has a positive side. There is a reason for all that growth in telephone marketing: It works.

One company that inadvertently got started in telemarketing attests to its success: "We had several salespeople who had worked for us for a long time, and they were getting older and having trouble traveling to different appointments," says Fred Kenner, president of Arrow-Magnolia, a distributor of chemical cleaning products. "They started making sales calls from the office, and we found that the success rate was the same over the telephone as it was in person, but now they were making four times as many calls. All of a sudden we had senior, aging salespeople producing more business than they had ever produced in their lives."[1]

But where does telephone marketing fit into the Customer Relationship Management process? It doesn't have to be intrusive. A call center can provide the best opportunity for creating dialog with customers, listening to customers, answering their questions, satisfying them, collecting valuable customer knowledge, building customer relationships and loyalty, and making additional sales.

Call centers are the next important step for marketers in customer service and CRM because every contact between the company and its customers is an important opportunity to collect valuable information, deliver value-added services, and extend the company's relationship with the customer. The American Telemarketing Association (ATA) recognized this in late 1998 by changing its name to the "American Teleservices Association." At the time its president of the board of directors, Gene Gray, said, "We selected a name that truly reflects the new diversity of our membership. ATA founders had a primary investment in outbound telemarketing. We now have an inclusive name that fully represents an industry involved in inbound and outbound sales and service. There are many companies with call centers that don't think of themselves as telemarketers. Many have call centers they use for customer service in a very professional way."[2]

One expert points out that, if designed with the customer in mind, most telemarketing programs will have no trouble gathering information on inbound calls that can be transformed into powerful database marketing information. She says, "The simple rule is that most consumers will answer a *few* questions if those questions are *relevant* to that particular transaction. Air New Zealand can ask if a consumer has a valid passport and will get a yes or no without the consumer blinking an eye. Princess Cruises can ask if they have ever taken a cruise before. Isuzu can ask when the consumer intends to purchase a new vehicle. But none will have success asking questions that are not relevant to their own transaction [relationship] with the customer."[3]

Author Jacques Werth believes that with the right "relationship inquiry" process, telephone dialog can build a *Relationship of Mutual Trust and Respect* (RMTR) that grows deeper with each contact. He says, "The RTMR enables both parties to be completely open and honest with each other. The bottom line for relationship marketing," he says, "is that a deep authentic relationship of the most meaningful kind can be initiated. True relationship marketing can build on a very strong foundation of Mutual Trust and Respect [on the phone]—immediately."[4]

In the *Harvard Business Review* study of customer relationships, one respondent complained, "Sure they can call me at dinner, but I can't reach them on the phone. They send me 100 pieces of mail a year, but I can't register one meaningful response with them."[5] Customers do have meaningful things to say to us, and they do want to talk to us. We must find new ways to listen by whatever means they use to contact us. It's part of the dialog that is critical for CRM, and the telephone is just the start. That takes us back to the Web.

Art Schoeller, an analyst at Gartner Group, says, "Although only about 10 percent of U.S. corporations are testing systems now, organizations that can't handle voice, e-mail, Web communications, and chat sessions on one system by 2001 will not be competitive."[6]

An efficient, integrated call center can provide long-term customer satisfaction and increased revenues. Al Subbloie, president and CEO of Information Management Associates, Inc., says, "To accommodate the needs of today's sophisticated consumers, the call center must become a 'customer interaction center,' supporting multiple channels of access and integrating with other departments within the company."[7] He addresses Art Schoeller's challenge, suggesting that a Web-based customer interaction system can deliver seamless integration of the Web call center applications, relational databases, and legacy system data to the call center agent, employee, or self-service customer. By providing access to the exact information needed, the agent can best respond to or fulfill a request. "It is a multimedia world," he says, "and customers are demanding to contact businesses on their own terms and timelines. Effective customer communication requires that businesses develop technological solutions that will interact with customers on their terms, will deliver the right end results and will keep customers returning time and again with additional business. This is no short order, but the technology is now out there to make this vision a reality."[8] What Al Subbloie describes is now called *real-time marketing*, the process that enables the marketer to determine appropriate action to take with individual customers through the use of technology. *Real time* means the shortest possible lapse between idea and action. Technology solutions sound easy, but it is important to remember technology is good only when it has a high impact on the customer. The customer doesn't really care about your back room.

While customers love toll-free customer service numbers and information-rich Web sites, they get frustrated with long waits on the phone and not being able to get the exact information they want on Web sites. To achieve real-time objectives, companies can no longer survive with customer information stored in separate departmental silos. Real-time CRM requires a global customer view with all customer information available to all of the company's representatives. A call center can't survive today if agents have to flip through 15 screens of data in a two-minute phone call.

Web-enabled call centers will help improve customer relationships by eliminating much of this frustration. Reps in Web-enabled call centers have the world at their fingertips. All applications on the desktop can be quickly accessed through a Web browser, giving reps a common desktop interface. A single unique data point, such as a phone number or an account number, can be entered to access all relevant data about a caller.[9]

Web-enabled call centers use what is called *Internet Protocol Telephony* (IP Telephony). Until now this protocol has been used mainly by hobbyists and Internet fanatics, but at the Call Center '99

Conference and Exposition, February 1999, in Dallas, a customer contact strategy integrating the telephone, Web, e-mail, and faxes was a recurring theme.

One expert explains, "The Web-to-phone interface works via a Web browser plug-in which can be downloaded from a Web site in minutes. A company with a Web site can distribute the plug-in on its home page for free. The plug-in is programmed to call fixed numbers as defined by the company. By clicking the plug-in button, users can connect to the company's staff or wherever the company wishes to route calls. The Web-to-phone interface gives both the company and the Web surfer what they really want—an interactive experience, in fact the first true interactive, real-time Internet experience."[10]

He gives this example:

> Perhaps a user browsing an online catalog is interested in placing an order for clothing. The user wants to know if a sweater comes in blue but cannot call the usual toll-free number because he or she has only one telephone line currently being used for the Internet connection. Typically, the person would either send a request for a callback by e-mail or disconnect the Internet connection and use the telephone. The Web-to-phone plug-in overcomes this barrier by opening up a separate channel for communication over the active Internet connection. After clicking the plug-in button, the call is routed over the Internet and through the telephony gateway into the company call center. The caller is given immediate access to the services needed, and the company gets one step closer to a sale.[11]

According to the Gartner Group, 35 percent of call center access will come from "nontraditional" electronic technology by the year 2000.

Selecting and implementing the right call center solution can be complicated. It may involve 6 to 10 interrelated technology components, integrated voice response systems, automated dialers, telephone switches, intelligent call routers—all, perhaps, coming from different vendors requiring new integration to link to each other and to existing data systems.

One integrated system is Customer Now, an enterprise-class Web-based sales and customer service software from SiteBridge Corporation that provides one-click access to a customer's past session transcripts and e-mail messages. It has the ability to automatically e-mail complete transcripts to customers at the end of sessions. The technology with open application-programming interfaces, ensures that any customer with any browser, hardware, or operating system can communicate with a live customer service representative.

Push-to-Talk technology from eFusion provides call centers a nice way to offer voice-enabled Web pages. Web shoppers can direct an immediate voice contact to call center agents without terminating their Internet session or waiting for a call back. A telephony application gateway works with the single phone line installed in most residences.

Using a combination of rich databases and Web browsers, reps can access needed information in seconds. Speed like this helps shorten the length of calls, thereby easing customer frustration and, not so incidentally, resulting in significant savings on long-distance costs and staffing.

More than that, real-time capability can turn selling into customer service by offering the customer something of real value in the customer's terms. If a customer calls her bank with a question, a real-time system develops dynamic customer scoring on the fly. While the agent answers the question—usually in less than a second—the system finds the special benefit or benefits most meaningful to the calling customer. As an example, once the original query is satisfied the agent can say, "I notice you have had $10,000 in your checking account for three months. If you had held that in one of our CDs you would have earned $125 in that time. May I transfer some of that money for you?" Or, if the agent sees several recent problem calls, she can refer back to those to make sure the customer is completely satisfied. Personalized real-time actions like these can often halt possible customer attrition. As an added benefit, successful real-time dialogs like this provide positive feedback for the call center agents.

Customers are always more satisfied when they have shorter wait times and can get answers faster or solve problems with a single call. Companies that don't have some form of IP telephony and can't handle voice, e-mail, Web communications, and chat sessions on one customer interaction system will fail to be competitive, perhaps even sooner than Mr. Schoeller's 2001.

Establishing a state-of-the-art call center is not a simple task. Those already involved can attest to the problems of employee turnover and the shortage of qualified labor. Add to that the capital cost of keeping up with new technologies, and many companies will shrink from the challenge. The good news is that there are many very qualified outsource options, and those call center outsourcers are transitioning into customer interaction centers developing offerings geared to specific industries. One recent study of the financial industry found that companies that fully outsourced their teleservice functions achieved a greater 10-year average return to investors, a higher average 10-year growth rate, and a larger average percentage change in annual earnings per share.[12] In Europe 50 percent of the call center market is represented by outsourced services, which are growing at 35 to 45 percent a year. And now there are some experts suggesting that major telecom carriers like AT&T, Ameritech, US West, MCI, or even British Telecom may soon get in the game.

This is not dream stuff. This is happening now. In the summer of 1998 the Thomas Cook Group launched Thomas Cook Global Services in the United Kingdom. The global service is very much a part of the company's CRM objective intended to simplify life for customers by offering a single toll-free number to track all services. That number and the Thomas Cook Web site funnel all service requests, from trip reservations to travelers' check orders, through one user call center.

The technology provides a unified view of customer accounts and pending queries whether they are via e-mail or telephone. The next step will be to turn each customer inquiry into an object that will be dropped into the Thomas Cook database. Agents will use Java-based clients to access the system.[13]

Mercedes Benz is on target to add new computer telephony (CTI) software for its European customer assistance center in the Netherlands in Maastricht. The new software will streamline customer communication in the new call center, which will serve as a central contact point for customers in 17 European countries.

The center provides customers with 24-hour service for all emergency calls, catalog requests, price inquiries, and other questions or complaints. With the new CTI software, Mercedes will be able to improve its Customer Relationship Management by delivering individual attention to each customer regardless of which medium is used—telephone, fax, postal mail, or e-mail. The full-featured call center is expected to be operational with about 500 customer service agents by 2000.[14]

Automakers seem to be leading the way. In 1998 Lexus implemented Clarify's FrontOffice integrated call center solution that allows each customer request to be handled from start to finish by the same call center agent with information at hand. Previously agents had to hang up with the customer, research files for information, then call the customer back. The Clarify system automatically routes each incoming call to the appropriate agent and creates a screen with the customer's name, account history, and all relevant information.

Lexus calls data from the calls "Voice of the Customer" data, and it is reviewed monthly by executive management to help the company improve its response time to new trends and customer issues.

Carroll Gordon, Lexus' customer satisfaction operations manager, says about the effort, "What differentiates us from the competition is service, the way we handle our customer relationships. We want to be sure their experience with Lexus as a company matches their experience with the car they buy." Lexus has been a leader at managing customer relationships since the launch of the first model.[15]

There is more to CRM on the telephone than just IP telephony and other high-tech tools. It's important to remember that what we are about is developing and managing *relationships*, strengthening the bond between the customer and the company, maximizing the value of the relationship to the customer. A human touch can be important.

While many companies are implementing customer service with automated answering systems, Sears Home Central is turning to the human touch for CRM. Live agents staff the nationwide number 1-800-4-My-Home, which supports Sears' repair business.

"We are in the service business and are trying to keep a very high touch component to everything we are doing," says Elaine Bolle, vice president of marketing and sales for the home services division of Sears. "We have a relationship and back it with our satisfaction guarantee. These people have a tie with Sears, and we build a two-way dialog. That's what is working to build this business."[16]

The company is marrying database information through call centers and retail to execute CRM with mail and inbound and outbound telephone campaigns. "We will be doing more and more work on relationship marketing because it is a significant and growing segment behind our efforts," Bolle says. She concludes, "This is truly an example of relationship marketing because people want to know who is coming into their home."[17]

Some marketers are finding good reasons to move their direct-mail CRM programs to the telephone. Atlanta and Winston-Salem–based Wachovia Bank moved its well-established direct-mail program for communicating with customers in order to obtain or seek even more customer feedback over the telephone.

"We didn't change the concept, we changed the methodology," said Fred Koehl, senior vice president and manager of market information. "We switched to the telephone because of the immediacy of it. We felt that in addition to obtaining the kind of information we were getting, it seemed that if issues needed to be addressed immediately, we would have the ability to do that." Koehl made the point that the callers try to make sure that they are not wasting customers' time, that they are asking the questions to help the bank serve them better. In most cases customers are more than willing to give their opinion because, as Koehl says, it is part of an ongoing relationship. To shorten the time of the calls without cutting down the amount of data they can collect, Wachovia rotates the questions. Because they are making 4000 calls a month, they are still able to get good numbers without burdening the customers by keeping them on the phone. Koehl gives the phone program high marks, saying, "I think there have been situations where our ability to be responsive has held onto a relationship."[18]

Managing customer relationships on the telephone is a two-way street, more than just outbound telemarketing. Companies have told me that when they first offered customers a toll-free number to call, they received more calls in the first few weeks than they had projected for the first year. While that suggests the call center can become a large expense item, the fact is that it usually becomes a profit center.

A recent study by consultant Booz, Allen, Hamilton found that cross-selling on inbound calls can lead to response rates three times higher than traditional outbound telemarketing, direct mail, or in the case of banks, branch visits. David Howe, vice president of Booz, Allen, sees three ways inbound calling is unique:

"The customer is calling the bank so they feel in control of the transaction. The bank is all they are thinking about at the moment, and they are ready to discuss banking issues. And the two-way communication allows the call center representative to learn something about the customer and maximize the relationship profitability of each call." Interestingly, Howe says, "The ones who are really leading edge have typically been at it for at least three years. This is something in which you won't become world class in a few months or even a year; it's an evolutionary process."[19]

Technology keeps changing our marketing world and our communication options. Up to now the technology architecture has dictated what tools individuals must use. That will change. Peter Keen, coeditor of the newsletter *You2Know*, suggests that whichever tools users prefer will soon dictate the architecture. "People like to talk," he says, and "voice is the medium of human exchange." The cell phone hit the 10-million-user mark faster than VCRs, PCs, or the Internet. The human voice, not the keyboard, will be the tool of choice, and companies will have to respond.[20]

David Bradshaw, senior analyst at Ovum, Inc., an independent analysis group, sums up the case for call centers: "Call centers are where corporations talk directly to their customers, discovering their requirements, persuading them to do business, and ensuring their demands are satisfied. Call centers also have a crucial advantage over self-service media—they allow corporations to be proactive in ways that would be rejected or ignored if self-service media were used."[21] So the new function of the call center is more than just telemarketing, it is an important part of establishing and maintaining a dialog with customers, a critical element of CRM.

The technology surge doesn't end with the cell phone or IP telephony. Even the print process is in revolution.

14

Things Gutenberg Never Dreamed Of

On-demand printing and digital prepress

The Internet, e-mail, and IP telephony are exciting, but some are saying the next killer application for Customer Relationship Management winners who want to communicate with customers one on one is digital color printing. Sometimes referred to as *print on demand*, digital color printing is the process of producing high-quality four-color printing directly from digital files without the creation of printing plates and with the capacity to reproduce up to 100 percent variable content.

Digital printing has revolutionized direct mail. It is now economical to print four-color direct-mail pieces that are completely tailored for each individual customer. Using this technique, companies can use detailed customer information to customize each direct-mail piece.

This technology can be employed to deliver personalized communications using varying levels of customization to create completely customized direct-mail pieces. This process incorporates selective customer and product information to create a true 1to1 document based on individual customer specifications. This means that a direct-mail piece can be created with specific messages, products, and offers for each customer. Each individually printed piece is uniquely personalized by varying the customer name, blocks of text, pictures, and/or the style of the design.

An additional capability is that these pieces can be produced in small quantities. The economics of digital printing enable a company to schedule the printing and delivery of each direct-mail piece when it becomes most relevant to the customer. As a result, these personalized communications are received by customers at their specific moment of interest.

Rab Govil who heads the industry spokesgroup, Print On Demand Initiative, says, "This process where each printed page is different, with the variations determined by relating print element options to customer information in a database linked to a digital engine, is driving sales, changing behavior, and building long-term relationships with customers."

Producing custom four-color, 1to1 messages is impractical using traditional offset printing methods. While prepress equipment has been getting better and faster, even the most advanced systems require a plate produced from either film or direct-to-plate technology. Since each new version of a document requires its own plate and the costly plates on the press must be changed for each new version, the cost to produce custom 1to1 messages has been prohibitive. With digital printing, however, creating a personalized version is easy if the proper systems are in place to make it happen right when it is needed.

For many of the details in this chapter I am indebted to James Morris-Lee whose advertising and public relations firm, The Morris-Lee Group, works with many organizations involved with digital and traditional printing and related technologies. He gave me this background.[1]

Digital printing is not really one process, but many. Its proper name is *digitalography*, which encompasses the multiple processes used in the growing array of digital equipment. Digital printing has been around for a while, but the recent addition of color capabilities has changed everything. When Indigo and Agfa announced the first commercially available color-capable variable-data printing presses at the International IPEX Graphic-Arts Exposition in Birmingham, England, in 1993, Morris-Lee says the process soon became the most written and talked about new product in the history of the printing industry. Today the speed of the front-end *raster image processors* (RIPs) is making possible the variable four-color printing of images and offers.

When the tools change, the rules change, and the development of digital printing has turned the printing world upside down, opening a whole new world of opportunities for CRM marketers. Here's how good it can get.

Novartis Seeds sells seeds that can cost up to $125 a bag and are purchased by farmers in quantities ranging from 5 to more than 1000 bags per farm. "Farmers are tough businessmen," says Jim Lewis, president of Relationship Marketing, Inc., the marketing agency for Novartis, "but they are fair. If they commit to a seed brand, they keep their word. That's why we have to build strong relationships. That's the key to our success."

Novartis builds its relationships with its base of farmers through its 3000 independent representatives and dealers, and these reps and dealers know their customer—what he plants, where he shops, the products he prefers and why, where he banks, his favorite sport, *and* the color and make of his tractor, red for International Harvester, green for John Deere.

Each season the reps and dealers send scanning sheets for their farmer customers to update this valuable information for Novartis. When the farmer returns these sheets, they are scanned within 48 hours of receipt, and thousands of personalized "product guides" are printed and sorted on an Agfa Chromapress digital printing system within days. The product groups offered are selected from 750 possible versions to be relevant to each individual farmer.

Using the additional information from the field, each mailer is customized to match each farm and farmer. A livestock farmer who uses green John Deere farming equipment gets a mailer with a cover showing a green John Deere tractor on a livestock farm, and the products featured are the types of products a livestock farmer in that specific farming community will be interested in purchasing. Response rates doubled expectations when this customization was first introduced, and dealers who participated in this program achieved a 21.7 percent increase in sales compared to 0.7 percent for those who did not.[2]

Results like this from database mining used to produce customized digital printing are not exceptional. The CAP Ventures Personalization Study looked at several key metrics to measure the effectiveness of personalization. Through effective database mining, they found that there was a 35 percent increase in response rates and a 25 percent improvement in average order size.[3] Also, according to CAP Ventures, the number of pages printed using digital color technologies grew by more than 100 percent in 1997, on track to meet a projected 1000 percent growth in the retail value of digital color pages from 1997 to 2000. One writer predicts that "with print vendors and their clients investing larger sums of money in digital printing, other marketers are going to have to get up to speed on digital output or be left behind."[4]

Digital printing fits in well with the Internet. Customers visiting an Internet site are able to specify exactly which products or services they are interested in, and on-demand printing makes it possible to produce and mail a personalized document for each customer. Progressive digital service providers are using the Internet to take in work and help their customers track jobs in progress.

Corporations of all sizes are using the Internet as a new way of disseminating information to customers.

With all this Internet activity, will printing become obsolete? Another CAP Ventures study in 1998 showed that print customers who use the Internet for marketing anticipate a 21 percent increase in direct-mail and personalized printing due to their presence on the Net.[5] With the Internet it is not that the volume of print will change but, as one writer said, the where, when, and how of print will be increasingly controlled by customers—making a strong case for CRM.

Examples of digital printing successes are plentiful. A European furniture company sends a customized follow-up mailer six months after a furniture sale showing only the pieces the customer did not buy accompanied by a discount coupon to encourage sales.

Crown Mercedes, an automobile dealer in Columbus, Ohio, uses digital printing to reach customers as their current lease nears expiration and they begin thinking about a new lease. "The project is designed to stimulate growth in the re-leasing market as well as hold on to market share," says Bill Black, director of marketing for Kreber, a company in Columbus, Ohio, offering turnkey solutions in the creation and printing of marketing materials for businesses nationwide.

The Mercedes mailer is printed digitally using Kreber's *SmartSeries*, a digital content management software system and an Indigo digital printing press. The campaign reaches customers as their leases approach expiration. Crown sends customers a self-mailer picturing the exact model of the car they leased. Other personalized elements include the customer's lease expiration date and the original salesperson's name and phone number. Mailings are sent 90 and 60 days prior to lease expiration.

KPN, the Netherlands-based telecommunications company that owns both the Dutch phone company and the Dutch Post mail system, has a service called "Toets 9290" (Dial 9290) which enables consumers to request information about products and services through an interactive voice response system and receive a customized catalog in the mail within 48 hours. The consumer receives a customized selection of articles, expert advice, manufacturer specifications, test reports, and dealer or supplier addresses. Information is always up to date as the information booklets are printed only after a request has been received. Customers are in control of the information they receive, and they love it!

With Toets 9290, when a customer requests information on electronics, the technology selects all the products and services that fit the customer's electronic profile. Then these valuable data are sent to a Xeikon printer, and the custom catalog is produced and delivered to Dutch Post for overnight or same-day mailing.

More than 3000 36-page books are produced each week. One-fifth of the Dutch population is picking up the phone to dial 9290, and response rates average 5 percent.

When K-Mart was ready to open its first New York City stores, they decided that their traditional opening campaign showing a blond soccer mom pushing an overflowing shopping cart to her car would have made no sense in Manhattan. Instead, for the New York City campaign, K-Mart used digital printing to show local neighborhood-specific graphics and copy for each store.

At Whirlpool Corp., inbound customer assistance telephone operators prescreen callers and gather information on the products a customer has expressed interest in. The operator can put together a custom brochure of up to seven digitized items to reflect the customer's interest. Uploads from Whirlpool's customer assistance center to the printer are made daily. The customized brochure—including appropriate products, closest dealer locations, a personalized letter from the operator, and a special number to call back—goes in the mail within 48 hours.[6]

Toys "R" Us uses digital production for traffic-builder postcards. Peggy Foxman, director of print production for the company, says, "Babies grow very rapidly. You want to mail offers appropriate for them every three months." This means having the flexibility to do short, seasonal runs and to track and coordinate mailing efforts as children move from Babies "R" Us to Kids "R" Us to Toys "R" Us.[7]

A toy retailer could even use digital printing to send parents personal wish list reminders "from Santa's Headquarters, North Pole," complete with color photos, text, and price for each toy the child has selected in the store's gift registry.

There is a lot more to this than just ink on paper. Digital printing facilitates us an entirely new method of reaching individual customers with messages that show companies understand their individual preferences or desires. Although the per-piece cost for customized printing is higher than traditional offset work, the potential for far greater impact and response gained can easily justify the expense. In fact, digital printing can often save money. Sending out Whirlpool's 8- to 10-page customized brochure is much cheaper than sending out the full Whirlpool catalog. Whirlpool reports a savings on mailing costs of between 25 and 50 percent.[8] Furthermore, digital printing can save time. One firm announced technical changes in its product after 300 pieces had already been printed. The printer made the changes, the client approved, and the presses were up and running again within 15 minutes. With an offset printing press, plate changes could easily have taken up to 24 hours—assuming press time was still available.[9]

According to recent studies, more than 90 percent of corporations' direct communications with customers is through documents, and the process of creation, design, document management, production, finishing, and distribution consume a significant and growing portion of corporate resources. Recent Datamation studies indicate that the creation, management, and production of documents account for up to 40 percent of a company's labor costs and up to 15 percent of its revenues—more than most firms spend on R&D.[10]

This is especially true for business-to-business marketers. Personalized documents at the consumer level seem, at first glance, to be the fastest route to widespread adoption of the digital printing technology, but there is even greater short-term opportunity in customizing and personalizing documents targeted at businesses. A business-to-business marketer has far fewer customers than a consumer marketer, which makes the low print quantities, enabled by on-demand printing, attractive. Because businesses buy products and services differently and in greater quantities than consumers, business sales have a much higher value by making increased per-piece printing costs quickly justified.

With digital printing and print-on-demand established and accepted as the most versatile and feature-rich imaging technology of the day, we can expect lots of changes. John Stuart, president and CEO of IKRON Office Solutions, believes the new technology will lead to more outsourcing. He says, "Companies considering outsourcing should step back and ask themselves, 'How are we doing things today?' If the answer is, 'The same way we were doing them five years ago'—and in a lot of cases this is the case—then by definition they are not doing them the most efficient way."[11]

Morris-Lee believes printing service providers will change as well. They will continue to provide traditional and on-demand printing, but many will be taking on new roles to serve the CRM marketer. They will become direct mail and database marketing consultants, data librarians, archivists, graphic designers, and advertising and fulfillment specialists to suit the needs of their clients.

Prepress shops are becoming digital printers, and some are even calling themselves "digital-asset managers" as much as "color houses." But general printing firms wishing to enter the dynamic digital market must also begin to understand the language of and many disciplines involved in the marketing process, just as creative people must now get to know the software that drives variable imaging.

Moreover, CRM winners will need to learn to develop a central content management system for all of a company's images, text, and pricing for distributing offers and other information to their customers over the Web, print, fax, kiosk, and so on. Retailers, catalogers, and corporations need to start thinking of their promotional information as a tangible asset that needs to be captured and managed. The new paradigm of state-of-the-art advertisers will be: organize, author, manage, publish.

Once the promotional information is organized, it can be published for any event, to any media—print, Internet, e-mail. In addition, any good asset management system will tie together merchandising and advertising to allow smart marketers to find the Holy Grail—tying automated information systems to advertising to create on-demand personalized promotions. *SmartSeries* asset management software from Kreber in Columbus, Ohio, embraces this paradigm with the Oracle database engine interfacing with the largest corporate information items to deliver personalized promotions via printed direct mail and the Internet.

The side benefits of a system like this are outstanding. Designers can spend as much as 30 percent of their time looking for the digital assets they need. Digital asset management systems offer a way to organize, capture, archive, retrieve, and reuse digitized information including text, graphics, photos, full pages, and complete projects. Experts have said digital asset management systems cause productivity to skyrocket and cycle times to shrink.

A digital asset management system requires a database that can manage item information, item relationships, multipurpose content, item hierarchal levels, table data, and multiple index criteria. One of the most important criteria for managing item information is the ability to relate content to more than one item. An item that comes in multiple sizes and colors will have a unique SKU for each item in each size and color, but items within that group will share common descriptive copy and images. Further, a good digital asset management system will take full advantage of cross-selling affiliations to help the creative team seize these selling opportunities.

To realize these benefits, another paradigm shift must occur. The point in the life of an SKU where promotional content is created must change. Advertisers will need to create promotional content at the moment an SKU is promoted, not when it is advertised.

Today, businesses retain huge staffs in their advertising department to author promotional content for print. Therefore, Web departments must go to the advertising department for promotional content, and the content frequently is not there since an SKU will probably be advertised on the Internet before it is in print.

The smart marketer will author multipurpose content for all media at the very beginning of the life of an SKU. Corporate product managers will be involved, and they will be linked electronically to the *content management system*. Some content will even be created by the vendors!

Digital printing won't mean every communication is personalized to an audience of one. The smart marketer will use a blend of CRM techniques. James Morris-Lee gave me these definitions:

> A *personalization* refers to a true 1to1 document tailored to individual customer specifications, where text unique to each recipient is printed on a digitally preprinted sheet called a *shell*.

> A *customization* refers to a document created as a template and characterized by both graphics and text that are changed for each piece based on database-resident information about a particular customer. Copy automatically reflows around each new image—referred to as *full variable* in variable-data printing jargon.

> *Versioning* refers to using broad demographic, psychographic, and purchase history data to produce a generic document that appears personalized but is identical to that produced for others with the same profile.

Because four-color variable printing is so new, the most important requirement for the CRM marketer will be some very original thinking. The CRM marketer winners will utilize the best of printed direct mail in concert with fully customized color catalogs and personalized messages delivered on the Web. Think about it. With the proper asset management system, CRM marketers can use printed direct mail for prospecting and then bringing in the Web to deliver messages to their best customers once a relationship and an e-mail address are secured.

Most marketers are only beginning to discover how to use digital printing to best advantage. One thing is certain. To maximize the value of this exciting marketing tool will require efficient mining of the data in customer files.

CHAPTER

Hi Ho! Hi Ho! It's Off to Work We Go

Data mining: The hot buzzword

Winners have learned that many pieces of information have a concrete dollar value, and as the information becomes more accurate, the corporation's ability to compete increases. Information is distinct from data. The process of extracting information from data is what data mining is all about. While a database includes the data about a customer, data mining provides information about the characteristics and trends that lead to customer retention and profitability.

The data warehouse is a *place* where the customer information is kept, and data mining is a *process* that turns the data warehouse information into knowledge. Data mining is simply a modeling technique, and models are not the answers to business problems. They are steps along the way. For Customer Relationship Management, they are steps along the way to learn more about customers' needs. A 1998 study by Two Crows Corp. showed that the top three end uses of data mining are, not surprisingly, in the marketing area: customer profiling, targeted marketing, and market basket analysis. Data mining can also be a technique for *contribution analysis*—that is, examining the profitability of specific products purchased by individual customers or customer segments.

In *customer profiling*, characteristics of good customers are identified with the goal of predicting who will become one. Data mining can find patterns in a customer database that will speed and simplify this process.

In the *targeting process*, data mining is used to help manage customer relationships by determining characteristics of customers who have left for a competitor so that the company can act to retain customers who are at risk of leaving.

The *market basket analysis* helps retailers understand which products are purchased together. Data mining helps them to know which products to stock in which stores and where to place them in a store. The purpose changes for CRM. By learning the mix of products a segment of customers is attracted to, we begin to learn what those customers value. With this knowledge we can mine the customer file for similar customers to offer suggestions they are likely to value.

This is what Amazon.com and Jeff Bezos have learned and why they are so smart to show customers "People who bought this book also bought." Data mining for market basket analysis gets us closer to Jeff Bezos' ideal: "The store of the future should be able to guess what he wants to buy before he knows himself." This gets to the heart of the CRM goal—to be very good at communicating and offering only those things that will have value to the individual customer in the customer's terms. This is what Martha Rogers means when she talks about "1to1 customization."

When Greg Osenga, senior vice president of information services, Cadmus Direct Marketing, addressed the audience at the National Center for Database Marketing in Seattle in 1998, he talked about data mining as a collection of buzzwords. He said the buzzwords and jargon were creating a lot of hype and confusion. He then gave us Webster's definitions of *buzzword* and *jargon*:

Buzzword: An important sounding, usually technical, word or phrase often of little meaning used to impress laymen.

Jargon: Obscure and often pretentious language marked by circumlocutions and long words.

The hype, Osenga said, is understandable because there are so many technology products trying to differentiate themselves, but his concern was that the confusion created by all the hype might intimidate people and discourage them from implementing what are very good marketing concepts.

With that background, let's look at the buzzword *data mining* with as few technical words and as little circumlocution as possible.

Exactly what is data mining?

Herb Edelstein, an internationally recognized expert in data warehousing and data mining and president of Two Crows Corp., says, "Data mining is among the most important applications of data warehouses. Essentially, data mining discovers patterns and relationships hidden in your data. It's part of a larger process called *knowledge discovery*: specifically, the step in which advanced statistical analysis and modeling techniques are applied to the data to find useful patterns and relationships."[1]

The folks at Information Discovery, Inc., a leader in data mining products and services, say:

> Any notion that data mining is just the next step up from query and reporting should be discarded immediately. In fact, data mining, in the context of intelligent databases, is the complex driving engine for transforming data into information, not just another data presentation vehicle.
>
> Data mining implementers should prepare themselves to deal with data mining as an application that needs as much underlying theory as a field such as semiconductor design or quantum mechanics. Although data mining end users do not need to understand quantum mechanics, semiconductor design, or the structure of the influence of domain algebra, the algorithm designers, system implementers, and design consultants need to know these topics in depth.[2]

You won't need the dwarf's pickaxe and shovel, but you will need a capable statistician.

Greg Osenga was right. There are a lot of hyped data mining tools from which to choose. If you walk the aisles of the next database marketing conference or expo, you will see things like "Loosely Coupled Symmetrical Multiprocess Systems," "Integrated Data Mining Systems," "MultiDimensional Intelligence Solutions," and "Genetic Architecture and Collaborative Personalization Solutions." What does all that circumlocution mean? The vendors' brochures will make enticing promises like "Almost all relevant patterns in data are automatically *premined beforehand* into a PatternWarehouse for end users" and "General patterns are automatically found with multitable analysis of large SQL databases with no sampling or extracts."

Beware. There are no magic tools. As Herb Edelstein says:

> The first thing you should know is that data mining is not magic. A data mining tool will not sit in your database watching what happens and, when it sees an interesting pattern, send you an e-mail to get your attention. It does not eliminate the need to know your business, understand your data, or know statistical methods. It does not find patterns you can automatically trust without verifying them in the real world. Data mining assists business analysts with generating hypotheses. It neither verifies a hypotheses nor gauges its value.[3]

What then is the purpose of data mining? It goes back to what Greg Osenga called the "real world": "Human beings and organizations do not act in response to reality, but in response to an internally constructed version of reality."[4]

Without data and its being analyzed to develop information and knowledge about the way things are happening in the real world, all we have is opinions. Every expert we have talked to gives the same answer: "Data mining is knowledge discovery."

Charles Berger, director of product marketing for data mining at Oracle Corp., says, "Many manufacturers adhere to the rule, 'Without data, it's just an opinion,' but marketers make important decisions to send offers based upon very poor utilization of available data. This approach is far too simplistic. In fact, the sophisticated solutions now available are critical to survival amid today's fierce competition."[5]

Berger predicts we will soon see what he calls "marketing engineers" who will use the new data mining tools to add discipline to the "craft" of marketing.

Despite all the fancy names for all the new technology tools, these tools are not different from statistics, and, remember, discriminant analysis was developed in 1936. *Decision trees* and *neural networks* are simply the latest iteration of statistical software.

Data mining tools differ from traditional statistical tools mostly in the quantities of data they can handle.

As more real-world knowledge is discovered, a company's ability to compete increases. For the purposes of CRM, the more real-world knowledge we can discover about customers, the easier we can make it for them to do business with us and the longer we will keep them as customers.

So, forgetting all the hype, *data mining* is just the term information professionals use for *data modeling*, but it is more sophisticated modeling with many new desktop tools. Data mining tools use data to build a model of the real world. The result of this modeling is a description of patterns and relationships among data that can provide knowledge to guide business decisions and make predictions.

Herb Edelstein describes six types of models that data mining can build to solve business problems: classification, regression, time series, clustering, association analysis, and sequence discovery. He says, "Classification and regression are primarily applied to prediction, while association and sequence discovery are primarily used to describe behavior that is captured in your database. Clustering may be used for either forecasting or description."[6]

In simplest terms, *classification* assigns instances to a group, then uses the data to learn the pattern of characteristics that identify the group to which each instance belongs.

Regression uses existing values to forecast what continuous values will be. *Time series forecasting* is the same, adding time factors to establish a hierarchy of time periods and an indication of how much of the past is relevant to the future.

Clustering tracks customers within the database into different groups to find groups that either differ from one another or have similarities.

Associations reveal things that occur together and can be used for market basket analysis, like the old cliché "Men who buy diapers buy beer at the same time."

Sequence discovery measures associations and predicts the spread over time—if a customer buys a big-screen television, 30 percent of the time he will upgrade his sound system within 90 days.

Traditional database marketing is concerned with *predictive modeling*. By using a predictive model to identify good candidates for mail offers or catalogs, the direct marketers are able to increase sales while reducing expenses. CRM is more concerned with *descriptive models*—models that describe patterns in the data you have.

In simple modeling the analyst generates a hypothesis and uses query tools to test and verify the hypothesis. The analyst guides all of the exploration using data mining tools to explore the data; the tools perform the exploration. The value of data mining tools comes from the fact that in large databases there are so many patterns that, practically speaking, the analyst can never know all the right questions to ask. A good data mining tool automatically searches the database for the analyst to find hidden patterns without a predetermined idea or hypothesis about what the patterns may be. So *data mining* refers to an automated process of data analysis in which the system takes the initiative to generate patterns by itself, thereby reducing the analyst's need to call in the statisticians.

Greg Osenga was right. *Data mining is* the buzzword, but there is a caveat. Data mining is not a wonder drug. It will not build perfect models on its own. It will not create sudden breakthroughs.

It will produce profitable returns through steady incremental learning. The better you understand your data *and* your business, the more effective your knowledge discovery process will be.

While various approaches to data mining seem to offer distinct features and benefits, just a few fundamental techniques form the basis of most data mining systems. The secret of success is not the tool, but the skill of the staff and their insight into the business challenge. No one data mining tool or set of tools is universally applicable. For any given challenge, the nature of the data will determine the right tool, which means data mining requires a mix of tools.

The most important thing to remember is that data mining is not a single technology—it is a *process*. Data mining is knowledge discovery. Knowledge discovery is building and using a data mining solution. Data mining is a piece of the knowledge discovery process. In the end, if you don't know your business, the data mining tool won't save you.

16
CHAPTER

"Everything That Can Be Invented Has Been Invented"

What can be predicted for the new century?

In 1899 Charles H. Duel, commissioner, U.S. Office of Patents, said, "Everything that can be invented has been invented." He missed the mark by just a bit. There were more patents issued between 1980 and 1990 than in the first 100 years of our nation.

What can be predicted for the new century? Some believe the new century starts in 2000. Some say 2001. But everyone agrees it will bring new technologies we cannot even imagine—even more inventions than we saw from 1980 to 1990. One thing seems certain: We will see an avalanche of new tools for Customer Relationship Management, and that will include even more sophisticated means of mass customization. CRM winners are looking for these things now.

The uncompromising customer will continue to press the manufacturer to produce precisely what she or he wants in the

color, style, and fit desired. The retailer shifting from market share
to customer share will understand customers' needs so well he or
she will buy only what is already sold; again, 1to1 customization.

Brian Amaral, president of Atlanta-based Image-Ware
Technologies, Inc., calls this "relationship selling." His company
already has software that maintains a comprehensive client database
that includes sizes and measurements, personal preferences, family
member data, and purchasing triggers. Garment selection is supported by a wardrobe survey and coordination system that stores and
prints digitally photographed images of customers' prior purchases.
The software includes an online tutorial for measurements and a garment design system that addresses the various style details of specific manufacturers. Will Image-Ware's next technology advance
expand the family member data to include a wardrobe survey for the
family pet, complete with digitally photographed images?[1]

In the retail store the sales associate won't even have to go to
the "old" point-of-sale PC register to find this kind of customer
information and complete a sale. Palm Pilot has already introduced
a hand-held POS device with a built-in laser to scan bar codes and
"ring up" the sale, and the device stores all of the pertinent customer history. One wonders, with the POS device in his or her hand,
where will the sales associate go to hide from customers?

In January 1998 Epiphany launched a new CRM software
application so simple the training for employee use required only a
10-line e-mail. The *e.4 System* application suite turns companies
into CRM enterprises by putting all customer data at everyone's
fingertips. Peppers & Rogers said of the new application, "This is
more than a product launch; it points to the future of information
technology investments around the world. Such new marketing
automation systems set the stage for a wave of CRM investments,
as soon as companies are through ransacking their IT budgets for
the Y2K problem."[2]

Epiphany's *e.4* connects information from every customer
"touch point," from the call center to the Web. As Martha Rogers

told a group of Epiphany users recently, "You are the pioneers of one-to-one, and Epiphany is your arms supplier, . . . selling high-powered bits and bytes instead of bows and arrows."[3]

Not far away are data warehouse tools that will eliminate the bothersome fussing over database design and quality analysis and maintenance procedures that make traditional warehouse projects drag on for months or years. David Raab, a Philadelphia-based consultant, predicts that new products from Norbert Technologies, Broadbase, Digital Archaeology, and Sand Technology will allow database builders to load all the data they want, straight from operational sources, and access it in any way they like in minutes, hours, or days.[4] With that ease of start-up we can expect to see many more CRM winners in the years ahead.

IBM has done a lot of work with Fingerhut, the second-largest U.S. catalog retailer, to manage customer communications longitudinally (more about longitudinal marketing in Chapter 29). Each customer or customer group is allotted a specific number of promotion dollars to control the flow into each home mailbox. Each week, data from 7 million customers is downloaded to an IBM SP2 computer dedicated to organizing the mailings.

Fingerhut's president sees this as transforming his business. Instead of sending customers catalogs containing ever more merchandise, the company can now feature merchandise that specific customers are likely to buy. Fingerhut's emphasis has shifted from catalog to customer, giving the company more opportunity to develop a relationship with individual customers that will encourage customers to keep coming back.[5]

The prediction here: In the new century tools like this will be developed in shrink-wrap versions. Right now it takes a 600-million-catalog mailer like Fingerhut to amortize the expense of this sophisticated technology. Tomorrow it may be affordable to help the corner store join the winners' group.

What about the cellular phone? Will we see a day soon when wireless will replace the regular wired phone? If that happens, what will it mean for the marketer? As ubiquitous as they seem, cell phones are carried by only 67 million Americans, about 24 percent, which is lower than in Finland, Israel, Hong Kong, and Italy, where the rates are 35 to 50 percent and climbing fast. Our guess is that the market will explode when the U.S. market finally moves from its five service formats to one standard as has happened overseas, and as service providers deliver the added convenience of cell phone log-on-Web services and other neat bells and whistles.

That time may not be very far away. In September 1998 Microsoft and Qualcomm each invested $25 million to form a company called "Wirelessknowledge" to deploy e-mail, contact lists, calendars, and even Web content to wireless phones, pagers, laptop computers, and all species of mobile devices. Observers predict that, if successful, the company can change the way society conceives of phones—devices not just for talking to other people but for communicating with other computing devices.

For example, Wirelessknowledge will make it possible for an individual to access e-mail and other information housed on his or her office PC, edit the information on his cell phone, then tell the phone to call the person who just sent the e-mail.

Surveys show that wireless phone sales will eclipse PC sales in the next few years. While there were only 2.2 million wireless data users in 1998, the research team at Yankee Group estimated 12 million wireless data users to generate $5.6 billion in revenue by 2002. Vodafone believes this will happen, and they are betting big bucks. Their takeover of Air-Touch Communications in January 1999 brought them 14 million new cellular customers—at a cost of $4300 each![6]

There is more out there than cell phones. On May 24, 1999, 3Com Palm Computing introduced the Palm VII in the New York market. For $599 stock traders can place orders from anywhere without the use of a phone. The user requests data from a Web site by touching an icon on the main screen of the Palm VII. The request is transmitted by a tiny two-way radio system to 3Com data via the

Bell South Wireless data network. 3Com receives data from the Web site partner and transmits it back to the hand-held device. By transmitting and receiving only the tiny amount of information the user needs, and not entire Web pages, the process is fast and requires only a small amount of radio communication.

Those ever-present Internet providers that fill your desktop screen are rushing to get access to the Palm VII, targeting Palm with everything from weather information and maps to the ability to buy goods from anywhere you happen to be. Starbucks was one of the first on board with a program to help its customers locate the nearest Starbucks location. Again, to save radio time, only the desired location goes over the data system. How long will it be before CRM winners can enhance the relationship building dialog to reach the customer at the customer's convenience anywhere, any time?

It's not just 3Com and its Palm VII. As the number of adults on the Internet increases, so does the number of users accessing it by alternative measures. In a study released in April 1999 by InteliQuest Research, 3.7 million respondents said they used a hand-held computer for access and 3.1 million used a television set-top box or Web TV. Technology and content companies including Netscape, Amazon.com, Excite, Microsoft, IBM, Cisco, CNN, and Reuters are all trying to claim a piece of this market. Developers can no longer assume that all users have 4.0 browser capability.[7]

Wireless e-mail pagers have been with us for a while, but up to now they have required a separate e-mail address, meaning that a reply to an earlier message went to your hand-held unit even if you were back at your desk. A new unit from BlackBerry (www.blackberry.net) functions like a remote control for your desktop e-mail. A message sent from your BlackBerry is routed to the Microsoft exchange server at your office, then forwarded to the recipient with a copy saved in your mail-sent folder. Incoming messages are pushed to the BlackBerry with a copy stored on your desktop.

As an aside, one would think that the old fax technology that dates all the way back to a late 1800s patent would be gone the way of the telegraph. Not so. Worldwide fax transmission minutes grew to 395 billion in 1998, up from 255 billion in 1995, and are predicted to jump to 647 billion by 2002. At big corporations the fax expense accounts for one-third of phone bills. The growth projection is based on the continuing drop in cost. The cost of sending a three-page fax dropped from $1.89 in 1990 to 92 cents in 1998. The growth of Internet faxing internationally should lead to even further economies.

The intersection of broadcasting and computer technology was supposed to create breakthrough opportunities for marketers. The intersection has been a long time coming, and some giant companies have lost millions trying to lead the way. It now appears interactive television is about to happen. Scientific-Atlanta now offers a set-top box, called "Explorer 2000," that processes 54 million instructions per second for high-speed Web browsing, phone calls, shopping, and games. They shipped 126,000 boxes in the final quarter of 1998, twice as many as planned. Needless to say, 126,000 set-top boxes will not change the face of marketing, but it does suggest another CRM opportunity to watch for in the days ahead.

It took Bill Gates and Microsoft quite a while to appreciate the value of the Internet, but when the Microsoft giant moves, we can expect even more interactive solutions.

How big an opportunity will this be for CRM? Quite possibly a new communication stream to reach known customers or target prospects—one of many we will be seeing in the years ahead.

Are electronic books—e-books—the next 1to1 medium? Today NuvoMedia's *RocketeBook* at $499 and its competitor *SoftBook* at $599 can download e-books at prices roughly comparable to their printed counterparts. It is predicted that prices will plummet when more of the big players get involved. In Japan, an Electronic Book Consortium, with more than 100 companies including Microsoft, is reportedly spending $90 million on a new vision of e-books. Microsoft has announced plans to bring audiobook technology to *Windows CE* devices. Microsoft's vice president for technology development says, "You're going to be able to play a book on every platform Microsoft makes."[8]

Since the content of each e-book download can be targeted to a single computer, think about the CRM possibilities of including a specific customer message in each book.

High-speed data networks already allow conventional newspapers to transcend geographical limits and publish anywhere on demand. What might be next?

Today's newspapers, by necessity, are one-size-fits-all entities. With the exception of zoned editions, all readers get the same ads and editorial content. When the on-demand digital printing we saw in Chapter 14 reaches the newspaper, the advertisers will be able to speak to an audience of one. If the Toets 9290 campaign can deliver a four-color personalized catalog to an individual consumer's door practically overnight, newspapers should soon be able to print individualized, personal messages in papers delivered to address-specific households.

Soon newspapers can have a print version of *My Yahoo* giving personalized news on the front page of every copy. It is now possible to print one column of ink-jet, personalized, late-breaking news at 40,000 copies an hour. More newspapers will become winners as they use these tools to develop new ways to serve CRM marketers.

The television industry will begin to find similar opportunities to reach individual households. It won't be a matter of viewers' choosing from 100 channels. It will be broadcasters' presenting a menu of programs tailored to an individual's tastes and values. When that happens, the advertiser will be able to personalize messages to specific customers and specific prospects. Moreover, the broadcasters will be able to help marketers find the best prospects. Amazon.com now tells us what people who bought this book also bought. Broadcasters will soon be able to tell us what viewers who liked one show will like next.

As Jeff Bezos of Amazon.com said, the store of the future should be able to guess what the customer wants to buy before the customer even knows. "We can do that online," he says. "We can make it your store, tailor-made for you. The Internet can bring the personal touch back to commerce, only this time on a mass scale."[9]

Finally, we may see magical new toys to help us build and manage customer relations. Technophiles in Japan now have virtual matchmakers. A device called "The Lovegety" is an egg-shaped electronic toy on a keychain that singles are toting to nightclubs and social events. When a man carrying his blue Lovegety gets within 15 feet of a woman and her pink one, the gadgets emit simultaneous beeps suggesting each owner is in the mood to mingle. Lovegety's can be programmed to sound off three ways to indicate whether someone nearby is interested in chatting, getting to know one another better, or having a romantic interlude. More than 1 million of the electronic icebreakers were sold in the first six months they were available. CRM winners may next be looking for ways to persuade customers to carry similar toys to "beep" when the customer is ready to buy.

A century ago Charles Duel was wrong. We are certain to see lots more inventions. We can still dream of new ways to manage customer relationships. What will be needed to make these dreams come true? It won't require more inventions. All the tools we need are either here or on the way. All we will need is the creative management to use these new tools to develop CRM in the ways that will be most valuable for the consumer. This will require what Martha Rogers calls "active 1to1 Learning Relationships."

Welcome to the New Digital World

Technology.com.
e-mail.telecom.fridge.digital

We have talked about the Internet. We have talked about e-mail. We have talked about the new telemarketing. We have talked about digital printing, and we have talked about some new technologies yet to come.

What does all this mean to CRM? It means that we are entering a digital world. Technology will be the defining weapon, and winners will have to be on the cutting edge.

The Internet is the single most important development for marketers since the U.S. Postal Service. It is a most important piece of the CRM revolution. Over time a portion of practically every transaction will touch the Internet, but it is only a piece. The gestalt—the magic bullet for CRM—is technology in all the forms that we know today plus those just on the horizon.

Of course we have to start with a closer look at the Internet, the ubiquitous medium that represents our period in history. In the 1920s radio was recognized for its importance when Calvin Coolidge used it to deliver his state of the union address. In the 1960s Nixon and Kennedy secured the place for television with their decisive debate. In the 1990s the Internet came alive with the Starr Report.

The Internet has become a powerful influence in our lives, and the number of ways it affects us personally will grow even more in the future. Our journey through the digital world promises opportunities that will eclipse anything we have known or even imagined—not just for selling more goods but for building the kind of relationships that will help us bind customers to our brands in ways that will add value for them and add sales and profit for us.

Just how important is the Internet for consumers today? Roper Starch Worldwide conducted a study for AOL in August 1998 that gave some answers.

Almost half of online consumers said that being online is just about a necessity in their lives. Almost 9 out of 10 said their online access would be missed if no longer available. More than three-quarters of consumers who go online said that being online has made their lives better in some way. Almost three-quarters of those online regularly or occasionally go online for information about products to buy. Half of online consumers go online between one and five times a week to get the news, and another 20 percent go online 6 to 10 times a week to get news.

We agree with Jim McCann, the Internet *is* going to make everybody a relationship marketer, or at least those that survive and prosper, but in the rush to the Web, there are three questions every company should ask:

1. Why is our company online?
2. What is our promise to our customer?
3. What do we want our site to do?

Let's look ahead, again, at what we will be dealing with or, better stated, what will be available to us.

The Internet is a narrowband, circuit-switched network. Some say its days are already numbered. The next revolution is a broadband, packet-based public network—a completely new, much bigger network that will have a far greater impact on our communications capabilities and our lives. Broadband will make today's Internet seem like playing in your child's sandbox.

Today's circuit-switched network will not scale to handle the traffic needs of applications ahead. The new network will look like the Internet, but it will also offer the scalability to allow for the more sophisticated applications and the rich media—that of audio and video and very rich graphics.

Attendees at the @d:tech Internet advertising conference the first week of May 1999 in San Francisco heard one overriding theme: rich media, rich media, rich media. Seminars on *rich media*—the ability to add sound, video, and transactional capabilities to online communications—had standing-room-only audiences, and it was the rich media vendors who were drawing the crowds to their booths.

The builders of the broadband network are combining the best from the data world with the best from the traditional telecommunications world. They will capitalize on *Moore's law*—computer power doubles every 18 months and costs halve. New software will offer 50 to 100 times the performance we know today.

As of December 1998 the number of Web sites accepting rich media was up 90 percent from the previous year, but still most users of narrowband sites fear the glitches that result from messages that take too long to load, don't work properly, or don't load at all.

With broadband in place (in common use), rich media will bloom, and it will be important for marketers to learn to handle the creative firepower of Java banners and other tools of rich media advertising. In March 1999 @Home Network released a study based on online surveys with 3000 respondents over @Home's high-speed Internet service.[1] The study showed broadband advertising to be much more effective than narrowband. Measuring one narrowband ad against three broadband ads, the study found that recall for the broadband ads was 34 percent higher than for the narrowband ads, broadband advertising was at least 30 percent more effective based on questions concerning how the ads shifted a user's understanding of the brand, and in 60 percent of the cases over half the visitors spent between 30 seconds and 5 minutes interacting with the ads. All this suggests that broadband offers a lower cost-per-brand impression than narrowband as a result of the higher recall rates, but, in 1999, experts were predicting that widespread use of sound and video online is still a year away.

One company, MatchLogic in Westminster, Colorado, offers advertisers broadband capability now to reach users able to access the rich media. A service called "SpeedSelect" determines users' access speed before delivering a banner they can view, allowing the advertiser to deliver the richest possible media based on access speed. Mitchell Bennett, president of MatchLogic, says, "Based on our changing role, Web advertising that was funded for branding is now moving into retaining customers [CRM]."[2]

Targeting customers on the Internet does work with click-through rates increasing 20 percent over nontargeted messages, but with click-through rates often less than 1 percent marketers must still learn better CRM techniques. Interactive agencies that have been stuck on the publishers' side serving ads to the Internet are now signing on third-party ad servers like MatchLogic to help them get under the hood to look at all the data that can help them measure ROI. However, their real need is to learn how to build 1to1 relationships on the Web.

Anu Shukla, CEO of Rubric, a company that provides Web-based enterprise-marketing automation software, says:

> E-businesses are not taking advantage of the Net as a communications medium. The Web offers an opportunity for real-time dialog that can lead to repeat sales. Internet *marketing* is the missing link.

The Web should facilitate communication. It is uniquely suited to foster one-to-one relationships with customers. E-business demands a new strategy. Beyond crunching demographic data, Internet marketing is about using the Web to build customer relationships and turning them into measurable results.[3]

Business-to-business marketers are beginning to heed this advice. At the 10th Annual Direct Marketing to Business Conference in Orlando in February 1999, the overriding theme was that of the Internet and other new technologies letting customers take charge of the sales and marketing process. Conference speakers made the point that the Internet is reversing the way business-to-business marketers reach customers and that role reversal is occurring on intranets, private networks, and extranets.

When Dell Computer Corp. tested its Web site, they found that seven of eight customers couldn't navigate through it to make a purchase. They listened to problems, and the company now supports 12,000 personalized customer extranet sites with intuitive navigation systems based on customer tasks. Dell is able to put customers in the driver's seat because its sales force has the tools to build a personalized site in 20 minutes.[4] Dell understands CRM.

The ability to learn faster than your competition will be your only sustainable advantage, so you must stay focused.

One thing every company should remember: Using the Internet to establish dialog with individual customers is what CRM in the 2000s is all about, and e-mail will be the catalyst. We talked, in Chapter 12, about e-mail having gone from a questionable practice to an accepted marketing medium—accepted not just by marketers but by consumers as well. It may prove to be the magic tool that gets us beyond the cycle of telephone tag produced by the infamous answering machine.

The Roper Starch study for AOL tells us that one in four online consumers owns a laptop computer, and three-quarters of those with laptops take them with them when traveling on business—just under half when traveling on vacation. One-third of all online consumers check their e-mail while traveling on business, and over one-quarter check their e-mail while on vacation.

When asked whether they would want a telephone, television, or computer connected to the Internet if they were stranded on a desert island, more than two-thirds of online consumers said they would want a computer connected to the Internet.

Finally, e-mail is the preferred method of communicating with business associates for over half of online consumers, while slightly fewer than half prefer e-mail for communication with coworkers. Over two-thirds agree that being online brings family and friends together with 90 percent going online to communicate with friends and family. The goal for CRM marketers is to be one of those "friends."

The e-mail opportunity for CRM marketers *is* enormous, and it *will be* enormous for the customer. It *is* direct mail on steroids. As we learn to use it to manage customer relationships, it will be important to remember the 84 percent of @ONCE survey respondents who wanted customized e-mail, the 76 percent who wanted their e-mails to include new product information and availability, and, most important of all, the 89 percent who wanted their e-mail communications to recognize them as a preferred customer.

In this look at CRM and technology opportunities, it is important to revisit the call center. We spent some time with Peter Berczi, president, North Direct Response, a customer communications company operating state-of-the-art call centers in Canada. Berczi believes call centers are the next important step in our gathering and using customer knowledge to manage customer relationships. He describes the call center as the "front line," the chance for the customer to communicate the way the customer wants. He showed me how companies are turning the inbound 800 number from a cost center to a profit center.

Think about these facts, and think about our quest to reduce customer attrition: Over 25 percent of customers who had a problem never told the company about it. Often those who did make contact reported that it took too much time and trouble to get the problem resolved. A recent Hepworth Company study measuring customer satisfaction reported top-quartile companies are averaging 2.6 contacts to resolve customer problems with the figure for the bottom-quartile companies about 3.0. For companies receiving 1 million calls a year, this represents $100,000 in additional service costs.[5]

Customer loyalty is more than a feeling. It is a set of behaviors that produce revenue: purchasing, repurchasing, and purchasing other products and recommending them to others.

Satisfaction is a precondition to loyalty but cannot guarantee it. Research shows that many of the merely "satisfied" will happily switch to a competitor tomorrow. The Hepworth study also showed more than 8 percent of a company's revenues are at risk as a result of poor customer contact handling, but customers who have experienced a problem and who have had it resolved successfully by a call center come away from the experience more brand loyal than those who have experienced no problem at all.

Telemarketing contact management is more than a mechanism for handling complaints. It is a means for establishing a connection with customers—answering their questions, listening to them, satisfying them, and building their loyalty. It provides opportunities for sales and the collection of valuable customer knowledge that can pay off in relationship building and in future sales. It provides an opportunity for the important dialog with customers.

Peter Berczi tells me that every 12th call in one successful call center includes a short survey, taking less than a minute to turn the call from an information "consumer" to an information "producer." With call center direct customer contact, businesses can learn more from customers who say no because the customers will say why they are not interested. This information can produce instant results. One outbound call center changed its incentive offer and learned, in minutes, the change was a mistake.

The Hepworth study concludes, "Effective customer contact management establishes a cycle in which customer feedback drives process improvement. It is a rich source of customer data and offers opportunities for upselling. And, if well managed, it can become a profit center, with ROI potentially exceeding 100 percent."[6] That feedback cycle is what CRM winners call "dialog."

While the customer feedback dialog is a vital part of CRM, the outbound CRM phone call can also be a giant sales producer. The Jan Bell fine jewelry departments in 499 Sam's Club discount store locations in the United States use telemarketing campaigns to invite previous buyers to attend VIP jewelry shows, and their success is impressive.

In the first quarter of 1998, 50 percent of the 54,000 customers called agreed to attend a show. Of that, 25 percent showed up and purchased jewelry, with sales averaging $250 to $300 per person. Jan Bell had a 50 percent increase in sales in the first year of the campaign. According to Brent Reck, account manager, TeleQuest Teleservices who make the calls for Jan Bell, "The campaign's success rests in the company's relationship with its customers which is based on flawless service. If Sam's Club started to get complaints from the customers, they would make one phone call and stop the telemarketing campaign. That has not been an issue. We have received no [telemarketing] complaints."[7]

In the next chapter you'll learn that the Tesco supermarket chain used CRM to move ahead of Sainsbury's to capture the number 1 spot in UK food retailing. As part of their CRM program, Tesco is setting call center benchmarks for the other major chains to emulate.

Established in August 1996 as part of the company's ongoing commitment to the development of service quality and concepts, the Tesco customer call center has grown rapidly from a starting staff of about 180 to today's 650 and is evolving into a productive profit-driven operation. The Customer Engagement Company (CEC) partnered with Tesco to develop the call center. Peter

Morris, CEC's managing director, reports, "The very success of the system has meant that it is already close to capacity. As callers get accustomed to the level of service offered, they tend to expect more and become more demanding—and work is now in hand to increase capacity substantially."

Interactive voice response (IVR) *units*—those systems that tell us if you want *x*, press 1, if you want *y*, press 2—allow the Tesco customer service representative to determine the nature of the call, contact history, club card membership status, and purchasing history. A pilot for IVR and *computer telephony integration* (CTI) will soon be trialed to enable operators to retrieve data from corporate databases prior to being allocated a call.

Tesco's next step should be to add Web enablement. Today nearly 15 percent of call centers are Web enabled. It is estimated that by the year 2002 nearly a quarter of U.S. companies will have improved their customer service operations by adopting multimedia technology in their call centers. Within the span of the next five years, customers visiting a company's home page will find that, with a click of a mouse, they'll be able to talk directly to representatives while they are online. With additional corporations unearthing the customer service benefits associated with multimedia operations, the call center industry can expect a surge in online customer service.[8]

With all of this technology available, how much should a marketer invest to be state of the art? A recent study of the call center industry had this advice:

> The cost and performance of a call center can be critical to its success. Spend too little and perform poorly, and the center becomes a business liability that consistently drives away customers and creates market damage. Spend too much and overperform, and the center again becomes a financial loss to the company.
>
> Spend efficiently and perform effectively at the level just better than your competitors, and your center can be a profit center for the company—gaining and retaining customers.[9]

It is important to remember our earlier comment: There is more to CRM on the telephone than just high tech.

Finally, in our look at the fast-advancing techy future, we see Frigidaire moving the computer to your kitchen. In early 1999 Frigidaire introduced an online refrigerator. It comes complete with an indoor bar-code scanner with which consumers can reorder a fresh bottle of salad dressing, ketchup, or other products by scanning their used-up container across the door. The refrigerator picks up the UPC and automatically reorders a fresh supply.

Frank Britt, VP marketing and merchandising for Streamline, a consumer direct retailer that takes orders via the Web, says, "Automatic replenishment of grocery products could have a profound effect on marketing because it is the ultimate loyalty program for a packaged goods company."[10]

If all of this sounds frightening to you, don't read *The Age of Spiritual Machines* by Ray Kurzweil (Viking, January 1999). He predicts that by 2019 the average $1000 PC will be as powerful as the human brain. He says:

> We already have more than the processing power of the human brain on the Net, and soon we'll be able to call on that power through computational-sharing proposals. You'll be able to apply the computational ability of the human brain from your PC simply by pulling in power from other computers that aren't being used at the moment.
>
> During the 21st century the cutting edge of the creation of intelligent machines will move from humans designing intelligent machines to the more intelligent machines creating their own next generation.
>
> We will have machines that have the subtlety, complexity and depth of human response. Our more advanced computers will be based on the design of human thinking, and we will have machines that appear to be conscious, will claim to be conscious. In fact they will claim to be human and they will be very convincing, and ultimately they will be more intelligent than we are, so we will end up believing them.

Perhaps Ray Kurzweil's predictions are more than we need. The important point is that we are now living in a digital world, and as technology continues to race ahead, we must learn to use the new tools to manage customer relationships, just as Don Peppers and Martha Rogers predicted in their first book, *The One to One Future: Building Relationships One Customer at a Time*, back in 1993: "The interactive strategies of successful companies will have to change."

Winners need to know that what they must be about is developing and managing *relationships*, strengthening the bond between the customer and the company, maximizing the value of the relationship to the customer.

It's not just the Internet or e-mail or telemarketing or any single one of the new technologies. As we said at the start, the magic bullet for CRM is the gestalt— technology in all the forms that we know today plus those just on the horizon.

In *Business @ the Speed of Thought* (Warner Books, March 1999), Bill Gates admonishes, "The successful companies of the next decade will be the ones that use digital tools to reinvent the way they work—to make digital information flow through the Web as an intrinsic part of the company." He predicts a "Web-workstyle" with a company's middle managers and line employees, not just high-level executives, as part of that digital information flow. Every worker will be a knowledge worker as the Internet transforms the way we do business.

He cites a new information system being installed at McDonald's that uses PCs and Web technologies to tally sales at all McDonald's restaurants. "As soon as you have a Happy Meal," he says, "a McDonald's marketing manager will know."

Bill Gates sums up our message for this technology summary when he says, "Companies that invest early in digital nervous systems to capture, analyze and capitalize on customer input will differentiate themselves from competition."

It's still about getting the right message to the most important people, but we will have to learn to deliver the message in new ways. CRM, to be effective in the high-tech 2000s, will require all of the parts and pieces of what Bill Gates calls "the digital nervous system."

QUICK TIPS FROM PART TWO

CHAPTER 9: New Tools Require New Skills

- You must change from a mass-media-only outlook to include all customer contacts.
- Because relationships are built on trust, any information control problems can be as serious as any financial control problems.
- Don't get lost in the enterprise data warehouse.
- Use data differently; use it to gain a better understanding of what a customer will value about a relationship with your company.

CHAPTER 10: The CRM Blueprint

- Don't start with technology. Focus first on where the real value is.
- Too much data are as troublesome as too little.
- Value is your customer's value to your organization and your organization's value to the customer.

- Develop or hire the right professionals: constructors and creators.
- Give the professionals the authority to get the job done.
- Take a long-term budget view.
- Establish firm objectives before investing any money.

CHAPTER 11: But What Is It Good For?

- Understand and accept the new economic order of the Net economy, but think of it as more than just e-commerce. The Web is not about technology. It's about what it does for people.
- Use the Internet to establish dialog with individuals—getting information and listening. Develop active 1to1 Learning Relationships.
- Use the Internet to provide information that has unique value to individual customers.
- Use technology as a customer-facing infrastructure.
- Always ask how you can make it easier for your customers to do business with you.
- Learn to react in real time.
- Remember the service imperative. Let customers feel their interaction with you is within their own control.
- Don't think transactions. Think relationships.
- Don't think only ROI. Think R&D.

CHAPTER 12: You've Got Mail

- e-mail is the next big thing.
- Consumers *want* e-mail services.
- e-mail *is not* a passive medium.

- Think of e-mail as customer intimacy on a mass scale.
- e-mail must factor into the whole business system.
- Don't think mass marketing. Think relative marketing.
- Keep mailings simple, short, and to the point.

CHAPTER 13: Should Telemarketing Be a Four-Letter Word?

- Call centers are the next important step. Don't think of tele-marketing as a four-letter word.
- Build telephone relationships with mutual trust and respect.
- Make your call center a complete customer interaction center.
- Put up the "No Waiting" sign, and use state-of-the-art tools to deliver the promise.
- Don't be afraid to outsource.
- As Lexus says, "Make sure the customer experience with the company matches the experience with the car they buy."
- Maintain the human touch. The high-touch component is important to CRM.
- Don't expect to become world class the first year.

CHAPTER 14: Things Gutenberg Never Dreamed Of

- When tools change, the rules change.
- Learn how to use customer information to customize your offerings.
- Customized digital printing can drive sales, change behavior, and build long-term relationships.
- Remember the study that showed a 35 percent increase in response rates and a 25 percent improvement in average order size.

- The color of your customer's tractor *is* important to him.

CHAPTER 15: Hi Ho! Hi Ho! It's Off to Work We Go

- Information has a dollar value.
- Information is distinct from data. The process of extracting information from data is what data mining is all about.
- The data warehouse is a *place*. Data mining is a *process*.
- Models are not the answers to business problems. They are steps along the way.
- Data mining reveals patterns and relationships hidden in your data.
- Data mining is not magic. There are no magic tools.
- Data mining is knowledge discovery.
- The better you understand your data—and your business— the more effective your knowledge discovery will be.
- The secret of success is not the data mining tool but the skill of the staff and their insight into the business challenge.

CHAPTER 16: "Everything That Can Be Invented Has Been Invented"

- Learn how to accomplish "relationship selling."
- Tomorrow's digital advances will put customer data at everyone's fingertips.
- CRM marketers are pioneers, and their technology vendors are their arms suppliers—selling high-powered bits and bytes instead of bows and arrows.
- Be ready for new capabilities of cell phones and unified message services.
- Watch for wireless to replace the regular wired phone.

- Interactive television is finally happening. Be ready.

- Learn how to reach customers inside e-books.

- The one-size-fits-all newspaper may be history.

- We should be able to guess what the customer wants before the customer even knows.

- We won't require more inventions. All we will need is the creative management to develop CRM in the ways that will be most valuable to the customer.

CHAPTER 17: Welcome to the New Digital World

- Technology will be the defining weapon of the future.

- Over time a portion of every transaction will touch the Internet.

- The Internet is going to make everybody a relationship marketer.

- The three questions every company should ask:
  - Why is our company online?
  - What is our promise to our customer?
  - What do we want our site to do?

- Broadband will make today's Internet seem like playing in your child's sandbox.

- The Internet is uniquely suited to foster 1to1 relationships with customers.

- The ability to learn faster than your competition will be the only sustainable advantage.

- The e-mail opportunity for CRM marketers is enormous and it will be enormous for the customer.

- Contact management establishes a cycle in which customer feedback drives process improvement.

- Call centers are the next important step in the gathering and use of customer knowledge to manage customer relationships.

- The successful companies of the future will be the ones that use digital tools to reinvent the way they work.

PART THREE

WINNERS.COM: REAL-WORLD APPLICATIONS

Here comes the fun stuff. In Part Three we'll have a look at winners in industries from retailers to packaged goods to banks to media to hotels and business to business, how they are implementing CRM and how they are using new digital technologies and applications.

Detailed case studies will showcase U.S. and international CRM leaders.

Ideas from the many different companies will provide specific concepts that can be applied even to other kinds of businesses whether they have been practicing CRM for years or are just starting out.

CHAPTER

Can CRM Save the Brick-and-Mortar Folks?

It's not about providing larger selections of shelved products.

Not so very long ago the retail industry had 10 square feet of store space for every person in the United States. By 1998 that figure doubled. Also in 1998 retail store sales dropped from a former $200 a square foot to about $150. In 1999 *The International Journal of Retail and Distribution Management* reported that consumers' shopping time per month was down 31 percent and monthly mall visits were down 47 percent with stores visited per mall trip down 57 percent.

At the same time online retailing has come out of nowhere with its threat to represent a $20 billion competitor by the year 2000. Many are predicting the demise of the traditional retail store. Can a company still doing business in a brick-and-mortar location use the tools of CRM to succeed?

Some are saying the marketplace of the future for retailers is Anything/Anywhere/Any time, but that doesn't have to mean catalogs and the Web will take over the world. These darlings of the 1990s are not really as easy to use or as inexpensive or, for sure, as entertaining as they are made out to be. Not everyone will want to spend an extra $10.95 to have a $19.95 book delivered to her door, and there is no certainty that "The Market," one of the oldest institutions in existence—where people get to meet other people and share important social experiences—will cease to exist.

Moreover, the notion that the marketplace of the future for retailers will include "Anything" may, in fact, be exactly the wrong prediction. In a 1998 column for *Direct Marketing*, Murray Raphel, developer of the outrageously successful and respected multimillion-dollar Atlantic City pedestrian mall, Gordon's Alley, and one of the nation's brightest retailers, quotes Al Meyers of PriceWaterhouse: "The days of retailers being all things to all people are over. The high-performance retailers of the future will be those who carry products specifically selected for their own customers."[1]

I always enjoy asking retailers who they think has the largest selection of men's clothing in New York City. The answer, invariably, is Barney's. It is true Barney's probably hangs more suits than any other New York retailer, but they do not have the largest *selection*. If a man likes the style of suits Brooks Brothers is so famous for, he will find the largest selection of these styles at Brooks Brothers, not Barney's. "Selection" is in the mind of the customer. Al Meyers makes the perfect case for CRM: Tailored product selections, services, and values to known customers are the very thing that can save the brick-and-mortar retailers.

But the in-place retailers will have to realize that since the rules have changed, they will have to change. Some experts suggest that will be difficult at best. Stan Rapp and Thomas L. Collins in their excellent book *Maxi-Marketing* (McGraw-Hill, 1991) maintain: "Far too many marketers remain ill-prepared philosophically to

deal with today's world of constant risk taking, customer empower-
ment, and the complex process of turning likely prospects into long-
term customer relationships. Many marketers still don't get it."

When it was published, the book made a powerful point that
"not getting it" is to risk putting a business at a tremendous disadvantage in the remaining years of the last decade of the century. The
decade has ended, and we see little change. Too many marketers,
and particularly too many retailers, are still unprepared; too many
still don't get it. It is no longer just a matter of putting a business at
a disadvantage. It's a matter of survival.

Sometimes the need to change can be the best thing that can
happen to a company. From the mid-seventies into the early eight-
ies Southeast-headquartered Lowe's became the largest home
improvement store in the country. In the mid-eighties, warehouse
clubs and The Home Depot changed the rules. The rollout of the
warehouse concept resulted in consumers' being preoccupied with
price. They began defining value as price, displacing other components of the value equation in favor of low price. High-volume,
low-cost operators swept into power, and Lowe's stumbled.

Robert Tillman, chairman, president, and chief executive officer of The Lowe's Companies, says, "I think it's fair to say that one
of the best things that ever happened to Lowe's was The Home
Depot. As the saying goes, a good scare is worth more than good
advice. We changed. Others didn't. We had to change the way we
do business. We had to change our pricing, improve our systems,
modify our policies, change our operating procedures, enhance our
training programs, augment our assortments, intensify our commitment to service, and dedicate sufficient resources."[2]

Did changes save this retailer? In the 1990s Lowes achieved a
compound sales growth rate of 20 percent and a compound earn-
ings-per-share growth of 24 percent. With sales exceeding $10 bil-
lion, they are one of the nation's top 20 retailers with one of the
cleanest, best-managed balance sheets in retailing.

So change can save a retail business. But what changes can CRM help the retailer make? How can the Internet and other new technologies help?

The Internet doesn't have to be the enemy of brick-and-mortar retailers. The Web produced more than 6600 vehicle sales and $150 million in revenue for AutoNation during the first quarter of 1999, but John Costello, former senior executive vice president for Sears Roebuck & Company and then president of Republic Industries, AutoNation's corporate parent, said, "Dealerships remain central to our strategy. The Internet provides an opportunity to generate greater traffic and revenue, but the physical dealership will continue to play an important role in the sales and ownership experience."

His experience with Sears convinced him the Internet should be used to drive in-store traffic, not replace retail outlets. "Some customers who gather research on the Internet still would rather come to a store to make a purchase," he said.[3]

Tests are proving Costello right. In Denver, where AutoNation tested a new brand marketing campaign in 1999, 50 percent of AutoNation's customers would not have visited the stores without the Internet presence, and 35 percent said they wouldn't have bought from AutoNation if it hadn't had a Web site.[4]

AutoNation learned in Denver that the Internet could triple the size of a dealer's sales territory. Promoting a Web site can expand a dealer's territory from the normal 10-mile radius to a 30-mile radius.[5]

The American Booksellers Association (ABA), the nearly 100-year-old nonprofit association of independent bookstores, is thinking young and thinking digital to help its retailers compete against Amazon.com and Barnesandnoble.com. In August 1999 the ABA announced an e-commerce initiative called "BookSense.com" for its members. The Internet storefront will contain a common, fully searchable database of 1.6 million books and a means to purchase those books with an electronic shopping cart.

Participating booksellers have access to a password-secured area of the site where they can update customized information like in-store book readings and newsletters, check on the status of orders, set their own book prices, and deal with returns. Richard Howorth, owner of Square Books and president of the ABA, welcomes the new e-commerce initiative. "I'll certainly make more profit than Amazon does," he says. "It would be really hard for us to lose as much as they do."[6]

Barbara Thomas, advertising manager at Seattle's Bay Book Company, understands that the initiative is to strengthen the independent book stores' capabilities for Customer Relationship Management. "Who better than the neighborhood store to make one-to-one marketing a reality," she says. She argues that local booksellers already have the type of customer relationships Barnes & Noble and Amazon boast about, without sacrificing intimacy to efficiency. "We're built on a link of individual relationships," she says. "If there is any difference between what we do and what the others do, it's that we want to have a relationship. Those stores want to minimize the relationship and make you think you're having the same relationship from anywhere."[7]

When the national consumer electronics retailer Circuit City launched its online E-Superstore in July 1999, it integrated all of its 550 brick-and-mortar stores with the Web site so that customers can order merchandise from home and pick it up at their nearest store to save shipping and delivery costs.

CRM and the Internet combined will put brick-and-mortar retailers in the winners' circle.

Nordstrom uses next-generation technologies on the Internet to strengthen its fashion image. In spring 1999 the store worked with the 3-D service provider 3Dshopping.com to produce a fashion show featuring a number of new pieces for spring. The 3-D technology allowed customers to view the fashions from virtually every angle—even change the colors. A shopper interested in seeing a sweater in pink rather than green could make the change, or even zoom in to see texture, with a simple mouse click. Narrowband transmission means the viewer must still wait up to a minute for the images to download and be fully operational, but that will be resolved with the coming of phone companies' digital signal lines and cable companies' modem services that will offer download speeds 50 to 100 times faster than current 28.8K modems.

When broadband is available, Nordstrom expects to add a talking salesperson to help describe the fashions. The Nordstrom experience is just one more example of what John Costello learned at Sears, that the Internet can be used to drive in-store traffic, not replace retail outlets.

It's not just the Web that is bringing fresh excitement to brick-and-mortar stores. Advanced digital systems are being used to transform the shopping experience by transmitting audio and video to stores.

Foot Locker is working with ITEC Entertainment, which has developed technology for major theme parks that runs everything from rides and show controls down to the media and the special effects that happen like P2 or Jaws. ITEC transmits programming over the Internet to store-level engines that broadcast it throughout the store using ITEC MV2 technology. Because the technology is digital and versatile, Foot Locker can send virtually a different package of content to each store in the chain to target different customers. So far, Foot Locker has 230 redesigned stores using the network's distributed media. The chain plans to extend the service to other stores as they are redesigned.

Companies of every kind are turning to exciting in-store experiences to win customers. Discovery Communications spent $20 million to build what has been called a four-level Taj Mahal of a store in Washington, D.C., complete with a life-size *T.rex* skeleton and the fuselage of a World War II B-25 bomber.[8]

As Robert Tillman says, "The secret to true innovation lies not in doing things just to be different but in doing things to be better. The future of retailing isn't about providing large selections of shelved products. It's more about providing smart solutions to the customer." The business of providing smart solutions to the customer is what CRM is all about.

Frank Britt, vice president of marketing and merchandising at Streamline, Inc., the home shopping and delivery service, echoes Robert Tillman's thoughts about the power of customer solutions. Talking about today's opportunities for retail innovation, he says:

> One major move to watch will be power retailers known as "solution killers" as opposed to category killers. These providers understand that the retailer asset with the maximum leverage is the consumer relationship, not their products or store infrastructure. They focus on "value aggregation" around a specific target customer. As a result, their strategic intent is on pooling demand, not supply, to acquire and grow a profitable *relationship*. This focus significantly changes the retail emphasis from getting new customers to selling more to the same customers.
>
> In this model the retailer becomes a horizontal brand that bundles highly relevant products and information for a well-defined clientele, developing active 1to1 Learning Relationships. This fundamental shift in strategic orientation moves a retailer away from push-based selling toward pull-based customer relationship management. In the process, the logic implies profound changes in traditional retail business practices that alter the entire system of delivering value, including how a retailer selects customers, defines offerings, and configures resources to create utility for the customer.[9]

Retailers have always known what is selling by SKU and by store. With CRM they can know *who* is buying. They will know which customers spend $5000 a year in their store and which customers spend $50. They can identify the 10 percent of customers who account for 40 percent of the business, the 20 percent that provide 60 percent of the business, and the 30 percent that account for less than 5 or 10 percent. With the knowledge gained from the CRM program, it is a simple matter to focus inventory on the product categories that are favorites of the "best" customers—the

$5000-a-year folks—moving open-to-buy from the categories bought mostly by the $50-a-year customers. CRM allows them to fully exploit the process of pooling selected demand, not supply, to grow profitable customer relationships.

As Robert Tillman says, the *future* of retailing isn't about providing large selections of shelved products. It's more about providing smart solutions to the customer. Capturing customer information through CRM and sharing it throughout the retail enterprise provides the power to create smart solutions for the customer.

Wal-Mart shares customer information throughout the company to create solutions for the customer. I have been told that Wal-Mart's database is second in size only to that of the U.S. government. Wal-Mart's "market basket data," showing what products are likely to be purchased together, has enabled the chain to address customers' frustrations by placing products in the store to help people find things they didn't even know they needed. Kleenex tissues are in with the paper goods but also mixed in with the cold medicine. Measuring spoons are in housewares and also hanging next to the Crisco cans. In October flashlights are in the hardware aisle but also with the Halloween costumes. No wonder sales at Wal-Mart stores open at least a year are consistently rising faster than at its competitors.

When we talk about sharing customer information throughout the retail enterprise, it is vital to include the sales associates. STS Systems in Montreal provides sophisticated software for retailers to capture, analyze, and use customer information for CRM. I asked Leo Rabinovitch, vice president of new product development at STS, how many of his retail clients are really good at driving this valuable information to the sales associate level:

> It is still a problem in most stores that the CRM activities are aimed at getting the customer information directly to the head office, bypassing the sales associate.
>
> I believe we should be looking at systems and processes that strengthen the sales associate–customer link, thereby making it an

integral part of the retail cycle. To initiate this link, information about customers should be captured at point-of-sale by sales associates, then forwarded to merchants and marketers to supply the store more effectively. Sales associates are a key element of the enterprise-wide CRM program.

Even in the types of stores that don't lend themselves to service differentiators, sales associates should nonetheless be kept informed of all communications with the customers since they are the first point of contact for the customer.

For a really effective CRM program, more effort has to be made to carry head office strategies down to the store level, to inform store personnel and make them true partners in the CRM effort.

Today Leo Rabinovitch's dream requires direct access from the database directly to the POS terminals, which STS Systems' MarketWorks provides, or replicating the customer data from its central location to the POS terminals, thus enabling the use of that information at the time the customer is shopping. Advances in communications (especially the Internet) will allow direct access. Smart cards are also an option where direct access is not yet in place. This will allow the full complement of customer data to be stored on the customer's loyalty card to provide the information at point of sale.

The leading Dutch supermarket chain, Edah, has distributed more than 1.6 million smart cards to customers of its nationwide network of 315 stores.

When the customer's smart card interacts with the store's multimedia terminal, a chip in the system provides the customer with a completely personalized shopping list of special offers on products of interest to her. Initial results from the first installations show a typical monthly sales increase of about 5 percent compared to the prior year, showing yet another way the new technologies and knowledge about the customer can save the brick-and-mortar store.

For full-service stores, having this kind of relevant and actionable information at their fingertips can drastically change sales associates' understanding of what their jobs are all about. It can also help them improve their (and the store's) relationships with customers since they will be offering a better-informed service based on known customer values. They will be doing their jobs better by offering smart solutions and making their customers' lives easier. As another benefit, sales associates can use the customer information for personalized problem resolution with a set of escalation rules based on severity of issues and the value of each individual customer.

One retailer who understands the importance of customer information for sales associates is Neiman Marcus. Billy Payton, vice president for customer programs at Neiman Marcus, says, "We're talking with our customers constantly. We know a lot about them, and each of our sales associates has electronic clientele books that they keep in their POS registers to develop and maintain their individual customer relationships."

CRM *can* save the brick-and-mortar retailers only if the CRM program and interactive technology are integrated to involve the resources of the entire organization.

Where does technology fit, and will the Web replace the brick-and-mortar retailer?

Two final thoughts. First from Robert Tillman again:

> Is Internet shopping coming? You bet. Is it going to replace bricks and mortar or store shopping? Unlikely. Why? Because the future of retailing and Internet marketing is not mutually exclusive. This is similar to the predicted end of radio and the cinema when television came on the scene. Both industries have survived and prospered. In both cases it was, and is, purely a matter of adapting, adjusting, and accepting change. Again, it's a great opportunity for those who are willing to make the investment.[10]

And from Frank Britt:

> It is the new consumers' demand for convenience, choices and control that is at the core of the emerging retail revolution. When a brand moves from a cluster of values around a product to fulfillment

of customers' needs, this creates meaning, which then modifies behavior that generates deeply felt attitudes.[11]

Frank Britt is echoing Martha Rogers' counsel that you can help your customer to create her own barrier to exit.

When a retail brand moves from a cluster of values around product to fulfillment of customer needs through CRM, we will see that CRM and technology and the Internet can save the brick-and-mortar folks.

If CRM and technology can, indeed, save the brick-and-mortar retailers, what other industries can this combination help develop? We'll start with one you might least suspect: packaged goods.

19

Managing CRM with Faceless Customers

How can packaged goods marketers use the disciplines of CRM?

It has been well documented that companies whose business brings them face to face with the consumer can, indeed, manage the customer relationship. But what about the brands that must reach the consumer's hands through channel partners—particularly packaged goods brands?

Packaged goods brand marketing has always relied on mass media to build the brand with consumers, but that was before the Internet arrived and gave us a new kind of mass media that can reach out and interact with individual customers. Now consumer and business trends and new technologies are changing everything we ever thought we knew about consumer marketing. So, too, will they change brand marketing.

These trends involve virtually every link in the marketing chain, from the manufacturer, through the retailer, to the customer.

They are tearing apart the efficient, delicate marketing process that has worked for the past 60 years. The packaged goods brands are facing the strongest test.

The packaged goods industry introduced another 24,000 new products in 1998, up 2000 percent from just 15 years ago. With this number of new products introduced into an already overcrowded marketplace, companies are finding brand loyalty more and more difficult to defend.

Over 9000 supermarkets in the United States alone have card marketing programs in place gathering consumer data. Vons with its 350-odd stores has more than 4 million members in its preferred shopper program, and I'm told the program is growing by an average of 25 percent a year. Vons' objective for the program has been to increase its private brand penetration—the very thing brand marketers fear.

One example makes the point of the new test for packaged goods brands. While store brands of breakfast cereal hold a market share of only about 11 percent compared with Kellogg's 31 percent, Kellogg, the world's leading maker of ready-to-eat cereal, reported a serious sales drop through the third quarter of 1998, reducing third-quarter earnings 31 percent and putting 2000 jobs under review for possible layoffs.

One typical customer in a Midwest supermarket gave her reason for the brand's problems. "Store brands of cereal are cheaper, and they are just the same. I buy the expensive brands only when I have a coupon."[1]

Vons' senior management has called the Vons Club (and its objective to increase private brand penetration) one of the company's most important strategic initiatives.

Of the 7 million households who shop Tesco in the United Kingdom each week, 75 percent have signed up for the company's loyalty program, and Tesco has used the club card program to vault over Sainsbury's to the number 1 spot in food retailing in the United Kingdom.

Boots the Chemists with 1300 stores in the United Kingdom has more than 9 million customers who show their Boots Advantage Card each time they shop to earn "treats."

Examples like this could fill this book.

Grocery mergers add more pressure. The new $36 billion "number 1," Albertsons and American Stores have almost 2500 stores. Will Kroger and Safeway be next to give us a $50 billion Goliath? And if one doesn't think the world is changed, think about the fact that suddenly 2 percent of all Chicago food sales are at Home Depot!

Just to raise the bar even higher, we're facing a new consumer—the smartest shopper we have ever known, better informed than ever before, intent on value, hungry for information, starved for time. Marketers will have to keep changing to keep up with this savvy consumer's interests and her changing perception of value.

In today's environment, winning success for the brand marketer, just as for others we have looked at, will require an intense focus on the customer and breakthrough tools and techniques for maximizing customer relationships.

Packaged goods marketers will have to learn the micromarketing disciplines of CRM—to target and build relationships with the *most profitable* customers. Forty-five percent of customers in a supermarket at any given time are value shoppers. Mass advertising sometimes brings in the wrong customers. Targeting profitable customers requires customer knowledge, and customer knowledge requires a customer database.

Garth Hallbrook, worldwide director of differential marketing at Ogilvy & Mather, in his great book *Not All Customers Are Created Equal*, talks about the importance of targeting the most profitable customers:

> It is a proven fact that in category after category, the largest brand is the one that has made the greatest inroads with the small group of highly profitable customers. Invariably, the brand leader has attracted the largest number of category high-profit buyers. Winning over

and building the loyalty of these high-profit consumers is the most productive path for profitable growth for most brands.[2]

This is the most important book any packaged goods marketer can read!

Companies will no longer waste advertising dollars on non-prospects. They will learn to talk to their high-profit segments—even to individuals within these segments—and they will learn to use the new tools we have been talking about in new ways. Admittedly, this kind of custom marketing adds incremental cost, but companies are finding ways to make these efforts scalable.

Supermarkets spend heavily for frequent shopper programs to find and target their best customers because they know that, in the United States, the average customer spends $390 a year in her supermarket but the *best* customers spend $3674!

Garth Hallbrook points out that 36 million of the 95 million households in the United States buy Folger's coffee at least once a year, but just 4 million households account for nearly half the brand's annual volume. That's the kind of statistic that shows the need for packaged goods brand marketers to find and target their best customers.

So what does all this mean to the packaged goods marketer when it comes to execution?

It *doesn't* mean suddenly addressing each and every customer by name, but it certainly does mean targeting best customer segments.

For *sure it doesn't* mean moving all coupon efforts from free-standing newspaper inserts to 1to1 targeted direct mail. That's already been proven.

Coupons do not build a relationship. Coupons have a very important place, but they don't build relationships, and they don't buy brand loyalty. Brand marketers should continue to distribute coupons at the lowest possible cost, but they should use their targeted customer relationship investments to build the brand.

If brand manufacturers can find ways to deliver personalized coupons targeted and timed to attack specific customers' brand switching behavior, couponing will have a new value. It is possible the Internet will now provide that opportunity.

Internet coupon firm CoolSavings.com began a concentrated effort in spring 1999 to help consumer packaged goods manufacturers develop this new kind of coupon value. CoolSavings can now let manufacturers use detailed customer information to deliver targeted offers to its Web site and to its members' e-mailboxes. CoolSavings members will then download coupons, rebates, or other offers redeemable in stores. Visitors to the company's site at www.coolsavings.com supply names, addresses, area codes, and e-mail information. They have the option of telling CoolSavings the number of homes and cars they own, household income, profession, age, number of children and pets, household birthdays and anniversaries, and more—with the promise of getting offers tailored to their interests.

Adding to this the fact that CoolSavings will let advertisers list recipes, post store events, and carry on interactive focus groups, it may be that CoolSavings has found a way for packaged goods marketers to use the Internet to reach out and interact with individual targeted customers.

Brand equity built through customer relationships is the best weapon, and perhaps the only recourse, against the private labels of multi-billion-dollar powerhouse chains.

So today's marketing challenge remains what it has always been—build the brand. The new rules of marketing mean only that you must build the brand in new ways.

One of the ways will be to work within the scope of the supermarket customer programs—finding new ways to work with these channel partners.

And it's not just supermarkets. The Web is now an important part of the food business. That smart, young Web upstart, PeaPod, tracks customers' purchases, which brands they prefer, how often they shop, and whether they respond to promotions. PeaPod knows they sell five times as much Keri hand lotion by running a banner ad whenever a customer clicks on bananas. Kraft, Bristol-Meyers Squibb, and Kellogg use PeaPod to test consumer taste and behavior. They have seen an average of 10 percent to 15 percent increase in sales when they run a targeted banner ad—twice that of targeted electronic coupons.

From all the reports I see and hear, retailers are interested in help from their brand manufacturer partners, and 60 percent of manufacturers recently surveyed think spending on frequent shopper programs will increase.

The 81st Annual DMA Conference in San Francisco had a panel discussion titled "Harnessing the Power of Grocery Stores' Frequent Shopper Programs for Brand Marketing." Laura Henze of Willard Bishop Consulting, Ltd., Barrington, Illinois, offered these caveats.

In setting out to work within the scope of supermarket customer programs, most brand marketers need to spend more time at the start on formulating their objectives.

1. They should ask, How can we participate strategically to benefit our brand and the retailer and the consumer?

2. How can we use the program to increase total sales rather than just a channel switch?

3. It does not make a lot of sense to work with grocers, only to teach them how to be better ("private") brand marketers.

4. Profitable involvement for the brand must be more than just "renting a page" in the monthly mailer.

5. A brand marketer buying into a grocer's loyalty plan deserves, and should demand, exclusivity.

6. It should always be remembered that the retailer's goal is shopper loyalty to the store; the brand's goal is a greater share of the store's customer.

Right now there is a big gap between grocers' tactics and strategy. Most know how to use the discounts to drive card use, and most are still at this tactical level. Few have developed any strategy for building customer relationships. Most retailers don't have the right data to give the brand marketer the answers he or she really needs.

The brand marketer can help the retailer by bringing his or her consumer understanding and insight. Working with the retailer and his or her customer knowledge, the brand marketer can even help the retailer with category management and result measurement.

The Coca-Cola Company is a leader in working with retail partners and their frequent shopper data. Don Hodson, consultant to retail partners at The Coca-Cola Company, works with the retailer data, assuring the retailers an objective analysis to identify growth opportunities across the total store, not just the carbonated soft drink category.

Hodson uses the POS data to learn customers' needs and to develop customer insight to serve three objectives:

1. To identify growth opportunities, storewide
2. To provide assistance to retailers with weak IS capabilities
3. To develop relationships between The Coca-Cola Company and its retail partners

Some retailers provide The Coca-Cola Company with weekly uploads and maintain two years of data. Others are just starting in the analysis process. While the data identify individuals, the company gets only an identification number for each customer, not a name and address. Hodson reports that he sees lots of bad data.

The Coca-Cola Company helps the stores measure promotion effectiveness by studying which featured SKUs bring in the high-quality shopper. One set of items may bring in the most traffic while another set may bring in higher spenders. Another measure of promotion effectiveness is which price points prove most profitable. For example, bananas on sale at 49 cents a pound filled 29 percent of baskets; at 39 cents a pound, 32.8 percent of baskets; and at 29 cents a pound, 34.5 percent of baskets. However, the 29-cent-a-pound buyers spent $3 less per basket. Forty-nine cents attracted 84 percent of core customers, 39 cents, 82 percent of core customers, and 29 cents, only 69 percent. The 39-cents-per-pound price point rewards the better shopper. The 29-cents price attracts the wrong customer.

When The Coca-Cola Company first started on this program, they had to pound the pavement to persuade retailers to share data. Now retailers are coming to them. The company is certainly a leader in teaching retailers how to use customer intelligence rather than price to drive business and to provide value in terms that mean the most to core customers. They are now in the process of creating aggregated data to give retailers benchmarks against which to measure their activities. The program is active in Canada, South America, and Europe in addition to the United States.

In helping the retailer, the brand marketer will be helping his or her brand maintain shelf position. Activity-based costing and data mining of supermarket frequent shopper card programs now enable retailers to make the decision to eliminate underperforming brands.

Supermarket consultant Brian Woolf says, "Loyalty cards are key to helping broad-line retailers make correct assortment decisions because they provide real-world data on which products and brands are important to the high-spending customers who account for most of the retailer's profits." He also sees some supermarket chains reshaping categories based on loyalty card data, citing a chain that doubled the size of its baby care category and halved the size of its candy section based on loyalty data.[3] This is all part of the CRM process to make it easier for customers to do business with a particular company. It will be important for the brand to find ways to work with the retailer's customer information for survival and growth.

There is just one problem: At the start, most brand sales reps don't know the term "customer decile." CRM must be taught to the field force before a brand's CRM can begin to work within the scope of the supermarket customer programs. But there is no question that the ones to get a handle on all this customer data in scalable size and usable form will be the winners.

Another way brand marketers can reach out to build customer relationships and build the brand is by providing the consumer with *information*. A recent Cox Direct study reported that almost all methods of coupon distribution either maintained or slipped in popularity among consumers with the exception of couponing at the store electronically. But direct mail ranked highest (52 percent) among consumers as a medium *to convey information* about grocery and/or health and beauty care products.[4] Information is often more important than price and can help build customer relationships and brand loyalty.

How are some folks using information to build increased use, customer retention, and loyalty, and how many are doing it?

John Cummings, whose firm John Cummings and Partners tracks these things, reported at the fall 1998 DMA Annual Conference that newly launched programs in the packaged goods industry are at their highest level in five years. Ninety-four new loyalty programs were launched during the 12 months ending September 30, 1998. Although 51 companies ran at least three programs, Cummings ranked Kraft's Miracle Whip Cooks! as the top-ranked program.

Miracle Whip Cooks! is a relationship marketing program specifically designed for the heavier users of Miracle Whip. The program, utilizing a newsletter format, centers on food preparation needs and offers recipes and ideas featuring Miracle Whip as a helper and friend. The program is a recipe strategy and has proven effective due to the highly receptive audience of the product per serving. I'm told the program has proven very effective over several years in building incremental volume and nurturing brand loyalty.

The Kraft Crystal Light program that started almost a dozen years ago is still a classic. It carried some coupons, but it was the *information* in the newsletter and the "membership" relationship, developed by the club and the catalog, that was meaningful to the million-plus heavy users of Crystal Light.

Direct-mail programs like this do carry coupons, but the coupons are not the main thrust of the message to the customer.

Once more I have to quote my friend, Arthur Hughes, our customer lifetime value expert. He says this about coupons and relationship building:

> Where mailing programs are built on discount coupons as the core, instead of building a relationship focused on the product or the manufacturer's established name and reputation, they are doomed to failure.
>
> Solid relationships built through database marketing are immune to discounts.
>
> Your customers prefer you because you are an old friend who recognizes them, who provides personal services and delivers a well-known quality product. You would be insulted if a friend gave you a tip for doing a favor. A database should aim at that same kind of relationship.

Some marketers will be able to address their best customers in new ways. Even television is getting in the addressable target game. Next Century Media, a new media consultancy, is planning a year-long test of addressable advertising. The first test will involve 3000 homes in the Detroit area. Two-thirds will get targeted ads, and the remaining 1000 households will constitute a control group. Up to five different commercial messages can be sent out during each of the commercial breaks, enabling advertisers to send messages based on values that are important to specific customers. Next Century has planned a heavy research component of the test to measure how effectively the messages are being delivered to the advertisers' target homes.

Over 30 years ago AdTel, run by John Adler, developed a system of sending different television commercials (and constructing control groups) to individual households in the same market. The sales results were tracked by grocery store audit before, during, and after the test period. The system was used by major advertising agencies and packaged goods companies, but purely as a test mechanism to learn which commercials performed best at moving the products.

With the arrival of digital television, the technology is now available to create even finer targeting to specific households. Kraft and cable-television operator Tele-Communications, Inc. (TCI), are already exploring this. TCI has converted most of its systems from an old analog platform to a more advanced digital one allowing for micromarketing and even interactivity with its more than 14 million subscribers. Don Miceli, Kraft's vice president of media services, says, "With digital technology, we can now use cable more strategically and inventively to develop a closer relationship with our consumers." Alee Gerster, executive vice president of media services at Grey Advertising, New York, which is working with Kraft to create the targeted ads, poses an exciting challenge: "Our goal with the program is ultimately to be able to deliver one message to the cook in the kitchen and another to the family in the den."[5]

While we're talking about delivering information on television, we have to ask if "infomercial" is really such a dirty word. Can the infomercial be a tool to build relationships with customers?

The financial troubles of many of the industry's infomercial leaders have been well documented. Some have declared bankruptcy while others are hanging in until the business makes a comeback. Infomercials made a bad first impression on Madison Avenue because of the bad acting, fake audiences, and screaming pitchmen in the early versions. Mention the word *infomercial* and most brand managers still cringe, while creative directors still snicker.

But Charlie Breen, co-chairman of Mayhew/Breen Productions, sees a big comeback on the horizon, and he says it's not all mops, amazing car waxes, and exercise gadgets. Kodak, The Sharper Image, even Cheseborough-Ponds are on the air with infomercials. Cesari Response Television, Inc., a producer of infomercials and direct response television, was named the fastest-growing company in Washington State in 1998. Between the years

1995 and 1997, the company showed a revenue boost of 2398 percent.[6] By using an infomercial, automaker Lexus received tens of thousands of calls from people who wanted to know more about its preowned vehicles. Taylor Made, the golf equipment manufacturer, was swamped with inquiries from golfers who wanted more information about the Burner Bubble driver. Wouldn't it be nice to have half-sold customers calling you?

Charlie Breen thinks the infomercial business is simply undergoing a major transition and the current shakeout will result in a stronger industry. Used properly, the infomercial can be the ultimate sales representative, building the brand while building customer relationships and transforming viewers into buyers and advocates. Two things have been proven: The 800 number responses will build a customer database, and the medium *can* drive consumers to multiple sales outlets.[7]

Just so you don't think of this as such an off-the-wall idea, there is another reason I urge marketers to reexplore the infomercial now. In the interactive future (which is really here now) and with the development of broadband transmission, infomercials will migrate from traditional broadcast to the Web, where consumers will watch them on demand. One expert suggests that a Web infomercial, perhaps 5 to 10 minutes long, will become an integral component of most advertising campaigns.

All of this leads us to a further consideration of the Internet and where it fits in the process of branding and building relationships with consumers.

A quick review of a few key players:

A fine example is the recent Quaker Oats "Meanies" promotion. For those of you who don't have small children who know all these things, Meanies are a line of fuzzy collectibles for kids, and at the time of this campaign they were *hot* in stores across the country. Up front the Quaker Meanies promotion was a typical cereal promotion with a mail-in offer, but the promotion was supported by a specially designed Web site (www.meaniescrunch.com) targeting high-tech-oriented kids ages 6 through 12. Kids could go to the site—featured on all 20 million Cap'n Crunch boxes—to learn more about the promotion, the Quaker brand, and the Meanies clan. Quaker did not collect any data on the site because of its kids' target, but they believe the Web program will help them communicate and build lasting relationships with customers.[8]

Power Bar, who makes "energy" food bars sold in supermarkets, drugstores, and convenience stores, reports that its site is now the firm's primary source of consumer data. The database is used (to quote a spokesperson) "to build brand loyalty and develop and announce new products."

Seagrams, who already has more than 10 million names in their brand building database, now has established sites they call "interactive communications platforms" for seven of their brands.

My favorite all-time online effort is the Ragu site. Ragu is now in its second generation of Internet marketing with what they call "salesworthy *edutainment*." The home page, called "Mama's Cucina," is bright and peppy, and takes little time to download. Offerings include a cookbook titled *What's New at Mama's*, *Goodies from Mama*, and phrases from Professor Antonio—Italian language nuggets in both print and sound.

And even grocers are on the Web. Kroger recently launched an experiment offering to send discount coupons on *house brand products* to visitors to its Web site at www.kroger.com.[9]

With respect to the Internet, someone has said we are about where we were in the early 1950s when large packaged goods advertisers made the move to television and really pushed that business forward.

Unilever has signed a deal to spend an estimated $30 million on America Online and Microsoft Network Web sites over the next three years. The AOL deal will take them into Canada, the United Kingdom, Germany, France, Japan, and, later in the year, Australia.

And, I guess, the real sign of the Internet's coming of age occurred in August 1998 when a big advertiser, P&G, hosted a summit at its Cincinnati offices, bringing together senior executives from other leading marketers, technology companies, and advertising agencies to figure out how to jump-start Web advertising effectiveness.

As the trade papers said at the time, when the big advertiser doing this is a *brander*, as opposed to somebody who is going to sell a lot of product from his or her Web site, that's big news.[10]

If you accept the fact that coupons reward switching behavior and that without targeting, you are pretty much rewarding all the heavy coupon clippers who switch back and forth between heavy-volume offers, then the Internet gets interesting because you will be able to pick your best targets for coupon distribution. The Web promise of personalized offers like CoolSavings may just allow brand marketers to use coupons to build brand and attack the switching behavior problem by hitting the right people with the right offer at the right time.

At the outset I urged brand marketers to use their customer relationship marketing investments to build the brand. As a last example, I want to take one more look at Kraft who is building brand loyalty through targeted mailings. They are pursuing an aggressive brand and loyalty building strategy by mail and breaking some of the rules along the way.

While the company has no objection to a bump in sales like the kind generated through coupon use, the focus of all their CRM mailings is more on building an image for featured products and building brand loyalty. The key factor in the mailings is the response card that enables Kraft to get input that helps in targeting and product development. More than that, the response card gives recipients a chance to voice their thoughts to Kraft. This is the kind of dialog that can, indeed, build brand and create brand loyalty.

Louis Bart, Kraft's director of direct marketing and database marketing, says:

> Our focus is not mailing out coupons for discounting. Obtaining customers through couponing is what I would consider antiloyalty.

If you focus your customers on coupons and get them used to price discounts, you have the potential to erode the equity or loyalty you have with them.[11]

One other CRM leader deserves special mention. Starting from scratch eight or nine years ago, Ralston Purina now has a dedicated staff of 18 professionals delivering outstanding results. So outstanding, in fact, that they have been ranked the number 1 or number 2 packaged goods company in 11 of the last 14 measured quarters through 1997 in John Cummings' DBMScan's "commitment to database marketing," swamping the competition.

I always talk about the "new rules of marketing," not just to sell more of my books but because we *are* facing a new consumer—the smartest shopper we have ever known, better informed than ever before, intent on value, hungry for information, and short on time. The purpose is to get marketers to think new thoughts about marketing brands to this savvy consumer.

The thing to remember about the new rules is that they represent a constant process of learning, continually acquiring knowledge, adapting, responding, and interacting with customers and the marketplace—that is, developing active 1to1 Learning Relationships.

Building relationships *from the customer point of view* will be the only way we will be invited into the household. However, this doesn't mean everything has to hinge on database marketing or on the Web.

My good friend, Northwestern Professor Don Schultz, said it best in his book *Measuring Brand Communication and ROI* (Association of National Advertisers, 1997). He defined *brand communication* as "encompassing all forms of communication, actions and activities that influence and impact the relationship between the customer and the brand." That's what micromarketing with consumer knowledge–driven initiatives must be all about for the packaged goods brand marketer.

Packaged goods marketers will have to learn to use the disciplines of CRM and the new technologies to become winners.

20

Because That's Where the Money Is

CRM leaders: Financial institutions master the tools for success.

Willie Sutton had it right: Banks are where the money is, and banks are where a lot of the money is today for hardware and software database marketing vendors and data analysts who support CRM programs.

For some years banks were slow to understand customers' needs and the potential profitability of CRM. They were content to spend up to $100 to acquire a new account and as little as $6 to keep it. As studies began to show a fairly typical 80 percent attrition rate among banks' most profitable customers, bankers began to realize that yesterday's product-focused business model would no longer work to retain and grow today's demanding customer. They were right. Twenty years ago, U.S. banks held more than 50 percent of household deposits, but that figure has slipped to 25 percent today.

The implementation of CRM programs has not been easy for most banks. Few had true corporate databases to bring together, in one place, the full view of a customer's history. One report had this to say:

> In reality, the data that many financial institutions hold is, in its current form, not very useful for marketing purposes. Many of the legacy systems encountered are account driven and product focused. Data are thin and patchy, and no customer view is available. The mere process of *identifying* all the transactions involving a single customer across 40 or 50 different product-oriented systems is daunting.[1]

Now savvy banks have been quick to solve this problem by consolidating customer information and developing data mining and other technologies to help them hold onto customers who have been moving money to mutual funds, online stock trading, and even online banking.

The Internet has produced a new phenomenon: banks that exist only online. CompuBank, with $600 million in assets, started from scratch on the Internet and was the first online bank to receive a charter from the Office of the Comptroller of the Currency. In the spring of 1999 Jonathan Lack, executive vice president of marketing and planning of CompuBank, boasted, "We've only been open since October 7th, and we've already been rated number 8 on Gomez Advisors' Web site based on the quality of our service. Online financial services is the only thing we do. We're not a division of another company or a subsidiary. We're an Internet bank only."[2]

By August 1999 American Express Co. and Bank One's First USA had launched online banks; E*Trade, the nation's second-largest online brokerage, had announced a plan to buy Telebank Financial Corp., the largest online bank; and Citigroup and Wal-Mart Stores were said to have e-banks waiting in the wings.[3]

The CRM efforts of offline banks are paying off. As early as 1993 we worked with the Royal Bank of Canada (then the Royal Trust) to implement a datamart to present a view of individual customers and customer segments for CRM. In a recent trade article, James Rager, executive vice president of the Toronto bank, reported that using the system, the bank has boosted the profitability of more than 1 million of its customers by an average of $100 per customer over three years.[4]

In July 1998 Fleet Bank, the tenth-largest commercial bank in the United States, implemented a new enterprise-wide open data warehouse to give Fleet a comprehensive view of its customers. Loaded with 350 gigabytes of information and expected to grow to 4 terabytes, the system keeps daily customer account, transaction, and demographic information from 34 internal and external data sources, including ATM, branch, deposit, loan, investment, and telephone banking systems.[5]

First Union, Charlotte, North Carolina, announced in 1998 it was adding final touches to a database system for CRM that has been in the works for two years. First Union implemented the data warehouse for its retail consumer banking, and it plans to add the commercial side of the business. The retail database maintains data on 16 million customers for 24 months and receives information from 20 sources. Naras Eechambadi, senior vice president of First Union's knowledge-based marketing arm, says the development of the enriched database was essential: "To maintain our business advantage, we need to differentiate ourselves from other institutions through service, and service comes from knowing your customers."[6]

One way First Union is differentiating itself from other institutions is by pioneering an effort in electronic bill presentment and payment as a benefit for its customers. First Union customers can now view their utility bills from BellSouth and Florida Power and Light online and then pay them at the bank's Web site. As one writer says, "For consumers, the appeal is convenience. For billers, there's a chance to cut printing, mailing, and processing costs— and, perhaps more important, build a closer relationship with customers."[7]

As part of its efforts to make bank customers' lives a bit easier, FirstStar Corp., Cincinnati, has installed software that remembers the amount of a customer's previous withdrawal from its

ATMs and immediately offers that figure to save customers' time on their next withdrawal.

Bank of America (BofA) has 25 data analysts supporting CRM for the bank's 11 million consumer households. A BofA retention program saved more customers than were gained from a new business acquisition program for the same period and delivered a four-time return on investment.

Other banks are moving just as quickly to centralize the data that will allow them to manage customer relationships. One writer says, "Propelled by technology, banking is transforming itself at a pace and scale that have no precedent."[8]

What has happened is that banks have finally come to realize that their domination is in product categories that have the least revenue growth potential—deposit accounts and mortgages—and core deposits are already showing declining growth as customers move their funds to other options.

The other options are not just online banks. Retailers and others, from Nordstrom to Hillenbrand Funeral Services, are expanding into financial services, and the Internet is making it easy.

Research shows that banking with nonbanks will be an easy sell. According to a survey of 125 bank customers in three major cities, when asked if they would open a bank account with Nordstrom, 30 percent said they would. The survey respondents would also be happy to bank with Blockbuster, McDonald's, Starbucks, and Mobil if they could. One expert believes this represents the power of capturing the imagination and loyalty of customers that banks typically have not been able to do.[9]

Nordstrom is following the lead of retailers in the United Kingdom where just about anyone can offer an unlimited range of financial services without a legal permit. Virgin and Marks & Spencer were early players, and more recently the giant supermarket chains, Sainsbury's and Tesco established in-store banks with almost 1.15 million deposit account holders between them with total funds under management approaching 2.4 billion pounds.

The vast network of Sainsbury and Tesco retail stores are a ready-made billboard and service point for financial services customers, and the constant interaction these retailers have with their customers removes the need for extensive advertising for their banks. With their powerful databases of customer spending information, supermarkets believe with good reason that they have the potential to be key distributors of financial service products by the year 2005.

There are many benefits for the retailer:

Increased customer loyalty, because shoppers have another reason to come into the store each week—customers change stores more frequently than they change banks

Enhanced sales, because shoppers who stop at the bank may also pick up food while they are in the store

Increased store traffic, because bank customers who may have never shopped in the store before now have a very convenient reason to come

Increased bottom-line profits from rent and additional sales

Many retailers have learned that the in-store bank employees are ambassadors for the store assisting shoppers when they are in the store aisles and talking to shoppers about becoming bank customers.[10]

All of this competition has forced traditional banks to concentrate on customer retention. Cross-selling is as important for customer retention in the banking industry as it is in the other businesses we have studied. Research has shown that banks keep those customers with whom they maintain multiple relationships three or four times longer than those with whom they have only a single relationship.

Banks have not had a brilliant history of cross-selling customers to multiple products. In the 1980s many banks jumped at the idea of creating "financial supermarkets" to offer brokerage services, insurance, and even travel. When customers failed to respond, the concept was soon abandoned.

What's different this time is that the new approach is based on sound CRM principles. Banks' cross-selling efforts are now much more tailored to customer interests. Banks are not rushing out to create points programs, as have so many other businesses. They are learning they must deliver values that are meaningful to the customer in the customer's terms, and they are using customer information to create dialogs and learn what values are important to individual customers. They are finding ways to develop relationships starting with the customer's first account.

There are already some big success stories.

Citigroup (the merged Citicorp and Travelers Group) has restructured its worldwide call center operations for cross-selling. The company has added 700 positions where new customer knowledge segmentation has shown potential. When Citibank call center agents were cross-trained to sell insurance products from the Travelers Property Casualty insurance business, call centers that had traditionally handled Citibank's credit card operations sold approximately 3000 auto and homeowner insurance policies in 1998.[11]

How big is the cross-sell opportunity for every type of money product under one roof for other recent mergers—BankOne Corp./First Chicago, BankAmerica Corp./NationsBank Corp., and Wells Fargo/Norwest with its 20 million customers and financial service stores or branches in all 50 states?

The data warehouse that supports the CRM effort at Chase, New York, has become the central point at which information from separate databases of credit card, deposit, auto loan, and other account holders and transactional data are gathered, analyzed, and then disseminated across the bank, often in real time.

Denis O'Leary, chief information officer for Chase, says, "Having a branch across the street is less effective than having a terminal next to a salesperson." Investment in information technology, which reached $2 billion in 1996, has helped Chase maintain 92 percent of its deposits despite cutting the number of its branches from 900 to 500.[12]

In another case, Key Corp., with $66 billion in assets and nearly 7 million customers, found its profitability per customer was lagging. They were spending millions to promote their broad base of services through direct mail, telemarketing, and media advertising with disappointing results. They had no way of focusing on the bank's best customers because they had no way of knowing who those customers were.

They launched an ambitious CRM project supported by a state-of-the-art data warehouse designed to collate all the information about bank customers in one place to support every sales and marketing decision made throughout the company. They decided they could not succeed unless they became a customer-driven company.

They first identified 150 elements—age, checking and savings balance, outstanding loans and when they come due, number of children, frequency of ATM usage—that could be used to answer strategic marketing questions. Their list included what kinds of customers purchase each product, when they purchase them, why they purchase them, the extent to which other customers with a similar profile might be interested, the names of the most profitable and least profitable customers, the distribution channels different customers prefer, and the circumstances under which a customer is likely to defect. Their stated goal is to develop fewer and better relationships with customers rather than have more customers that use only single products.[13]

Has CRM worked for Key Corp.? In 1996, Key Corp. was rated number 1 in customer satisfaction among top banks included in the annual University of Michigan/American Society for Quality Control Survey published in *Fortune* magazine.

Key Corp. executives have credited the success of the CRM program to some of the things we talked about in Chapter 3. For example, there must be a champion at the top. "If the bank's top executives hadn't been in accord about the overall strategy, the critical role of the data warehouse and the reorganization that followed to fit the new technology, the entire project could easily have fallen apart," they said.[14]

Key Corp. learned that people, processes, and technology must change. The technology will (and should) change the business model, organizational structure, and job descriptions.[15]

First Tennessee Bank has been rated by *Forbes* magazine as the most profitable regional bank for the last five years (total shareholder return average 36 percent) because of its record retention rates. First Tennessee's goals are to retain 97 percent of high-value customers and 95 percent of high-potential relationships. This retention program works, they say, only because of the full support of top management for the project.

It has been reported that one-third of all banking data warehousing and CRM projects have failed because they didn't have the full support of top management and/or the firms didn't change product-oriented structures to take full advantage of the warehouse's power to consolidate customer information and drive customer focus.

Other financial institutions are jumping on the CRM bandwagon, and in some cases they're bringing in CRM marketing experts from banks to make it happen for them. In February 1998, Fidelity Investments tapped Stephen Cone, chief marketing officer at Key Corp., to be the president of its customer marketing division so that its retail group could bring a more personalized marketing style to the financial company.

In less than a year, Cone had in place a number of initiatives to move Fidelity's marketing focus from products to customers. Fidelity has now developed a segmentation strategy for its 6 million customers splitting the file into top investors and further defining it by generation: seniors, boomers, and young professionals.

Following the sound CRM principle of developing specialized products to meet the needs and serve the value requirements of individual customer segments, Fidelity is now creating products like a tax advantage stock fund that will benefit high-net-worth investors by focusing on the potential tax consequences of an equity fund. It has also started an instant broker service with trading through a pager for its most active traders.

Cone promises more ahead to better target Fidelity's communications—mail, phone, e-mail, and Internet—including personal pages on the company's Web site. "We're doing more personalized messaging of our products and services that we think are the right ones for each individual customer," he says, "because our job is to create services and products that will give customers more reasons to buy from us.[16]

When London-based fund management group Mercury Asset Management replaced its generic magazine with a mass-customized version for the top 20 percent of its client base, the 7700-version customized guide attracted 141 percent more business in its first three weeks than the previous generic version had in four weeks. More importantly, the generic version, sent to 5 percent of the top client group as a control, did not generate any new business in that time frame.[17]

However, not all banks are up to speed on CRM. A survey of 1000 bank customers by Deluxe Corp. suggests that financial services firms don't know their customers well enough to practice CRM and present relevant offers.

Forty-three percent of responders said their financial service provider does not know their special needs "well at all." Sixty percent said the offers they receive are not relevant to their needs. Thirty-nine percent said they did not receive offers at all. It will take time for the industry to meet the demands of its sophisticated customers who expect the same personal treatment on the phone, in the mail, or on the Internet that they receive at their local branch office.[18]

As Internet banks invent new offers and services, traditional banks will have to respond. The Peppers & Rogers Group gives us some idea of the kind of new offers we can expect to see from online banks. In May 1999 they asked their newsletter readers to send in their best ideas as to how a 1to1 Internet bank should function. Here are four of the best suggestions:

1. Use real-time e-mails or pager alerts to notify customers when they are in danger of bouncing a check or when their account balance is dangerously low. Alert customers when selected deposits and registrations become valid and when contributions or records should be reviewed for tax or other planning purposes.

2. Put the entire loan process—whether for a new car or house—online. Offer an online payment calculator, and provide hyperlinks to real estate agents, home or auto insurers, and movers. Notify online billers of a new home address. In other words, approach the customer with an integrated solution to his or her relocation problem—not just with a collection of products suitable for relocating customers.

3. Post IRS tax forms online. Inform customers of new and revised tax laws specific to their needs. To the extent possible, complete these tax forms automatically, using information already carried within the bank account records.

4. Give customers an online personal finance program that will track their transactions according to purpose, category, or tax deductibility. It should allow them to prepare summaries of their assets and liabilities and, by comparing their financial ratios and assets to other customers, it could even give them a certain amount of "automated advice" about their personal financial situation.[19]

One more good reason to subscribe to *INSIDE 1to1*.

It is safe to say we will see some of these offers come to market from Internet banks, adding to the challenge for traditional banks to use their customer information to get much better at managing customer relationships.

The view of the customer is in place. The hurdle of data delivery has been jumped. The next hurdle is learning to use the information to manage customer relations intelligently. This will require creativity from management and will involve using customer information to identify new opportunities to create customer value in the customers' terms.

Randall Grossman, senior vice president of Fleet Financial Group's Data Management and Analysis Division, says, "The changing face of banking is like a glacier. It doesn't make big movement overnight. The big challenge is customizing each interaction with each customer—no matter what channel—so as to maximize profitability . . . by offering the most appropriate and most profitable products to each individual."[20]

Randall Grossman's goals for Fleet's efforts summarize the purposes of CRM:

> First, we'll get payback from improving the efficiency of our target marketing. We spend $20 million a year on direct marketing, and it's the fastest-growing component of our whole marketing budget, so improving its effectiveness can yield major profitability improvements.
>
> Second, we want to improve the profitability of our cross-selling efforts. On average, 40 percent of customers never use a product profitably. We want to improve that ratio.
>
> A third priority is developing retention strategies aimed at keeping the loyalty of our most profitable customers. Many tried-and-true bankers' assumptions about where profitable customers can be found simply don't hold up when you really analyze your markets.
>
> The final goal of our customer data vision is to understand how customers are using our services and recalibrate our product offerings accordingly.[21]

Improving the efficiency of target marketing is not just a payback for the bank. It gets to the heart of CRM, providing a giant benefit to customers. It's all well and good that this element of CRM can save postage expense and increase response, but its ability to eliminate all those unwanted offers in the customer's mailbox adds even more value to the customer relationship.

The same is true for the cross-selling benefit Grossman lists and the suggestions from Peppers & Rogers' readers. Customers will appreciate offers that meet their individual value needs.

Gains in customer retention will be a big profit payback for the bank. A recently published study found that a 2 percent increase in retention could mean a 10 percent reduction in costs. It is easier and often less expensive to expand an existing customer's use of a bank's products and services than it is to attract a new customer.

Finally, recalibrating product offers to match customers' needs and values is really what CRM and 1to1 is all about and may, after all, be the biggest profit payoff.

All of this is easy for banks and other financial institutions that have a direct facing to the consumer. What about companies that sell to other companies. Can they practice CRM?

21
CHAPTER

But Who Is *Really* Your Customer?

Business-to-business CRM marketing

If you are selling headlight parts to General Motors or washing machine motors to Maytag or office supplies to Wal-Mart, who is your customer? Not General Motors or Maytag or Wal-Mart. Corporations don't buy. People buy.

One of my favorite quotes about business-to-business marketing came from Denny Hatch, editor of *Target Marketing*, who said, "A business person is simply a consumer at work."

It has always been fundamental that business-to-business sales have been built through relationships.

Back in the best days of "Big Blue," when IBM owned the computer business, those IBM salesmen in their white shirts and wing-tip oxford shoes were the ultimate relationship builders. No sale ever ended with the installation. The IBM rep was back in the customer's office or plant regularly and consistently to check on his customer's needs— more than that, to ask about things that interested the customer: his Little League son, his college daughter, or simply his golf game. IBM executives didn't call this CRM. They really didn't think about what it meant. They really cared about their customers, and they were just showing it the way Tom Watson had taught them.

It's still a fact that business-to-business sales, from the very start, deal with real, individual people, not averages and not corporations.

Finding ways to respond to the solutions needs of these real, individual people is what business-to-business CRM is all about. We learned from Carolyn that "loyalty marketing" does not necessarily build relationships or customer loyalty for consumer marketers. The same is true for business-to-business marketers. You can't buy customer loyalty.

John Groman, executive vice president and cofounder of Epsilon, said it best at the DMA's Direct Marketing to Business Conference in Orlando in February 1999 when he called "loyalty marketing" an oxymoron. He said, "'Loyalty marketing' implies we can market to people and make them loyal to us. The truth is that loyalty is the result, not the object, of a successful relationship in business and in life. When we try to make another person loyal without providing a relationship that works for him or her, we waste time, money, and trust. Customers require a reason to concentrate their spending on you. Brands are made at every point of contact with the target audience. Introduce a personalized relationship building program, not a loyalty program."

Managing business-to-business customer relations is really much the same as managing consumer customer relations. It is still a matter of engaging individuals in interactive dialog to learn what they truly value and to learn their needs for solutions.

The only difference is that managing the customer relationship is a greater challenge in business-to-business programs than in consumer efforts because the relationship is more complex involving both an individual and a business. In business-to-business marketing, the value of any individual is directly tied to the business application he or she manages. It is the individual acting on the business applications with the product that creates value for the customer. Therefore, the business-to-business marketer must focus on the individuals at his or her accounts and business applications rather than on the company or simply "the account." Sometimes in business-to-business marketing, the most important targets are individuals who don't actually buy anything from your company but are the ones who most strongly influence the final purchase decision. In the business-to-business world, CRM is even more important than it is in the business-to-consumer world.

Are we saying this is the end of mass trade media advertising? Not at all. But it should change the targeting process for media selection and other communication. Corporate accounts are really a collection of many individuals. Targeting at the broad "account" level is generally done with the hope that we will reach someone, somewhere within the company who will raise a hand and say, "Yes, I'm interested."

If one accepts the fact that the interest of any individual potential buyer is tied to the business application he or she manages, it becomes apparent that broadly targeted trade ad messages without direct business applications, while perhaps building awareness, will produce few solid leads or sales.

This is not to say that every communication must be a sharp-shooter's rifle shot. When marketing efforts are too narrow, opportunities are missed because it may require more than one individual within the prospect account to initiate action. In all but the smallest businesses, individual influencers, specifiers, and decision makers come together in a buyer group for the acquisition of products and services they require for business solutions.

So it is important to track transactions by individual and by site. Because so many executives change jobs every year, it is not uncommon for sites to have three times better customer retention than individual buyers. The best place to prospect for new cus-

tomers is within the site of an existing customer. Increasing individual purchasers at a site from 10 to 20 is a supercharged way to
add profit.

The challenge of keeping track of all the players in a buyer
group suggests that a business-to-business database must be larger
and more complex than a database of consumer customers. Happily
that's not the case. A 1998 database survey by *Direct* found the
average business-to-business database has only 36,000 records
compared with 460,000 for consumer-focused marketers. The difficulty lies not in the size of customer lists but with their rate of
changing people and titles. With constant turnover in the workforce, promotions, restructuring, and mergers and acquisitions, the
average business-to-business list has a turnover of about 1 percent
a week, making it difficult for marketers to manage their lists.

One expert says, "The main reason B-to-B marketers have a
hard time managing their customer data has nothing to do with zip
code changes, company mergers, or restructurings. Rather, most
marketers do not have ongoing relationships with their customers.
As a rule, marketers don't have relationships that would cause customers to advise them when they may be moving within or outside
their company. And when they do leave, we may not even notice.
While we're all striving for relationship management, customers
retain the right of way."[1]

The CRM process does not exclude important mass trade
advertising, but it does change the message and the targeting.
Knowing the individual players, knowing the makeup of the buying
groups, and knowing what these folks value and the role they play
in the buying decision will serve to refine marketing communications and improve the ROI.

In the past business-to-business marketers have looked at
sales personnel, company reps, and competitors. Now they must
begin to learn to understand *customers*—their needs, their wants,
their business objectives. We must create dialog with these cus-

tomers, create conversations, and listen and learn—and that requires a fact-filled database.

One expert makes that point for us:

> Whether consumer or business oriented, the ability of any marketer to capture and then use current, relevant, and contact-based information is the key to the success of that marketer. Only in an environment that supports and takes into consideration all elements of customer and prospect activity can true relational marketing efforts be successful. A database configuration that supports multiple avenues of purchasing—and those address ramifications—is the key to successful business-to-business database marketing.[2]

In the business-to-business world, the kind of relevant information just described includes individual attributes like the type of PC a person uses and site attributes like the number of PCs at a business and the usual time between orders.

Business-to-business marketing is not that different from consumer marketing. The new rules of marketing still apply. The business-to-business marketer, like the consumer marketer, no longer drives the communication with customers. The customer has the power. Recognizing this, Ernan Roman, president of Ernan Roman Direct Marketing, suggests the newest breakthrough in achieving a true marketing database is a "Consensual Database," built by asking the customer the following questions:

- What are your information needs?
- Who are the other decision makers and/or influencers that should receive this information?
- What are your media preferences and media aversions?
- How often is it appropriate to contact you?[3]

Roman says his concept of the Consensual Database comes from consumer research. He says the idea was sparked by a research interview with the chief information officer of a large multinational firm regarding media preference and communication requirements. Suddenly, he says, she exploded, telling us:

> You marketers think that because I'm the CIO, all marketing material should be sent to me. Decision making in our company is very distributed. And I resent being your executive mailroom.
>   Once a quarter I will tell you who in my company you should be communicating with, . . . what information they need . . . and which medium is appropriate.[4]

IBM has found a way to use the Web to recognize the customers' power by putting its business customers in charge of the information they receive. The program called *isource* delivers sales and marketing messages inexpensively and very personally. With a simple registration service, the customer or prospect fills in business information and areas of interest. Interests are matched weekly with a content database that has been created by specific groups of people within IBM. They identify the content category and geographic area (globally) that should be sent, creating, in effect, a personalized home page for each customer. IBM reports these benefits: Prospects and customers *request* information to be sent to them. This is a nonintrusive method of communications as customers can read their e-mail at their convenience. It sends only the information that will be of interest to the customer or prospect. It costs the same to send 10,000 e-mails as it does to send just 1. And it does put the customer in charge.

IBM is also creating "Gold Service" sites, private Web sites for their individual best customers. The sites show IBM reps' photos and profiles, plus individual information, individualized prices, and services. Gold Service customers can speak directly to their reps in real time in video-chat format.

Another company using the Web to develop sales and manage customer relationships is Dell Computer Corp. Dell generates roughly 80 percent of overall revenue selling to businesses but only about half of its $2 billion annual Web sales are business to business. In 1998 the PC maker targeted business and government, setting up some 8000 custom pages that amount to a separate storefront for each of these customers.

Bill Morris, director of content and marketing for Dell Online, says, "Dell Online gives Dell a chance to have a continuing relationship by providing Web service and support to our direct customers. Have a problem with your Dell? Go to the site and plug in your PC code number. The site will then reconfigure to reflect only the information applicable to your system. These efforts develop long-term customers. Using the Internet, we get to personalize your experience with Dell, and that develops a relationship, an affinity, between you and Dell."[5]

Arthur Hughes tells the story of a manufacturer of building products that sells primarily to building contractors. The company conducted a CRM test, selecting 500 customers for a special CRM effort and 500 similar customers as a control group. The goal was to increase repurchase, purchase frequency, average order size, and annual account revenue by building close relationships with the personnel in the 500 test companies using telephone, mail, fax, and e-mail, while giving the control group no special attention.

They did not offer any discounts or special benefits, only friendship, information, and customer support. Fifteen more companies in the test group made purchases than companies in the control group. The test group delivered a 30 percent increase in orders over the control group in the six-month test. The average orders the test group placed were larger in size than the control group and larger than they themselves had placed during the previous six-month period. The overall difference was an increase of 28 percent in the size of the average order.

The combination of increased orders and average order size resulted in an 81 percent gain in total revenue. By spending

$50,000 over six months to build relationships with 500 customers, the company increased revenue by nearly $2.6 million.[6]

The business-to-business marketer will have to engage the individuals at his or her accounts in interactive dialog to learn what they truly value and to understand their perception of value.

To facilitate this relationship, Richard Barlow, president of Frequency Marketing, suggests that some traditional business-to-business incentive programs can be transfused into relationship building frequency programs. He warns of the three biggest mistakes that can be made in a business-to-business frequency marketing program—overreliance on discounts, underuse of communications, and inadequate database development. He then gives this sound advice:

> Traditional incentive programs are usually reward driven and characterized by one-way communication. True business-to-business frequency programs are data driven and distinguished by sophisticated two-way communication. Rewards aren't absent from these programs, but they're not the "star." Instead, the relationship is the star in that the rewards and other benefits are configured as evidence of the value of the relationship between the customer and the brand.[7]

The business-to-business marketer will have to learn how to target and find the companies that want what he or she can best provide for specific business applications and will have to learn to spend communication dollars to influence the most profitable, and potentially most profitable, customers. All of that requires customer knowledge, and customer knowledge requires a customer database that is very different from a list of customers.

This is the first message of CRM for business-to-business marketers. It is much more than technology. It is a whole new paradigm of understanding your customer, your customer's needs for solutions, and your customer's perception of value.

The second message is that CRM can help marketers move away from price incentive offers by building relationships that will mean more to customers than price. Today, more buying decisions are made on the total business solution cost than on the price alone. There is still a role for premium pricing if it can be earned. CRM is part of that process.

This leads to a final thought for business-to-business marketing. The keys to business success today, and in the coming decade, are to build a loyal customer base, ensure that product and service offers meet customers' *specific needs*, have an ongoing competitive intelligence system, have effective and efficient sales and distribution channels, and build new business around current customers.

This means being customer focused, but it means much more. It means changing the way you do business—moving from transactions to solutions, from getting the order to helping the customer. It means building an *interdependent relationship* with the customer in which each relies on the other for business solutions and successes. The customer values the relationship and believes in it. You create a common bond with the *individual customer* based on a shared win-win approach with the customer trusting you.

It all comes down to this. In today's competitive economy, no company can afford to operate only as product focused or cost focused or technology focused. Being competitive today requires a renewed focus on building long-term relationships with customers to build customer loyalty. The more customers value their relationship with you, the more you can show added value through the relationship, the more loyal your customers will become.

This is building and managing customer relationships, . . . and it is the future.

The Media Awaken to CRM

I gave at the office.

Can a case be made for media companies to practice CRM?

CRM is a fuzzy concept for most people in the media industry. They hear a lot about it and read all the articles, but few have any real idea about how it can apply to their business mission.

Simply put, CRM represents a more sophisticated way for media to do what they have been doing for many years—working to increase readership, or viewership, or listenership, and advertising revenue. That suggests winners in the media industry can look at the business case for CRM from two important perspectives:

1. As a cost-effective way to increase the depth of involvement with readers, viewers, and listeners so as to develop a stronger audience and reduce churn—the rate at which audience is lost

2. As a way to identify particular readers, viewers, or listeners who are best customers of or best prospects for particular advertisers

It is easy to think first of all the difficulties of capturing individual consumer data and creating dialog with individuals in a mass-media audience. For companies that sell products and services that are transaction based, the tracking of usage is easily managed. For the invisible product of broadcast, there has never been a method to track the daily transactions of individual viewing or listening on a mass basis.

For readers who would let that negative distract them, we'll interject a quick example here to show that tracking is possible, before we state the case for CRM for media companies.

The following is not yet CRM, and, sadly, it is a points program that may or may not build loyalty, but it does illustrate the real possibility of capturing lots of good customer information even in a mass-media environment.

For most radio stations the time their listeners spend listening is much higher in the workplace than in their home or car. The workplace is radio's big target. Stations realize having listeners turn on the radio at 8:30 A.M. and turn it off at 5:30 P.M. throughout the week is a tremendous opportunity for *time spent listening* (TSL). Workplace listening offers the potential of 180 quarter-hours a week covering three day parts.

In *The New Rules of Marketing*, we offered some database marketing solutions for broadcasters from Fairwest Direct, a loyalty marketing company specializing in interactive technology for radio and television companies. Fairwest is back with more new ideas and Reg Johns, Fairwest president, rushed to tell us about a new program, 18 months in design and rolled out to 42 radio stations in March 1998. While not yet a true CRM program, it certainly proves a station's ability to capture good listener data in important ways.

The "Listen-at-Work Rewards Program" from Fairwest is an innovative software-based promotion that continually encourages, tracks, and rewards daily workplace listening and captures lots of information about a station's listeners. Fairwest calls it "a totally new approach in attracting new cume (cumulative audience per week) and extending time spent listening loyalty."

Radio stations have always known their best listeners are those who listen the most, but they have never been able to know who these best listeners are and what they really value from the station. With listening "transactions" tracked on a daily basis, individually, with the masses, and with listeners providing personal profile and preference information, this rewards program begins to provide powerful marketing knowledge for participating stations.

The program targets everyone at the workplace with access to a computer. Listeners are provided a free Rewards disk that programs their computer with a variety of preprogrammed offers and listening reminders for up to one full year. The more listeners participate in the program and listen to the station, the more "Listener Points" they will earn. Listeners like the points because they have value in that they are treated as currency.

The program on the disk functions first as a screen-saver. Within the software of the screen-saver is a database management system acting as a 1to1 marketing department. An assortment of forced listening features and benefits are preprogrammed into the software with features changing on a daily basis for up to a year.

Built-in incentives motivate listeners to install the disk on their computers. Listeners are given incentives to listen to the station each weekday. Registration of listening for each individual listener is tracked on a daily basis.

Listener Points are awarded each weekday automatically to all listeners. The more people listen, the more opportunities they have to earn points. Points are treated as currency and managed with the "Cyber-Bank Account" of the software, which monitors growing point accumulation and point debits automatically. Participants can redeem their points by printing points coupons from their computers.

It seems Reg Johns is on the right track with his Listen-at-Work Rewards Program, not just to create station loyalty but to attract radio advertisers.

The personal nature of radio and its ubiquitous presence in the workplace have made it an extremely effective medium for driving people to specific Web sites on the Internet. These two attributes were central to the decision by CDNow.com, the Internet's largest music store, to make local radio its primary medium. "Radio is the most personal medium out there," says Mindy Sherman, vice president and director of broadcast buying for Hampel/Stefanides, CDNow's ad agency. "Radio is the only commercial medium in the workplace. Most of us now have computers at our desk with Internet access. This is the perfect convergence for CDNow—to reach their customers when they are able to take advantage of purchasing the product."[1]

Our hats are off to Reg Johns. He has kept Fairwest on the cutting edge of creative marketing technology. There is no question that the Listener-at-Work Rewards Program will increase workplace listenership for those 42 stations, and that begins to approach loyalty and involvement. Our hope is that Johns will read this book and put his creative team to work on strategies to increase the *depth* of listener involvement by finding ways to deliver personalized preprogrammed values and benefits to *individual* listeners in true CRM fashion.

Which brings us to the question, can the media industry use CRM, or in this case, *listener, viewer, or reader relationship management* (LVRRM), to grow profit?

Perhaps an earlier question should be, why do media companies need CRM?

CRM can serve the two basic marketing needs of the media industry: to increase the depth of involvement with their audience and reduce churn and to know enough about the individual members of their audience to help their advertisers target known best customers. Just how important are these challenges?

In the newspaper industry, statistics show annual churn to be anywhere from 30 to 70 percent of the reader-subscriber base. In radio the national average on exclusive cume is 8 percent. This leaves 92 percent of listeners aware of and perhaps sampling the station, but listening to other stations. Preventing more of these 92 percent from leaving should be the focus of radio's CRM strategy.

Why do media need to identify particular readers, viewers, and listeners for particular advertisers?

Advertisers are now looking at our changing world from a new point of view—the customer. Advertisers with CRM programs want to use what they know about their customers to strengthen customer relationships in all of their media communications. They are no longer willing to waste advertising dollars on nonprospects. They are looking at the efficiency of all media in reaching their target customers and prospects. They see the future of their media use in terms of their ability to achieve varying efficiencies of mass to micro levels of audience contact and targeting efficiency.

They have always considered the mass media efficient because they offered a nice low cost per thousand impressions. Now they realize that true efficiency lies in getting the lowest-cost-per-thousand viable customers and prospects as they define *viable*.

If newspapers and radio stations and TV stations don't find ways to have the information about their readers, listeners, and viewers they could be headed for lost revenue.

When supermarkets, for example, begin to mine their frequent shopper databases for information that can be turned into customer-specific loyalty communications, they become disenchanted with some of their mass-media investments. For Grand Union the use of customer data in their 237 New Jersey stores has proved so effective that the chain has cut back on millions of dollars of conventional media advertising while continuing to drive sales upward.[2]

And a program called "One-to-One Direct," a direct-mail program developed by Catalina Marketing Corp., now chooses people from supermarket customer knowledge files and delivers a magazine suited to the selected households' lifestyle—new competition for traditional media. Each magazine circulates to 2 to 3 million of the supermarket's top 25 percent most loyal and top-spending households, taking ad dollars that used to go to newspapers' free-standing inserts.

But media don't have to lose these advertising dollars if they will learn to work with their advertisers and their advertisers' customer knowledge.

The *Chicago Tribune* works very closely with one of our retail clients, allowing the chain to use its customer knowledge to fine-tune buys for prospecting. They work with the retail chain to help select zone distribution based on the distribution of the retailer's best customers, reevaluating the zone distribution each quarter based on ROI.

Each month the *Tribune* tells this advertiser how many papers they are going to put out in each zone and estimates copy sales. At the end of each month, they report copies actually sold. The advertiser's ROI measurement calls for $30 of annual sales for every paper sold in the zone. Below that level, a zone is dropped. Sales average $50 per copy, with best zones producing $100 to $150 per newspaper copy sold.

Our advertiser clients tell us it comes down to this. As advertisers continue to move forward with CRM programs and the development of customer knowledge, media that want their business must know as much about their own audiences as the advertisers know about their customers. Then the media must develop ways to cross-feed this information to support the advertisers' objectives.

Advertisers are now asking, Exactly how many of my best customers are in your audience? Who are they? How can I best reach them—where in your newspaper or when in your broadcast time? How many in your audience are *just like* my best customers? Can you help me find them and reach them? When media companies can answer these questions, they will have made the second part of the business case for CRM and will be able to make exciting things happen for their business and for their advertisers.

Happily, there are some who realize this. KABC radio in Los Angeles has used an interactive voice response system to build a club membership of more than 150,000 listeners they can identify for advertisers.

WARM 94.9 FM, in Tampa, has taken this to the next level by marrying radio and the Internet to build relationships with listeners. With a product called "Totally Interactive Radio," listeners can log on to the station's Web site and respond to music being played by the station. Listeners register their e-mail addresses, demographic information, artist preferences, and times they listen to the station.

For added listenership, the station can e-mail people who like a specific artist and suggest listening times. For those who usually listen only in the A.M. portion, they can send an e-mail about something really exciting that will be played during the P.M. drive time.

For advertisers the station sells banner ads on its Web site timed to the airing of the advertiser's commercial, and it can tell an advertiser when the most people with the advertiser's target profile will be listening.[3]

A 1998 study by Yankelovich Partners suggests that this is a strong strategy. The study reported that 66 percent of men and 62 percent of women listen to the radio while surfing the Web.[4]

In the newspaper industry, database marketing is fast becoming old news. At a recent Newspaper Executive Roundtable, Shawn Higgins, vice president of marketing for the *Spokane Spokesman-Review*, asked, "Why is it that database marketing is no longer being hyped? Was database marketing just a fad?" His answer: "Database marketing is alive and flourishing. It is not being hyped because it has gone beyond that infancy stage to be institutionalized by the industry. It is now the subject of very focused conferences and break-out sessions."

Yet many newspapers still have a lot to learn. In a May 1999 *Wall Street Journal* article, Kevin Gruneich, senior managing director for Bear Stearns and Company, expressed surprise that so few newspapers had effectively leveraged their local databases when it would be an obvious competitive advantage for them.

There are some who are learning to leverage their database by using their customer knowledge file to narrow in on a segment or segments of their subscriber base and use that subscriber knowledge for lots of actions to drive profit.

One paper used its subscriber database to distribute the Saturday Stocks Section to just 13,000 subscribers who were investors—a savings of more than 125,000 inserts.

This same paper learned to limit the distribution of *Parade*'s teen magazine *REACT*, to just the 15 percent of subscriber households with teens present.

Newspapers have all the marketing advantages. They already manage every street address and the most information about the marketplace. All they have to do is leverage it into new revenue sources.

Leveraging the newspaper database can mean much more than just refined insert circulation. Lauren Rich Fine, first vice president and managing director for Merrill Lynch, says, "Newspapers need to get into new revenue streams like direct marketing because I don't believe an investment in circulation will pay off. . . . It's better to simply hold on."

Jim Hart, database marketing manager at *The Arizona Republic*, says there is more to it than that:

> Database marketing is not direct mail. . . . Direct mail is largely a commodity business. Database marketing changes the rules for newspapers because we have a distinct data advantage, and a tremendous distribution advantage.
>
> Advertisers will migrate to a multiple-channel business model if they aren't already there. And newspapers are currently unwieldy in an integrated model.

At *The Republic*, Hart describes data-driven marketing as "points of entry." The first is targeted marketing. "This is simply list marketing. It's better than nothing," Hart comments, "but little or no analysis is done to develop the list and everyone on the list gets the same message." Hart points to the Advo ATZ program and most circulation mailers as examples of targeted marketing.

Hart continues:

> The second point of entry is database marketing. Here, the campaigns are truly data driven, and an incremental competitive advantage is gained. Analysis is based on historical detail, outside data sources often come into play, and dynamic segmentation occurs. Offers vary from segment to segment, and back-end analysis includes lifetime value measures, segment migration, up-sell and cross-sell success rates, etc.

The Republic has conducted several database marketing applications with auto dealers, home builders, and furniture stores.

Finally,

> The third point of entry is integrated marketing. Integrated marketing provides a view of customers across all sales channels including the Web. This enables targeting by any combination of segment, channel, transactional, or demographic data, and back-end analysis stretches across channels. Only 5 percent of *The Republic*'s database marketing revenues can be attributed to truly integrated marketing, but it is the "point of entry" that offers a sustainable competitive advantage.

Some newspapers are trying to build relationships with subscribers, but most don't seem to understand the process. Paper after paper has instituted some kind of a card offering restaurant discounts to people who will buy six-month subscriptions. One of the problems with this strategy is that they are rarely able to get the top-of-the-line restaurants as partners, and 20 percent off at Godfather's Pizza is not a big thrill for many of the newspaper's best customers. Of course, the real problem is what this book is all about. You can't buy customer loyalty.

One newspaper we are familiar with sends a newsletter to subscribers, but instead of showing that they understand customers' interests and needs, they talk only about themselves. They say, "Our ongoing goal is to enhance our relationship with you, our valued customer," but asking me to take my time to read about their investment in new presses or their editorial staff's recent awards is not satisfying any need I have for a relationship with them.

When a newspaper can speak to its subscribers about how the newspaper serves their special interests, it becomes much easier to convince them to become new subscribers (and it sure beats another discount).

Papers that delivered specialized content enjoyed the biggest circulation gains in 1998: Hispanic, alternative, and parenting newspapers and all newspapers reflecting customers' special interests. Spanish-language papers had a circulation leap of nearly 37 percent.

Why can't newspapers have a print version of "My Yahoo," giving personalized news on the front page of every copy, as we said in Chapter 16?

With CRM, newspapers can turn their promotion investments into real relationship efforts to increase and keep subscribers, . . . and they will be able to do this by targeting their most profitable subscribers.

One of the strengths of customer knowledge in a database is the ability it gives businesses to measure customer lifetime value, which is just as important to newspapers as it is for any other business.

As we've said, the central tenet of the lifetime value model is that not all customers are created equal. Some will deliver more profit than others will. Lifetime value is a calculation of the cost of attaining customers, which is then weighed against their value to the business and the length of their relationship with a company.

This is it. This is what customer knowledge is all about.

Customer knowledge will allow newspapers to get away from distribution-based decisions (most newspaper zones were designed for truck routes, not the value of the households).

The fact is the value of subscribers in some zones represent greater advertiser value than others do. Newspapers should really charge advertisers for the "value" of these "best customers," not just the number of households in a zone.

As we said at the start of this chapter, CRM is still a fuzzy concept for most people in the media industry. Their traditional strengths offer enormous potential for the building of relationships. They combine a powerful consumer base of readers or listeners or viewers with an unbeatable database of news, information, and entertainment, and a strong, well-accepted brand identity. Their primary business is to communicate news, information, and entertainment to consumers in a manner that is accessible, appealing, and relevant. In so doing, they create an effective mechanism for advertisers to communicate with their customers and prospects.

Newspaper executives are concerned about electronic publishing. Collin Phillips of *Editor and Publisher* told his audience at the Newspaper Association Convention in Coronado, California, in May 1999 that there were then 953 daily newspaper Web sites and 1271 weekly. However, the issue is not whether newspapers will go electronic but whether media organizations sufficiently understand and possess the necessary administration for interactivity.

Newspapers may easily extend their old top-down editorial and organizational paradigms into new electronic media without understanding the new concepts that are needed to build reader-consumer relationships.

The brand and the customer database are more important than the medium the publisher uses to relay his or her message.

It is not new media that threatens newspapers but the reluctance of some managers to understand and respond to the implications of interactivity, and *that* will require learning the lessons of CRM.

Our original definition of CRM still applies: CRM is a process of modifying customer behavior over time by strengthening the bond between the customer and the company. CRM seeks to add value to the customer relationship *in the customer's terms* to maximize the value of the relationship to the customer for the customer's benefit and the company's profit.

We see seven opportunities for media to develop the CRM process to add to their profit:

1. Don't underestimate the power of your customer knowledge when combined with your brand. All the things your advertisers are looking for you have or can get if you will only use them. There is nothing like it out there.

2. Stop fussing about the complexity of compiling data and find the time and the budget to make it happen.

3. Use CRM to reduce that awful and expensive churn.

4. Use customer knowledge to attract new advertisers and protect those you have.

5. Use your customer knowledge to create new revenue streams. Adopt the Honda theory—we want five Hondas in every garage, but they don't all have to be cars. Customer knowledge will help you develop a bigger portfolio of products and services.

6. You can't be afraid of change. You can't enter the same river twice.

7. For those who will say, "Yeah, but media companies are different," you're not. CRM can work for every industry.

23 CHAPTER

When You Care Enough

More than a points program:
The Hallmark Gold Crown Story:
A case study

We all know Hallmark Cards as the company that makes the greeting cards we send when we care enough to send the very best. We trust Hallmark with our passions grand and small at the rate of 8 million cards a day. They have been called the "General Motors of emotion." But not everyone realizes that Hallmark is also a giant retailer selling many products besides greeting cards. Hallmark Gold Crown stores represent the second-largest retail chain in the United States, second only to Tandy's RadioShack stores. Hallmark has 5000 stores nationwide, and they are all individually owned and operated by independent dealers.

Hallmark's CRM program is a world leader and a prime example of best practices in CRM. The present Gold Crown Card program was launched in 1994. Prior to that, the stores had a loyalty program built on punch cards. Each store had its own cards, and every time a customer made a purchase of $5, the card was punched, with enough punches earning a $5 gift certificate. This early program was not collecting any customer information for Hallmark, and it was a bother for customers since a customer shopping in more than one store had to carry more than one card.

The new program features a universal Gold Crown Card good in any one of the 5000 stores so that a customer can use the same card whether vacationing in California or shopping in Kansas City. Back in 1994 Hallmark expected to sign up 3 to 4 million customers in the first year of the program. They signed up 6 million. In 1999 they had more than 20 million permanent cardholders. The folks at Hallmark believe theirs is the largest active membership of any consumer card program. Ten million of these members have purchased in the last 6-month period, and over 12 million have purchased in the last 12 months.

The Gold Crown Card program *is* a points program, which could lead one to ask why we praise it here given our premise that points can't buy loyalty. The answer is that the program is managed totally as a *customer relationship program*. The points are used to make the program fun for the customers, but the customer contacts and communications are managed to create dialog and manage customer relationships. Hallmark uses the customer knowledge they gain from the program to learn what each customer values about the relationship, what core product or benefit has value to which customer and what the customer values about these, and what is the value provided to each customer that differentiates Hallmark from its competition—the very things we talked about at the start.

How does the program work? A customer joins the program by filling out an enrollment form in the store at which time he or she is given a temporary card for use that same day. A high-quality plastic card is mailed to the new member immediately with all the reminder details of the program and an offer of 100 bonus points if the new card is used within 30 days. Customers earn 10 points for every dollar spent and 50 points for every Hallmark card purchased. For every

300 points earned, they receive a $1 Reward Certificate good toward the purchase of any regular-priced Hallmark product.

Every customer who earns more than 300 points in a quarter receives a personalized point statement, a newsletter, Reward Certificate, and individualized news of new products and events going on at his or her local store.

In 1996 Hallmark added a preferred status for the top tier of customers who buy more cards and ornaments than anyone else does. The preferred level is limited to a little less than 10 percent of the membership because Hallmark wants to keep it special and make it an aspirational achievement so they can offer truly unique benefits to these most valuable customers. Notice of preferred status comes in an elaborate mailing piece complete with gold seal and enclosing a new membership card clearly identifying the customer as a preferred member. Preferred members enjoy preferred member bonus offers that are available for longer periods of time or allow them to earn more points than regular members do, and they have their own private priority toll-free 800 number.

Since these customers shop more often than regular members, Hallmark talks to them more often and talks to them about what they want to hear. A Keepsake ornament buyer hears the latest news about ornaments. A heavy buyer of cards receives a gift of three new cards to introduce a new line. Each customer is rewarded with the types of products he or she likes best. While these rewards are planned by the Hallmark team, they are not scheduled in the program materials. Members receive them as delightful surprises. So much so that Hallmark's corporate office is filled with giant stacks of thank-you letters from members.

And the customers talk back to Hallmark. Cindy Jeffries, Hallmark's director of advertising and the executive in charge of the Gold Crown program, says, "It is important to us to have an ongoing dialog with our customers. The Gold Card Program is really a relationship program, so ongoing dialog is really important to us." In addition to the 1-800 HALLMARK number where members can call and ask any question, the Hallmark Web site updates mem-

bers constantly on new product news and individual points earned.
Member e-mail is answered promptly by Hallmark's customer
affairs staff.

The Hallmark Web site is, indeed, a very friendly place. Here
are some examples of Hallmark attitude:

> We want you to have the best experience possible on Hallmark.com.
> If you have a specific problem—perhaps your order never arrived or
> you can't download an electronic greeting—please check our Help
> section and Frequently Asked Questions for fast answers.

I joined on the Web and got this immediate screen:

> Thanks for joining. We've created a Hallmark.com membership for
> Fred. [I was impressed they even picked up on the period I always
> use to show Fred. is really an abbreviation for Frederick.] We are
> sending a confirmation notice to your e-mail address.

And here's the light-hearted e-mail reply that arrived in minutes:

> Thanks for visiting Hallmark.com. We hope you return soon to send
> one of our electronic greetings, including over 1000 FREE greet-
> ings. Laugh aloud as you play one of our Shoebox animated greet-
> ings with sound. Browse through the large selection of unique
> Hallmark gifts. Or pick up a few ideas for your next party. It's all
> just a click away at Hallmark.com.
>> Have a great day!
>> Your friends at Hallmark.com.

They even offered to file the names and addresses of my family, friends, and colleagues so that I wouldn't have to retype that
information when I want to send a card. They offered to keep a
record of important dates and events I might want to remember and
to help me out by sending an e-mail reminder in advance of the date.

Several times a year Hallmark executives sit down with
groups of preferred and regular members to hear how they feel
about the program, what they would like to see added or changed,
and how they feel about product offerings.

On the technical side, member transaction data are updated
daily. Since not all of the 5000 independent stores have sophisti-

cated point-of-sale systems, about half the stores use separate
Trans-unit credit card readers to read member cards and record
transaction data. The card readers are polled every night to download the customer information to the corporate database. A licensed
proprietary software system called *Fast-Count* allows marketing
analysts to query the data to find special segments of customers like
those that bought one to five ornaments in the month of October.

The database is completely proprietary. Hallmark does not
share any of its customer information with any outside party and
does not rent names from the customer file. Cindy Jeffries says:

> We are using our data to learn more about our customers and give
> them what they want. Ornament lovers want to hear all about new
> product. They want to hear a lot of product information, and they
> want it as soon as possible. Knowing this, we are able to isolate
> them and give them just what they want. Other segments represent
> busy women who want the shortened version—tell me the short
> notes, the highlights of what I need to know for Valentine's Day, is
> there a bonus offer, where is my Reward Certificate? Our whole
> goal is to respond to what our customers are telling us with their
> purchases. It really is a dialog.

Has the program worked? From date of launch, the
Hallmark Gold Crown stores have had 51 consecutive months of
same-store sales gains, which the folks at Hallmark think coin-
cides quite nicely with the launch of the program. Listen to Cindy
Jeffries again: "Aside from that, our Gold Crown network has
become incredibly healthy over the last five years. We really
attribute much of that success to the Gold Card program. The percent of transactions and dollars represented by Gold Crown program members is amazing." And it truly is—more than a billion
dollars in 1997 and over $1.5 billion in 1998. Member sales now
represent 35 percent of total store transactions and 45 percent of
total store sales.

Hallmark encourages the individual stores to use the member
knowledge for local marketing events like "Family Fun Days," a

March 1999 event scheduled to attract more young parents. Stores receive a hard copy and a disk of all of their member information with a complete 12-month purchase history, and some have very sophisticated marketing programs to reinforce corporate CRM activities. The retailers have told the company that this is the best program that Hallmark has ever launched. They are incredibly supportive, and everyone involved agrees their support and energy is most important to the ongoing growth of the program.

Hallmark executives credit a lot of the success of the program to the sales force and the sales associates in the stores. They are the people who explain the program to customers and make it work. It's the sales associates who have enrolled over 20 million members. Hallmark has done no member prospecting by mail.

At the end of our last interview, I asked Cindy the tough question: "There are those who say you can't buy customer loyalty with points programs and discounts. How do you answer that?" Her reply:

> We do not perceive our program to be a discount program. To us this is a *relationship program* [her emphasis], and we look at it, as our consumers are some of the nicest people out there. They're considerate people who are in our stores all the time buying cards and doing nice things for other people. This is our way to reward them for that. And the more focus groups we've done, the more we've learned that these customers use the rewards to treat themselves. They buy themselves something they would not have otherwise purchased. We like to think of it as their way of being able to reward themselves for their nice behavior with everyone else.

I asked Cindy what Hallmark might do differently if they were launching the program today. In the first year, she said, they enrolled some customers automatically from an older direct marketing program. They learned it is much more important for consumers to raise their own hand and enroll themselves. The members the company enrolled automatically never responded or acted in the same way as the self-enrolled members.

Other than that, Cindy thinks the program has evolved pretty much as it should have. Here's her advice for others:

Your focus in the first few years has to be on growth. You just have to make sure you can enroll enough of a critical mass to get enough people in the program and get them interested and engaged so they will continue to participate. But after the first year or two you start building up enough data to look at customer behavior and to begin to segment to give special offers—to give customers what they want. Some of that just takes time.

I tell people to watch it, build it, plan for it—but it will evolve over a period of years. First you have to have the members, and you have to watch their behavior.

Finally, I asked Cindy about Hallmark's secrets for the future of the program:

We have no secrets. Only our consumers know for sure what the future developments will be because it's their behavior that is driving the development of the program.

We'll continue to become more sophisticated in our ability to model behavior and to try to predict behavior in ways that will allow us to be even closer to the marketplace and closer to the individual needs of our customers.

We're in this for the long haul. This is not something we look at as a promotional device that will come and go. This program now represents more than half of all our marketing investment for Gold Crown Stores. This is here to stay. It's not a program. It's a process.

We're in it to manage a long-term relationship with our customers.

One comes away from a study of the Hallmark Gold Crown Card program with a real understanding of the difference between this as a true CRM adventure and most card and/or points programs out on the market today. Part of the secret is the company's belief that their customers are some of the nicest people out there and Hallmark is dedicated to helping them to "treat" themselves to some well-earned rewards.

Reorganizing Using the CRM Initiative

Why the United Kingdom's largest health and beauty retailer calls their CRM effort their biggest marketing project of the last 10 years: A case study

In Chapter 10 we introduced Boots the Chemists and promised more. Here's the full story.

Boots is the United Kingdom's leading health and beauty retailer. It is a company with a long history, having been founded by Jesse Boot in 1887. Today there are 1300 Boots stores from small 2700-square-foot shops to almost 14,000-square-foot giants. With an annual turnover of about £3.6 billion, and serving 51 million different customers each year, they are deservedly called "Chemist to the Nation."

After watching the United Kingdom's Tesco supermarket chain launch a member card program and move from second place to first in market share in a bit less than two years by gaining insight about the Tesco customer, the Boots team recognized they had to get closer to the consumer for three reasons:

1. To gain customer insight
2. To build a database that would give them the ability to tailor offers to customers' needs to develop a CRM program
3. To develop incremental sales by building customer loyalty

As the program developed, they added a fourth objective: To use the customer knowledge to gain the ability to introduce new products and services that customer knowledge indicated their consumers would welcome. As a result of this initiative, Boots has now become a leader in health insurance and travel insurance and has entered the direct selling field with programs like "Mother and Baby at Home"—all new profit centers for the company.

The Advantage Card is absolutely a core issue for the company. Crawford Davidson, head of Advantage Card, calls it "the organization's biggest focus—the biggest marketing project in the last 10 years for Boots the Chemists." The program has been successful, he says, because of the company's solid commitment, with both the chairman and the managing director leading the way. He told me it would be impossible to achieve a project of this scale without that sponsorship.

"We have reorganized our entire business on the basis of this CRM initiative," Crawford said. "We used to be organized based on the differences between our large stores and our small stores. Now with this customer insight that tells us how our customers shop—multiple stores in a week or even in a day—we had to find ways to make our larger stores and our smaller stores work together to present a common brand to the consumer." As this is written, Boots is planning their second reorganization to capitalize on lessons they learned from CRM.

We said earlier that the folks at Boots did not rush into this program without a great deal of planning and testing. The Boots

Advantage Card was developed with two test markets. They ran the first test program in the East Anglia market. For a full year they ran the program with a 10 percent reward level (10 points for every pound spent). In their words, the results were "outrageously successful," with 40 percent of sales going to the card. While sales increases were sufficient to cover the cost of the rewards, the company decided to conduct a second test to evaluate a lower-value reward.

The second test in a southwest market was just slightly less successful at a 5 percent reward level, with sales increases and 30 percent of sales going to the card, leading to a final decision to launch in September 1997 at a 4 percent reward level.

The 4 percent reward level is still four times more generous than the supermarket programs in the United Kingdom. This is necessary, Boots believes, because the average consumer spends 50 pounds a week in the supermarket but only 7 or 8 pounds a week at Boots. To be even more generous, Boots rounds every purchase *up*. If a customer spends less than 25 pence, they still get 1 point. If she spends 26 pence, she gets 2 points—again different from competitors' programs.

So here we have what is obviously a points program in a book dedicated to the proposition that points and discounts can't buy customer loyalty. Que pasa? Crawford explains: "Our Advantage Card scheme is *very much not* about discounts for family shopping. It *is very much* about treating yourself!" Customers can use points to treat themselves to anything from the simple pleasure of tomorrow's lunch to a luxurious day of pampering at a spa.

The Boots team did a lot of research that told them women (93 percent of their cardholders) wanted something for themselves. They have learned that women like to shop for personal treats. Interestingly, the research reported that 39 percent of women prefer shopping to sex. Boots has learned that self-empowerment and guilt-free self-indulgence works. The Boots rewards are emotional rather than rational.

Boots made grand plans for the national launch of the Advantage Card program on September 1, 1997, complete with in-store and window signing, press parties, and extensive press coverage. They held off the television advertising for two weeks over the concern that more people might apply at one time than they could handle. To make a best effort to handle the surge of anticipated applications, they secured all the data capture capability in the United Kingdom as well as the two leading Smart Card manufacturers in Europe.

The only thing they had not anticipated in their risk assessment was the death of Princess Diana the day before the launch. They cancelled the press parties and coverage, relying only on in-store activity. With the nation in a solemn state, sign-ups were slow for the first two weeks until the television blitz that reached 100 percent of the UK television audience five times in mid-September. The first week of the television advertising, Boots received more than 1 million applications. They had been quite open with consumers promising personalized card delivery within 21 days. Their goal was systematically achieved, but, randomly, some customers received their cards after the promised date. In good CRM style, Boots rewarded these disappointed customers with special treats.

To be sure the 60,000 staff members were enthusiastic about the program, Boots signed all associates on as program members for six months prior to the launch. Associates are enjoying the treats so much they use the card more than any customers and sell the concept with genuine enthusiasm. Store staff are so involved with the program that Boots has had to install a special service phone line dedicated to the thousand calls a week from store managers looking for ideas to help them beat other stores in card use and from sales associates challenging the marketing staff with ways to make the card even better for the customers.

The CRM program has taught Boots that the more broadly customers buy, in more categories over time, the more they increase visits to the Boots stores. Boots has learned CRM can change customer behavior. "It's not just about customer loyalty," they say. "It's about customer development."

The marketing team at Boots is constantly seeking new ways to develop customer profitability. In February 1999, working with Interact of Norwalk, Connecticut, they started a pilot test of interactive kiosks in 16 stores. When a card member swipes her Advantage Card at the kiosk, she receives personalized offers targeted by life stage and past shopping behavior. The offers, which are a mix of points and price, are designed to change customer behavior. Because the offers are generated from the complete customer history file, Boots is able to manage the mix to increase the spending of low- and middle-range customers without overrewarding best customers. Personalized offers ask best customers to do more, such as move up to premium products, rather than just discount the products they already buy. Other offers get middle-range customers to buy new things. Some of the offers involve sampling for those who have never bought. Crawford calls this process "taking direct mail into the store to make offers only when the customer wants them." He says, "The customers choose to open their mail."

In the pilot test customers receiving offers increased their spending per visit 36 percent and started visiting the stores more often. Based on that success, Boots invested 14 million pounds to roll out the kiosks to 60 stores a week in September and October 1999 giving them 350 stores, which account for two-thirds of company sales. This will make the kiosks accessible to 90 percent of the Boots customer base.

Since the kiosks are interactive, Boots is able to ask questions that will eventually enrich the customer file. Realizing that there is an education process required, in order to have customers feel comfortable about giving information, they started with simple questions such as how the customers liked the offers. They are proceeding steadily to increase the dialog.

In our interview I asked Crawford the tough question: "There are those who say you can't buy customer loyalty with points and discounts. How do you answer them?"

His reply:

They are correct. You can't *buy* customer loyalty, but you can *grow* it, and that's what we're doing. We use our CRM activities to influence customer development. Influencing is the main part of what we want to do in tailoring what our offer is to the consumer and changing what we do to move forward to do different things and highlight the parts of our offers that are most appropriate for each customer to change customer behavior.

We know our card members spend 10 percent more, visit more often, and buy more categories than they would have bought without the card, but they were probably our best customers to begin with. The scheme is really a process of positive self-selection. We are asking customers to put their hands up. The customers who joined the first month are our very best customers. Those joining in the second month are our next best.

The important thing to realize is that we are not creating ways to buy loyalty. We are finding ways to develop loyalty that already exists.

One of the special ways Boots develops loyalty is by recognizing special customers' needs. The Boots catalogs and other communications are made available to visually impaired customers on audiotape or in Braille and to the hard of hearing through specially trained operators in the customer service center.

An added element of the Boots program is a special effort to strengthen the loyalty of top-tier customers. In September 1999 Boots launched the largest-circulation women's magazine in the United Kingdom; a magazine about health and beauty to rival the best high-street titles. In a United Kingdom first, this A4-size magazine will be mailed to the top 2 million cardholders four times a year. Boots' idea is not just to add another piece of direct mail but to create what Crawford calls "something with coffee table status," which women will be pleased to read and share with friends. Crawford says, "This is not a Boots magazine. It is a health and beauty magazine from Boots." The magazine provides Boots with an added means of rewarding top customers and of developing a stronger relationship through editorial content that addresses the issues women are interested in. The magazine carries a personalized letter pointing out key features to selected cells of the customer file and will also feature targeted offers.

I asked how difficult it is to keep up with the demands of CRM with 10.2 million card members to be concerned about. Crawford said:

> Queries and demands will always outweigh our resources. The prioritizing process is one of our most important skills. The customer database is a bit like the M25—a three-lane motorway that should have been built as a six-lane motorway. We expanded our marketing IS team by 100 percent in the first three months. We now have 20 analysts with 14 in business-unit-facing positions helping product decision makers. We could use 10 more tomorrow, but it's hard to find people with the proper conceptual thinking.
>
> We don't just want people who want to drive a database. We want people who actually want to drive our business. Analysts can spend most of their time driving the database to select information. They should be spending most of their time deciding the information they want, to be sure it is valuable to the company, and how they will use the information to make it actionable.

A great lesson for us all.

When I asked Crawford what he would do differently if he were starting again now, he replied with the obvious:

> If I were to launch again, in my risk assessments I would build in the death of a member of the Royal Family.

CHAPTER

Customer Involvement: RadioShack's Sophisticated CRM Programs

A growing depth of involvement: A case study

The overriding objective of CRM is to grow the depth of involvement between the customer and the brand or the store. One retailer who truly understands this process is RadioShack. RadioShack has the second-largest customer database in retailing today—1.4 terabytes of data—and they use it to develop CRM programs to grow the depth of customer involvement.

David Edmondson, executive vice president and chief operating officer of RadioShack, says, "The fact that 99 percent of American households have made at least one purchase from a RadioShack store in the past three years means that we have a huge base of occasional shoppers. We can't grow our business on a satisfactory year-by-year basis even by capturing 100 percent of that other 1 percent of households. Growing the depth of involvement with each individual existing customer is paramount."

RadioShack has been collecting customer data since the early 1950s because their heritage comes from the mail-order business. They used to be a catalog company. As they moved into the retail store business, they continued to collect names and addresses at the point of sale to grow and build the catalog business.

Over time, through the 1960s into the early 1970s, the company grew to 5000 stores. Where these stores went was based on the names and addresses in the catalog file showing where customers were coming from. There are now 7000 RadioShack stores—5000 owned and 2000 dealer franchised. Ninety-four percent of all Americans live or work within a five-minute drive of a RadioShack store. RadioShack captures 80 percent of all customer transactions regardless of form of payment, and the customer database has grown to include a five-year history of 142 million customers and 92 million households.

RadioShack has been developing its CRM program since 1995. They believe growing the depth of customer involvement translates into growing the frequency rate at which America shops, and David Edmondson reports that the frequency rate over the last four years has steadily moved in a positive direction.

At the start of the CRM process the company considered a points program but decided that the size of the average store transaction and the frequency rate at which even the very best customers shop would stretch out any point collection scheme over an unacceptable time for the customer. They elected to build the strategy around surprise-type communications that would be unexpected. Edmondson says, "We didn't want a program that would tell the customer you do this trick, you get this thing. We try to do things that are surprising and delightful to the customer." One result is that they receive a lot of mail from customers thanking them for these nice surprises.

RadioShack has a large number of customers with a huge involvement with the brand. As in most companies, a large percent of sales comes from a thin top slice of the customer base. Ten million of the very best customers receive monthly communications from the store. Other "surprise" mailings are triggered by customer behavior or an event that occurs. Customers receive a special birthday card designed by Hallmark Business Expressions, with a nice birthday discount check.

We're told that everything they do at RadioShack in terms of advertising and promotion strategy is driven by a basic understanding of what the customer wants and what the customer is doing and/or not doing. This is so widely embedded in the culture of the company that David Edmondson points out one of the dangers of having so much data is that you can do too much tactical moving and miss your strategy. They balance these two things well with a very precise business strategy.

They call the business strategy "POA"—"Participatory, Opportunity, and Anchor."

They talk of their anchor business like an anchor store at a mall, the reason a customer comes to that particular center. The anchor business for RadioShack is accessories—wires, cables, connectors, capacitors, and batteries. These are the things RadioShack is highly famous for, and they represent about a third of the total business. Eighty-one percent of people who walk in the door come for these things.

The next ring of the three concentric ring strategies is the opportunity business—hand-held recording devices, telephones, and radio-controlled cars. The company puts a disproportionately larger share of resources into exploiting these opportunity areas.

The outer ring of the strategy is the participatory area—computers, stereos, television sets, VCRs, and camcorders.

RadioShack uses all of its CRM activities to try to migrate customers out of the main anchor circle into the opportunity and then into the participatory areas. This strategy is driven by the knowledge of what customers do aligned with what the company would like them to do. At the same time, an equal goal is to develop product categories from participatory to opportunity to anchor.

A few years ago RadioShack had less than one-half of 1 percent share of the mobile phone business as a participatory category. They decided to exploit that business to try to move it to the opportunity area. By late 1998, with their alliance with Sprint Corporation and the development of a dedicated in-store area called "America's Telephone Store," they have moved wireless phones to an anchor business with 12 percent share of the total wireless business.

A recent alliance with Compaq and a similar alliance with Thomson Consumer Electronics, the makers of RCA, will move computers and digital convergence devices from participatory to opportunity, all based on understanding how customers move through the RadioShack brand.

This understanding comes from modeling individual customers against the POA model. A customer who is very loyal and even a very frequent shopper but is buying only in the anchor area will be sent special offers to invoke a first purchase in an opportunity or participatory category. Once a customer moves to the next ring, the customer's frequency of shopping is greatly accelerated.

RadioShack is not yet a leader in moving its CRM to the Internet, but they are seeking the lead as America's connectivity store. In May 1999 they acquired Amerilink Corporation, the leading installer of cable, telephony, and high-speed bandwidth products primarily for home use. The company goal is to tie RadioShack closer to the customer by demystifying technology for the mass market.

The dedication to CRM also allows RadioShack to spot trends in the customer relationships. As the company expanded the anchor area to include telephones and other less technical merchandise, they began to see a denigration of their loyal techie customer base. In quick response they created an area called "Tech America," which David Edmondson calls "RadioShack on steroids." The Tech America customers receive separate communications that recognize their special needs.

Management uses the CRM program to constantly watch trend lines on the size of the average store transaction, the percent of male versus female shoppers, RFM by category, and segments of the business. They measure success not just by same-store sales trends but also by watching returns. They believe that if a customer asks for a return, it means whatever the company did, wherever in the process it broke down, the customer wants his or her money more than he or she wants the product. They do lots of customer surveys, but an important daily measure of the success of the marketing process is asking why customers are coming to ask for their money back. They put enormous emphasis on reducing customer returns and understanding the reasons why customers are coming back. Returns were high in the early days of America's Telephone Store. That is normal for the telephone industry, but it was unacceptable to RadioShack management. Intense study of customer behavior and special efforts to improve customer satisfaction have dramatically reduced telephone returns, and now RadioShack has the lowest rate of returns in the industry.

With all this CRM success, we asked David Edmondson what he might change going forward. Rather than give away proprietary information, he said, "Retailing requires a great deal of discontent. Retailing is very dynamic and very interesting business that requires you to make changes. You either keep moving or someone catches up with you:

> The lion wakes up every morning in Africa knowing, in order to survive, he has to catch the slowest gazelle. The gazelle wakes up knowing he must outrun the fastest lion. The moral: When you wake up in the morning, whether you are a lion or a gazelle, you better start running.

To start running with CRM, it's not enough to talk the talk; you have to walk the walk. Famous ad-man David Ogilvy, who founded the agency that is now known as Ogilvy & Mather, had 50 tenets upon which he founded the agency. Number 34 was, "What you show is more important than what you say." Actions speak louder than words.

CHAPTER

Hopelessly Devoted to You. . . . Ta Da!

CRM is more than just database marketing—actions speak louder than words.

John Farrar in his seventies song "Hopelessly Devoted to You" reminds us how important it is to show we care. That must go beyond communications to include *actions* that add value to the customer relationship, and that includes communicating with our customer in the ways that best serve her or his lifestyle.

If you own a Palm Pilot hand-held computer, you can receive special e-mail offers, tips, and product news every week—one of the many reasons Palm Pilot enjoys fierce loyalty from its nearly 2 million owners. Andrea Butter, director of consumer marketing, says, "The idea of this online service is to keep a dialog going. We wouldn't have had the resources to keep updating all the new products and services. With this electronic service, we get the news out, and the customer doesn't get spammed by us." Right now Palm sends each customer no more than 2 e-mails a week. That's tricky because, according to Butter, most customers have registered for nearly every category. "We could easily do 5 to 10 messages per week," she says, adding that the company may adjust the system to accommodate those who want to receive more e-mails.[1]

Think about that for a minute: Most customers have asked for information for nearly every category of Palm's products. This supports what we learned in Chapter 4. Information is now an important value for most customers.

Palm is not actively selling via the e-mail service, but because many of the messages involve products, the service is driving sales. When the company announced a Palm III upgrade, three times as many of their e-mail subscribers upgraded than did their customers not using the service.[2]

One industry that should be acting to add value to the customer relationship is the hotel industry. One of the great annoyances in my much-traveled life is the hotel room in which I have to haul out the bed to find a telephone connector to use as a dataport for my laptop and then I have to stretch a cord across the room to find a power plug. Apparently I'm not alone. The 1998 Road Warrior Survey by American Express reports that roughly 57 percent of frequent flyers communicate via e-mail while traveling and 18 percent of them access e-mail three or more times a day. Yet a recent study by the Orlando-based research firm Yesawich, Pepperdine & Brown found many hotel properties lagging in installing the latest communication technology because of a concern for cost and the worry that their installation would be obsolete, requiring new equipment with more features before they could even send in their warranty cards.[3]

There are times I wonder if hotel executives know how important an Internet connection is to travelers today.

Fortunately some hotel managers understand the importance of the Net connection and other amenities that are valuable to road warriors and are building strong customer relationships by finding new and often exceptional ways to show customers they understand their needs. Steve Halliday is one. He knows how to care for his business traveler customers. He should—The Pan Pacific Hotel in Singapore, where he is vice president and general manager, has a clientele that is 70 percent business travelers. He says, "To survive in this competitive world, you're always searching for ways to be number 1 in the marketplace. We are constantly looking, each and every day, for ways to show our guests we care."

When I visited Steve Halliday's hotel in 1997, Pan Pacific had just leapfrogged into cyberspace to show their business guests just how much they care by bringing cutting-edge office automation to their guests with 133-megahertz NEC Powermate V series personal computers installed in 189 of the hotel's 800 guest rooms.

Halliday told me then, "This is one area we felt we could show our business traveler guests we care about them. We want to be the number 1 preferred choice in Singapore for the business traveler. It's just common sense if a business person knows he or she can stay in a hotel that cares enough to put the world at his or her fingertips, why should he or she not stay there, given that the other conditions, service, and location are good?"

The S$1 million computer installation was not simple, requiring that fiber-optic cables be laid throughout the hotel's 189 rooms, a process that began in March 1997 with 10 rooms a day being wired. To maintain the five-star-hotel ambience, about S$40,000 was spent to build wooden covers for the CPU boxes to match the room décor. "We didn't want to put this huge piece of metal in the room spoiling the integrity of the décor," explained Halliday. "We also had to create a mousepad with a few simple, clear instructions on how to get going on the machine. We describe it on the mousepad as 'a world of fun, education, and business.'" I found it fun. Each room had its own e-mail address according to its room number. The system listed 100 favorite Web sites, games, and books. There was even a 10-minute educational tour of how to use the machine.

"There's more to this than just showing we care," Halliday told me. "We've taken the tool and developed it so that it's easier for our employees to spend more time with guests providing the one-to-one service we want. We didn't want the 'hardware' element to overtake the 'software' element, which is still service and people. I believe this will become the hallmark of customer service in the information age."

Steve Halliday is truly a pioneer in CRM. As have pioneers before him, he has learned that the breaking of new trails is a challenging experience. Sometimes the mountain pass that looks like the most direct route ends at an impassable canyon, forcing the wagon train to return to the valley to try another option.

When I checked back with Steve Halliday, in 1999, to get his update for this chapter, he told me the computer systems had been removed from all the rooms.

What failed?

"NEC was great," he said. "Good product, good service. The guests loved the system. The problem was with the software support. The local software support company was great at the start and ahead of their time, but with technology changing every 42 minutes, they did not keep up. Then they escaped to London and New York to chase an IPO opportunity, leaving us with no support."

Halliday then listed some other lessons learned. Most business executives don't want to plop their proprietary and secure documents onto someone else's machine. They prefer to get into their own intranet, and they want to get there fast. A few other small problems included keyboards getting dirty, guests spilling scotch and sodas into the machines, and, in at least one case, a guest loading a Playboy screen-saver onto a machine, shocking the next room occupant with naked ladies staring at her from her bedroom computer. CRM is, indeed, a learning experience. He learned what the guests really want is a high-speed reliable Internet connection.

Steve Halliday is still upbeat, still the pioneer looking for the best pass through the mountain, determined to find the best solution to make his Pan Pacific the preferred social and business address in Singapore. He has no remorse, and he is not seriously out of pocket on the experiment since the software company funded most of the installation expense. He believes that as computer costs continue to drop, computers will be as common in guestrooms as television sets are today. "It will be like the early introduction of irons and ironing boards," he says.

Steve Halliday believes today's best pass through the mountain is DSL lines to provide high-speed Internet access to guests. With more and more travelers carrying their laptops and with the swift development of PDA access to the Web, high-speed ports will be the best guest perk. The Pan Pacific has targeted this installation for first quarter of 2000.

Steve Halliday has even revised his mission statement. He no longer considers it enough for his property to be the preferred business address in Singapore. He was proud to tell me his mission statement is now to be "The Business Hotel of Asia."

Another wonderful story of customer care comes from a different Pan Pacific hotel. In San Francisco repeat guests can keep a few suits and personal items in a "luxury locker" at the hotel. On their return to the Pan Pacific, they find their clothes drycleaned, laundered, and ready. The Pan Pacific even has a personalized pillow-fluffing machine that fluffs feather pillows to each guest's specifications.[4] This is far from Steve Halliday's hi-tech, but it is tops in high-touch.

It would be easy to fill this book with examples of customer care that make up the CRM strategy at Pan Pacific hotels. For my personal comfort, I don't like a feather pillow with any degree of fluff. I prefer to stuff a small terry towel in a pillow case to make the smallest possible pillow. On my last visit, the room service person at the Singapore Pan Pacific was quick to notice this and made up the bed the second morning with the appropriate "towel pillow." It almost seems as though these folks have thought of everything possible to make each visit positive from the customer's viewpoint.

Gary Seibert, general manager for Hilton Hotels Midwest Region, told my favorite Pan Pacific CRM story to me. He swears it's true. A guest whose suitcase had been damaged in transit called the floor concierge to ask for a screwdriver to pry open the broken locks. The concierge arrived quickly carrying a glass of vodka and orange juice on ice. "Oh no," the guest cried. "I needed a screwdriver tool to open the locks." "Ah yes," said the concierge bringing forward his other hand. "I brought that as well, but I thought the first would make you feel a bit better about the problem."

It's not just what companies say in their communications to customers. It's what they *do* to show they really care.

When a business traveler checks in to one of the top-level rooms at L'Hermitage in Beverly Hills, he or she finds personalized business cards printed with the personal telephone number of the L'Hermitage room.

Talking about hotels raises the big question. Why do some of the best lodging companies not care?

For many years, I have been an active member of the executive loyalty club at one of the South's grandest hotels. Recently I checked in from a late plane at about 11:00 in the evening. There was one woman at the reservation desk. That's OK at 11:00 P.M., but the man in front of me said he had been waiting there for more than 20 minutes for the woman to check in the person ahead of him. Hearing that, and realizing that might mean I would have to wait another 20 minutes for him to check in, I stepped to the desk and asked if she couldn't find someone else to help. She finally called someone else out from that magic back room. I thought I was all set, but it took 15 minutes for her to find my reservation and get me checked in. She didn't seem to care that I was a member of their premium loyalty group. So much for touting class and caring for the customer.

One of my favorite stories about CRM actions comes from Virgin Atlantic Airways. On a flight where the crew had to apologize for having just a single movie selection instead of the usual choice of 18, they printed a letter at 30,000 feet and handed a copy to each passenger departing the plane. The letter apologized for the inconvenience and offered a no-expiration 20 percent discount on a next Virgin flight.

In this chapter we've been talking about winning actions, but we haven't broached actions related to point-based loyalty cards, and by now our bias against these is obvious.

Research has shown that the operational element that makes these programs unfriendly is the delay experienced between earning points and being able to redeem them. Customers become frustrated. Unnecessarily, and too often, this delay is caused by operational systems that don't link to a central database until the night the details of points earned during a day are posted. Customers are sent monthly, or sometimes only quarterly, statements of points earned, and they often have to send a mail or phone request to receive vouchers redeemable on their next store visit.

UK–based WH Smith, one of the best-known names on London's high street as a seller of books, newspapers, magazines, and stationery, resolved this problem. When starting their loyalty card scheme, they wanted to put as much control as possible into the hands of the customer and remove as many operational barriers as possible between the customer and the stores.

They have managed to create an immediate electronic dialog for each of their 3 million cardholders. At any WH Smith store, when a customer swipes his or her card across the point-of-sale reader, the terminal dials the head office and pulls down instant information on the customer and his or her program points. The customer can decide whether or not to redeem them in the immediate transaction, and the new points are added to the account with details of the new points and their value printed on the register receipt. The folks at WH Smith point out that this is even better than bank ATMs, which give only a cash balance as of the end of the previous day. The information WH Smith customers get is right up to the minute.

A 1999 market study on loyalty cards showed that of all the reward cards reviewed, WH Smith's was the one most likely to change customer buying behavior. According to the report, 30 percent of customers will go to WH Smith first to look for something they want, while other stores only influence 12 percent of customers.[5]

WH Smith's operational actions add value to the customer relationship while saving the company the expense of producing and mailing customer statements. These case studies demonstrate that CRM is much more than database and 1to1 marketing. Some gurus are still singing just the database marketing song when what they need to add to their repertoire is that old 1970s song, "Hopelessly Devoted to You." They think CRM is still only about *talking* to individuals. They need to change their thinking: It's not what they *say*, it's what they *do*.

QUICK TIPS FROM PART THREE

CHAPTER 18: Can CRM Save the Brick-and-Mortar Folks?

- The marketplace of the future for retailers is not anything/anywhere/any time.
- The rules have changed, and retailers will have to change.
- Sometimes the need to change can be the best thing that can happen to a company.
- The Internet should be used to drive in-store traffic, not to replace retail outlets.
- High-performance retailers of the future will carry products specifically selected for their own customers.
- The retail focus must change from getting new customers to selling more to the same customers by customization that treats different customers differently.
- The future of retailing isn't about providing large selections of shelved products. It's about providing smart solutions to the customer.
- More effort has to be made to carry head office strategies down to the store level to inform store personnel and make them partners in the CRM effort.

- A successful CRM program must involve the resources of the entire organization.
- Retailers have to begin to pay more attention to the concept of integrated marketing communications.
- CRM *can* save the brick-and-mortar folks.

CHAPTER 19: Managing CRM with Faceless Customers

- It doesn't matter whether you sell face to face or through channels.
- The new consumer and business trends will change brand marketing.
- Brand marketers must learn micromarketing for CRM.
- Don't waste money on nonprospects and nonprofitable customers. Would you invest in a losing stock?
- Find new ways to work with channel partners.
- Watch for the coming of addressable television advertising.
- Think of coupons as antiloyalty.
- CRM is a constant process of learning.

CHAPTER 20: Because That's Where the Money Is

- Yesterday's product-focused business model will no longer work to retain and grow today's demanding customer.
- Service comes from knowing your customers.
- Banks keep those customers with whom they maintain multiple relationships three or four times longer than those with whom they have only a single relationship.
- It is more profitable to develop fewer and better relationships with customers than to have more customers that use only single products.
- For CRM to succeed, it must have a champion at the top.

- People, processes, and technology must change.
- Our job is to create services and products that will give customers more reasons to buy from us. That means active 1to1 learning in order to customize offers.
- The big challenge is customizing each interaction with the customer—no matter what channel—so as to maximize profitability.

CHAPTER 21: But Who Is *Really* Your Customer?

- Business-to-business marketers must remember a business person is simply a consumer at work.
- Business-to-business marketing deals with real individual people.
- Institute a personalized relationship program, not a loyalty program.
- CRM is not the end of mass trade advertising.
- You must understand customers—not just sales personnel, reps, and competitors.
- The customer has the power.
- Interactive dialog is the payoff to CRM.
- The right relationship will mean more than price.
- Change the way you do business. Move from transactions to solutions.

CHAPTER 22: The Media Awaken to CRM

- The business case to implement CRM in media companies offers two opportunities: (a) CRM can increase the depth of audience involvement to reduce churn, and (b) identify best customers and prospects for specific advertisers.
- Don't underestimate the power of customer knowledge when combined with the power of your brand.

- Advertisers are no longer willing to waste advertising dollars on nonprospects.
- If media companies don't find ways to provide advertisers with information about specific members of their audience, they will soon be losing revenue.
- Advertisers want media to know as much about their own audiences as the advertisers know about their customers.
- Media can use customer knowledge to create new revenue streams.
- Customer lifetime value is as important to media as it is for any other business.
- Find the time and the budget to make CRM happen now.

CHAPTER 23: When You Care Enough

Quick tips from an expert, Hallmark:

- Even points programs can be tailored to build relationships.
- Spoil the top-tier of your customers.
- Talk to customers about what they want to hear.
- Listen to customers when they talk back.
- The sales force and sales associates must be involved in the CRM effort.
- Let customers reward themselves for nice behavior.
- Focus on growth. Then build data.
- The customers must drive the program.
- You must be prepared to stay in for the long haul.

CHAPTER 24: Reorganizing Using the CRM Initiative

Quick tips from an expert, Boots the Chemists:

- Use customer knowledge to gain the ability to introduce new products and services.

- CRM is impossible without the company's solid commitment.
- It pays to test.
- Boots' program is very much *not* about discounts for family shopping. It *is very much* about treating yourself.
- Store staff must be involved.
- It's not just about customer loyalty. It's about customer development.
- You can't buy customer loyalty, but you can grow it.
- Boots is not creating ways to buy loyalty. They are finding ways to develop loyalty that already exists.
- The prioritizing process is one of the most important skills.
- You don't want technicians who want only to drive a database. You want analysts who actually want to drive the business.

CHAPTER 25: Customer Involvement: RadioShack's Sophisticated CRM Programs

Quick tips from an expert, RadioShack:

- The overriding objective of CRM is to grow the depth of involvement between the customer and the brand or the store.
- Growing the depth of involvement with each individual existing customer is paramount.
- Build the strategy around surprising and delighting the customer.
- Everything in terms of advertising and promotion strategy must be driven by a basic understanding of what the customer wants and what the customer is doing and/or not doing.

- Use CRM to migrate customers profitably through the business.
- Use CRM to watch trend lines and spot changes in customer relationships.
- You either keep moving or someone catches up with you.

CHAPTER 26: Hopelessly Devoted to You. . . . Ta Da!

- Actions speak louder than words.
- Find new ways to show customers you care.
- In developing your plan, talk to everyone—associates and customers.
- In the end CRM is about service and people.

PART FOUR

MAKING PRODUCTS INTO SERVICES: STRATEGIES FOR PROFITABLE DIALOG

Because products must become services if they are to inspire long-term customer relationships, we'll explore the word *prodices* and see what it means for CRM.

We'll have some final words to guide new players in devising and implementing a CRM strategy, and we'll share some important thoughts about our favorite word *dialog* and the importance of listening to the customer.

We'll see why the privacy issue creates fear and what marketers must do to protect customer information.

Finally, we'll take a closer look at the matter of loyalty, examine the business process required for CRM, and review the most important piece of all: Where do the profits come from?

27
CHAPTER

The Missing Link: "Prodices"

Customers want service—
not just stuff.

People don't really want quarter-inch drill bits. They want quarter-inch holes. That was the message paraphrased by Lester Wunderman, then chair of Wunderman, Cato, Johnson, the world's largest direct marketing advertising agency, in his keynote address for the Direct Marketing Association's 79th Annual Conference in New Orleans in 1996.

He reminded his audience that consumers increasingly want what products *do* rather than what they *are*. "They want the service, not the stuff," were his actual words. As is always the case, Lester Wunderman was ahead of his time. Addressing the same group as long ago as 1983, he said:

> Interactive systems will create flexible, data-driven, knowledge-based relationships in which buyer and seller will constantly serve each other. What we now call "direct marketing" should now be

renamed "relationship marketing." We no longer sell products or services alone. What we do is to market and manage relationships between sellers and buyers.

Now we take the term *relationship marketing* for granted, forgetting his introduction of the concept almost 20 years ago.

In his 1996 keynote address, he introduced another new word into our marketing vocabulary—*prodices*, things that look like products but act like services—explaining that people want the total ability to communicate more than they want just phones, faxes, computers, modems, and satellites. They want meals, not foodstuffs; entertainment, not cassettes or disks; clean clothes, not laundry products; healthy teeth, not toothpaste. He predicted a day when automakers would sell miles instead of cars.

In the late 1990s few had gotten his message. Businesses seemed to be going in the opposite direction, asking customers to provide the service.

One market watcher, commenting on that trend, said, "In recent years banks have turned us into tellers. The phone company has turned us into operators. Gas stations have turned us into do-it-yourself-gas-pumpers. Federal Express has turned us into shippers. We do their work, and they charge us for it."

Superfresh, a group of A&P-owned supermarkets in the Washington, D.C. area, offered "Superlanes," where customers swipe their own packages over the scanner, plunk their salads and produce on the scale, and punch in the price. They bag it themselves, press "end order" on the touch pad, grab the receipt, and pay the cashier.

That's not relationship marketing, and it certainly isn't delivering prodices.

Now, finally, it seems that companies, even supermarkets, are listening to Lester Wunderman's words. Customers of Safeway's Basingstoke superstore near London don't have to check out their own groceries. In fact, they don't even have to leave home or office to shop. These Safeway customers now use a modified Palm Pilot *personal digital assistant* (PDA) called "EasiOrder" to preselect their weekly groceries. Safeway loads a suggested shopping list into the PDA based on each customer's prior purchases.

When the order is ready to be placed, the customer connects the PDA to a telephone line and the order is in the store in 90 seconds where a Safeway team picks and packs the groceries for the customer to pick up and pay for at his or her convenience.

The PDA has several buttons across its face, all very helpful to the customer. The personalized list key displays items the customer has purchased within the last five months, and this list is updated each time an order is placed.

Another key brings up a list of in-store specials, again updated whenever the customer places an order. A third key displays loyalty card program information.

Other mechanisms include a shopping basket key, which shows the items selected with their individual and cumulative prices, an index button that brings up a list of products in walking-store order, and a scanner. Presumably a customer can enter orders for items by scanning the bar codes on near-empty packages in his or her pantry.

The system can make very personal recommendations. If you bought a birthday cake six months ago, and the store knew what was written on it, and you have been buying Huggies in a specific size, the smart folks at Safeway can deduce that you have an 18-month-old daughter and the date of her birthday. Six months later the PDA will ask you if you want to buy a birthday cake.

This UK Safeway has a points-based loyalty program, but our guess is the customized, convenient, electronic shopping service will do more to keep customers loyal to Safeway than the points program.

Many of the great service ideas that fit within Lester Wunderman's definition of prodices seem to be coming from the United Kingdom. While many supermarkets and online food services will deliver to individual homes in the evening, Waitrose Supermarket chain offers an even more convenient way for customers to buy their groceries. Using Waitrose@work, a free online ordering service, busy, hard-working people are able to order groceries via their Web browser and have them delivered to their workplace during one of two time slots available each day. The system allows customers to shop without leaving the office and have their groceries delivered to them at either 2 P.M. or 5 P.M. The system also allows them to keep the same shopping list week after week, to take advantage of special offers, and even to specify if they want green bananas instead of yellow. Personal information is stored on the individual's account and used to aid them in their choices.

Waitrose@work is available to any company provided that it has an intranet, surface car park, and is within 10 to 15 miles of one of the 115 Waitrose stores. More than 20 major companies have signed on so that they can provide this service as a benefit for their employees. About 30 percent of the staff at most participating companies have signed on, and many of these people had not shopped at Waitrose prior to discovering the convenience of the system. They are now loyal customers.

One might think that employers would not like their staff ordering groceries during workhours. The converse is true. They are happy to have their people relieved of the stress of traveling into town for lunchtime shopping with no guarantee of a parking space on their return to the office. Participating companies say the program helps employees to work better and use their time more effectively. Not having to shop after work also shortens the day and means workers are less tired and irritable when they get home.

While most systems delivering to individual homes incur substantial delivery charges from traveling to each separate home, the Waitrose system allows for several hundred peoples' shopping to be delivered at the same time with one stop, thus making the service free—a great benefit for consumers *and* for Waitrose.

In Newton, Massachusetts, Todd Krasnow, one of the founders of Staples, Inc., has started a *prodice* that he hopes to take national. He is betting that he can deliver more convenience to customers at a better price with guaranteed service quality. The company is Zoots, a dry-cleaning business with five locations as this is written.

Zoots promises a lot of nice things that will turn its dry-cleaning and laundry product into a true prodice. Customers can drop off and pick up their clothes at a drive-through window where Zoots employees exchange the dirty laundry for fresh pressed clothes. An "Express Service" allows customers to keep a credit card on file with Zoots, and this same file keeps track of customer preferences for how customers like their laundry.

Zoots gives customers bar-coded garment bags that customers can fill with laundry and drop off in the store or at the drive-in window. Zoots will even leave customers' laundry in a personal locker that can be accessed outside the store 24 hours a day. As a high-tech prodice, Zoots allows customers to monitor the progress of their order on Zoots' Web site and will also notify customers by e-mail when their laundry is ready for pickup. As a final "feel good," Zoots will forward used clothing to Goodwill Industries, earning customers a tax break.[1]

Noting the trend to added service offerings, *Entrepreneur* magazine declared concierge services the hottest business idea in 1999. Office towers, shopping malls, and apartments are adding concierges to fetch dry cleaning, arrange car tune-ups, and order birthday cakes for busy people. Some airlines offer concierge services at major airports.[2]

In this era of souped-up, stressed-out, overscheduled, high-stress living, Lester Wunderman's prodices will become more and more vital for the winners who want to develop long-term customers. Even families are seeking to outsource services, from grocery shopping to rides to soccer, and technology solutions will help them connect home, work, and community life. A recent *USA Today* article talks about parents who keep their schedules on his-and-hers Palm Pilot digital organizers that they synchronize at night. They update each other throughout the day by phone, e-mail, and paging as piano lessons get cancelled, games get moved, or business meetings go overtime.

The *USA Today* authors followed some Silicon Valley families, spending days watching moms, dads, kids, and nannies to see how they spend their time. They found some families outsourcing nearly everything. Here's just one case:

> The twins have a nanny, while the parents have personal assistants at work who do "everything for us," including paying the bills. At home groceries are ordered over the Web using PeaPod and delivered weekly. Dry cleaning is picked up and delivered by Italy Cleaning. Waiters on Wheels and Dine 1-1 deliver meals. A housekeeper cleans their house and a gardener takes care of the yard.
>
> It has gotten to the point that shopping is a novelty. A few weeks back they forgot to order groceries so they actually had to go to the supermarket. "It was like a recreational experience," was the quote. "It was exciting to saunter around the aisles."[3]

Today's customer wants the service, not the stuff. Winners will find it's the quarter-inch holes, not the quarter-inch drill bits, that will develop long-term customers.

28

It's a Matter of Degrees

Why developing CRM strategy is a learning process

It's still the planning of the strategy that counts, and part of the strategy development can be a matter of degrees.

By A.D. 150 the cartographer and astronomer Ptolemy had plotted lines of latitude and longitude on the 27 maps of his first world atlas, but that didn't mean our seafaring ancestors could use these meridians to find their way. Throughout the great ages of exploration, sailors, lacking the ability to determine their longitude, were literally lost at sea as soon as they lost sight of land. They could gauge latitude well enough by the length of the day or by the height of the sun, but to determine longitude at sea required knowing what time it was aboard ship and measuring that against the time at home port or another place of known longitude. Navigational accuracy demanded a clock that would not lose or gain more than 3 seconds in 24 hours, and no such timepiece existed until late in the eighteenth century when John Harrison invented a clock that would carry the true time from the home port, like an eternal flame, to any remote corner of the world.[1]

Today, as we enter the twenty-first century, many marketers are as lost as seventeenth-century sailors and continue to run aground on rocky shoals because of their inability to map customer contacts longitudinally.

The consultants at Kestenbaum & Company have trade-marked the idea of Longitudinal Contact Strategy, a strategy to plan customer contacts over a substantial time horizon. They make the point that companies dealing with a large customer base and especially those with infrequent purchase or service interactions face a challenge in developing and maintaining a long-term relationship with customers. In addition to offering products for sale, marketing communications can add significantly to the customer relationship and brand-building process. Communications can deliver vital information, recognition of customer importance, personalized attention, a sense of friendliness, and other elements that are meaningful to customers—all important elements of CRM that add value to the customer relationship.

Most companies, Kestenbaum believes, plan their marketing communications as campaigns, deciding for each individual event how many customers they will contact and how deeply into their file they will reach without regard to the individual customers and how much mail he or she might be receiving. This effort-by-effort approach, they suggest, may not be accomplishing either maximization of sales or purposeful strengthening of the customer relationship. If a customer is not selected for contact for a campaign because he or she falls a little below the cutoff point used for the decision criterion, the customer is not contacted. If this happens for continuing campaigns, the customer is inadvertently abandoned. Receiving no contacts for an extended period of time guarantees this customer's poor performance will become worse.

Companies practicing CRM must be proactive in reaching out to draw in former and potential customers. A single or occasional purchase or service contact experience is not likely to build much of a relationship. The folks at Kestenbaum arrive at their Longitudinal Contact Strategy by suggesting, "We need to take the conventional process of planning marketing contacts in vertical, independent time slots, turn it 90 degrees, and think horizontally about how to plan contacts longitudinally."

This Longitudinal Contact Strategy envisions a coherent stream of marketing communications planned over a substantial time horizon and adjusted as well as possible to fit each customer or prospect to add value to the customer relationship. A good contact plan should have goals, a clear approach to achieving the goals, and measurements to determine how well the goals are achieved.

When contacts are insufficient, Kestenbaum concludes, profitable sales are lost. So Longitudinal Contact Strategy is important to every market regardless of size, product, audience, or media used for communications.[2]

One multi-billion-dollar women's specialty apparel chain we studied understands Kestenbaum's Longitudinal Contact Strategy for CRM. The chain has 54 million customers. They know who their best customers are and what percent sales these customers generate. Research has given them a good idea of each customer's clothing budget and their share of each customer's wallet. They have added customer demographics to the file, and they know when and what each customer buys at their stores. Moreover, they know who buys full ticket versus on deal. In many cases they have learned when and what each customer buys from the competition.

With all of this knowledge, this chain manages relationships with each customer segment by developing specific longitudinal marketing plans differentiating communications, customizing messages, and planning individual contacts over specific time horizons to fit each customer segment, thus adding value to the customer relationship.

They allocate 60 percent of their marketing dollars to the 14 percent of customers responsible for 55 percent of sales, and these customers receive five communications each season including status-based loyalty benefits, advance notice of private sales, personalized gift with purchase, season merchandise previews, image-based mailings, and in-store recognition and special service.

Thirty-five percent of the company's marketing dollars are allocated to the 34 percent of customers who account for 35 percent of sales. These customers receive a minimum of three contacts per season including performance-based frequency programs, notice of sale events, bring-a-friend promotions, and gift certificate promotions.

Just 5 percent of the marketing dollars are allocated to the 52 percent of customers who generate 10 percent of the company's sales. They receive a maximum of two contacts per season including clearance announcements and gift certificate promotions.

A large department store chain has profiled the customers who spend more than $700 a year and generate 80 percent of the company's business and created a longitudinal marketing strategy for different segments based on key similarities and differences in demographics and lifestyles for each of its store markets.

For effective CRM there is a lot more to this, of course, than the number of degrees our communication contacts stretch from the prime meridian. The nature of the contacts must help to convince the customer that a company really cares. They must add value to the relationship.

Dick's Supermarkets, Platteville, Wisconsin, are good at CRM, and they are constantly conducting tests to improve their CRM program. One test used greeting cards to strengthen loyalty with grocery customers.

The rationale of the test was that relationships are built on a foundation of logic and emotion, facts and feelings, and within the grocery industry there is little differentiation among card-based loyalty programs—most simply provide price discounting. The test was designed to test the power of emotion in loyalty marketing and to test to find the optimum number of contacts to establish the appropriate longitudinal communication plan.

The campaign consisted of eight customized greeting cards sent over a six-month period to test and measure the impact of three key variables: offers, personalization, and frequency. The creative concept for the greeting cards was warm, caring, friendly; upscale, photographic format; subtle undertone of incentive messages and purchase suggestions. Hallmark produced the cards, and the Hallmark subsidiary, Irresistible Ink, produced the hand-addressed test envelopes.

Dick's learned that the offer, of course, was important. Better results came from cards with offers. Better results also came from handwritten mail. As for the frequency of contact, for the best longitudinal communication strategy they learned that five cards mailed to a customer performed better than three.

Lessons learned: Emotions and promotions cannot be measured in the same way. According to Ken Robb, senior vice president of Dick's, "This program taught us the power of using a personal touch in our business communications. We learned that while customers want price discounts, they also appreciate the fact that we take the time and effort to let them know we appreciate their business. We can't do that too much or too often."

When BMA, a Kansas City–based insurance company, wanted to adjust its offers to fit individual customers, it turned to IBM's Printing Systems Division to combine data mining tools with custom printing capabilities. They knew that increasing their share of customers would require understanding what their customers needed. Customer knowledge and digital printing allowed BMA to tailor direct-mail pieces to specific customer life cycles like growing family or looming retirement, offering specific products to fit individual needs. A mailing of 4200 pieces netted a 43 percent response.[3] Another great example of the value of customizing offers.

It's not enough to talk about 1to1 marketing. The new Y2K consumers want more than canned loyalty program discounts and rewards, and they want more than sell, sell, sell on your home page. They want to build relationships with companies that prove they care. Proving you care requires a dialog with customers.

29

Recognizing the Power of the Consumer

It's not about simply moving your marketing efforts to the Internet. It's about how well your company dialogs.

Dialog is the most important word in the CRM lexicon.

To manage customer relationships, we have to learn to listen to learn enough about each customer to understand the customized products and services that will provide individual solutions because CRM is all about selling solutions, not just products.

Seth Godin calls using dialog "Permission Marketing." Godin is vice president of direct marketing at Yahoo! and founder of Yoyodyne, a pioneer company in online CRM. In his book *Permission Marketing: Turning Strangers into Friends, and Friends into Customers* (Simon & Schuster, 1999), he calls this the first marketing approach that recognizes the power of the consumer.

With permission marketing, Godin says, "Customers volunteer their attention. Marketers take that attention, treat it like an asset, and then turn it into cash." He details the process in his book:

> Each of us is born with only a certain amount of time on this earth, and figuring out how to use it wisely is one of life's primary activities. Paying attention to something—anything—is, in fact, a conscious act, requiring conscious effort. So one way to sell a consumer something in the future is simply to get his or her permission in advance. You'll do this by engaging the consumer in a dialog—an interactive relationship, with both you and the customer participating.

Peter Brabeck-Letmathe, CEO of Nestlé, the world's biggest food company, understands this. In his earlier life, as group VP at Nestlé responsible for strategic businesses, he guided the company's first step into dialog communication with the Casa Buitony Club that collected detailed information about customers of Italian food. Club members were encouraged to turn to Buitony as a helpful expert for advice on all aspects of Italian cooking, and customers were invited to participate in recipe and new-product development. The budget for dialog communication has now risen to 70 percent of Casa Buitony's $7.6 million marketing fund, up from 40 percent of $2.5 million in 1992, and the concept has spread to other Nestlé divisions.[1]

Dialog clubs are now set up for Nestlé in France, Switzerland, and North America; Buitony in the United Kingdom; KitKat in Japan; Maggi in Germany; and Friskies in Canada.[2]

In Malaysia, Nestlé is using 1to1 communication and establishing dialog to learn about the buying population in a country of 19.5 million people who speak one or more of three languages, vary in their religion, and eat out only on special occasions, and consumers are responding. "As soon as we send out a mailing, people phone because they're so excited and want to call and say hello and thank you. It's an incredible way of finding out how people really feel," says a spokesperson for Nestlé. In 1998, 100,000 Malaysians answered detailed questionnaires on consumption patterns, lifestyles, race, religion, and feelings about specific brands.[3]

Brabeck says:

> I want to know what my consumer is feeling, how he or she is changing, what he is desiring— . . . those things, and afterward to see if I can find an answer, through my products, my services, and my communication. This is absolutely why we are using our own databases more than conventional research. We have to know our consumer in much more detail.[4]

Rance Crain, editor in chief of *Ad Age*, says:

> Nobody listens to consumers anymore. Well, maybe they listen, but too many ignore what consumers really want in favor of common platforms for look-alike automobiles and advertising designed to win awards and the approval of colleagues, but there is brewing a major reaction.

He quotes Simon Anholt: "The 20th-century brands were the 'shouting brands.' They had it easy. The 21st-century brands are the 'listening brands,' and sensitivity to culture is the new holy grail of global marketing."[5]

Nestlé understands this, and there are others.

GM's Buick Division creates a dialog with prospective customers with a series of interactive mailings with a response device that lets prospects provide feedback on features they are most interested in. A health care company sends clients a monthly e-mail message to show them how much they have saved, and every other month they include a short survey to enrich their database with self-reported customer information.

In addition to the Global Services office in the United Kingdom which we talked about in Chapter 13, Thomas Cook announced a plan to open a North American call center in late 1999 and another in Australia in 2000. The North American center will accommodate travelers to North America speaking English, Spanish, French, and Portuguese. The Australian center will serve all of Asia. This costly expansion of customer-friendly facilities is just another way Thomas Cook is reaching out to create dialogs with its customers.

Dialog with customers is teaching companies to change their reward systems for customer-facing personnel. They are learning the value of taking the time to learn and meet each customer's individual needs. One insurance company that had always recognized the "top" agent as the one who processed the most calls, gave out the most quotes, took the most applications, and produced the highest premiums later learned that this agent was not the most profitable to the company.

When performance was analyzed from the perspective of converted sales per 100 quotes, the agent with the least number of quotes, the least number of sales, and the least total premiums had the highest closing rate, highest average premium, highest premiums per 100 quotes, and highest number of retained customers per 100 quotes. This agent took the time to learn enough about her customers' real needs to convert quotations to sales and retain customers—not just handle calls and bind total premiums.[6]

CCG Online, a division of Customer Communications Group, whose clients include Fortune 1000 companies in the retail, financial services, telecommunications, travel, and health care industries, has developed an opt-in e-mail dialog program for Express, a women's apparel chain owned by The Limited, Inc.

Express sends monthly targeted outbound offers to its young, Generation X, computer-literate customers and also uses surveys to collect size and apparel preference information. They are masters at building dialog to build stronger customer relationships and even use the customer dialog to help store buyers be sure they are stocking the merchandise their customers most want. When an Express store buyer was unsure whether her customers would want a particular pant she was buying in linen or denim, she asked the customers by e-mail. In one week 50,000 customer replies told her to please buy it in denim, saving thousands of dollars in potential markdowns if she had made the wrong choice. When experts at the Direct Marketing Association's 3rd Annual net.marketing conference and exhibition in March 1999 shared ideas about ways to be sure companies are meeting customer needs, Tom Hoffman, manager of Internet Services, United Parcel Service, said, "Customer service is about strengthening relationships. The goal is to create mutual benefits—for UPS and its customers—to increase repeat business." He recommended continuing surveys (dialog) to see whether a company is measuring up to customers' expectations and to find out what its customers are doing and not doing.

Office Depot's Elizabeth Van Story agreed, saying, "It isn't necessary to measure yourself against every benchmark and online retailer. All you need to do is know your customers and their expectations and find your benchmarks there." She recommends hiring an outside firm to survey customers at your Web site and when customers make a purchase, to place follow-up calls a week later.

The Internet offers exciting new opportunities to create dialog with customers, but it will bring new challenges. It doesn't cost much to e-mail to millions of people. It is relatively easy to put up a Web site, and consumers are moving to the Internet in droves.

Acknowledging this, Steven Krein, cofounder and president of Webstakes, says, "The problem is the many advantages of the Internet are already becoming major disadvantages for marketers. The minimal cost and accessibility of the medium are helping drown consumers with clutter."[7]

Krein says, "So what's a marketer to do now that mailboxes are full in the 'post office' world and 70-plus million people are deleting your e-mail already? It's not about simply moving your marketing efforts to the Internet. It's about how well your company dialogs." He harks back to the time when the storekeeper actually knew us, when people shared information with each other, when they dialoged. He calls using dialog to build relationships "marketing circa 1801."[8]

Krein sums up his case for dialog marketing with these comments:

> Many marketers will continue to look for short-term ways to generate results, but they will be surpassed by a new breed of dialog marketers who embrace the concept of ongoing dialog to build relationships.
>
> Dialog over time. It takes time to prove yourself and build loyalty with consumers. Over time, your dialog will evolve and become more focused. You will get to know your prospects, and they will get to know you.[9]

All businesses love their customers, but it will be unrequited love if you don't talk to them *and listen to them.*

Finally, remember one thing about Steven Krein's friendly storekeeper circa 1801. He was wise and circumspect. He respected confidences and respected each customer's privacy.

30

Information Is Knowledge, Knowledge Is Power, and Power Can Be Frightening

Some people believe companies have power over them because of the information they collect.

Privacy!—a hot topic for politicians and the press, and for marketers.

Privacy was one of the hottest topics in speeches, lecture sessions, and breakfast roundtables at the DMA Telephone Marketing Conference in June 1999.

DMA president and CEO, H. Robert Wientzen formally opened the conference by warning that while the industry is booming, the consumer environment in which it operates is becoming increasingly inhospitable, and precautions must be taken to maintain consumer trust.[1]

Garry Meyers, CEO of the children's magazine *Highlights for Children*, understands this:

> The privacy issue taps into a powerful emotion: fear. It's fear that helps elect politicians, sell papers, and capture the anxious imaginations of television viewers. The public's fascination with (and fear of) privacy violations is reinforced by a never-ending stream of real-life instances in which people are stalked, are victims of stolen identity, or are denied credit, insurance coverage, or employment.[2]

He saw this consumer fear firsthand when a mother called his company to complain that her young daughter had received an inappropriate lingerie catalog. The mother was sure *Highlights* had been the source of the name since the children's magazine was the only thing the child received in her own name. As Meyers said, by the time the mother got to him, she was livid. *Highlights* had not provided the name to the lingerie catalog and, in fact, never releases children's names for any use, but Meyers was able to track the name release to a company specializing in thank-you cards where the girl's uncle had purchased cards and had them sent to the young girl. The mother's faith in *Highlights* was restored.

Meyers makes the point that people are afraid of what they don't understand, and they generally don't understand much about database marketing. People believe that companies have power over them because of the information they collect, and they fear that power. He says:

> Consider what might have happened if the card company had made its information policy known to consumers beforehand and provided an opportunity to opt out. The uncle might have realized that his niece's name was subject to being rented, and he might have opted out. The whole situation could have been avoided. Even more to the point, the card company should have been more selective and not released the name to the lingerie company. It was not providing a valuable service to its customers.[3]

A fundamental of CRM is providing valuable services to customers based on knowledge of what customers really value, but it is vital to remember that relationships must be built on trust. The increasingly refined technology that enables us to compile ever-richer information about customers helps us build and manage customer relationships, but if the relationship is not something the consumer values, it becomes a liability.

Information about our customers and our potential customers is the fuel of our business, but great care is required to guard against the kind of information leaks and surreptitious data capture that makes privacy advocates scream. Patricia Fraley, reporting for the Direct Marketing Association (DMA) at the 1999 Supermarket Industry Convention in Chicago, listed some of the worst examples:

Judge Robert H. Bork's video selections were made available to the press; a credit bureau reported an entire town in Vermont as deadbeats; a list of children was sold to someone who used the name of Polly Klass' killer; Hallmark cards had an accessible online file containing not only the e-mail addresses but intimate messages of customers' electronic cards to loved ones; and Microsoft released *Windows 98* with an identification number unique to individual computer owners and embedded in both hardware and individual documents created by users—without their permission. And when Intel introduced their new Pentium III chip in 1999, it contained an embedded serial number that allowed the company to trace equipment.

In June 1999 the Minnesota Attorney General sued U.S. Bank for improperly releasing customers' private banking information to telemarketing firms in exchange for fees and commissions. The information allegedly consisted not only of customers' names, addresses, and telephone numbers but also confidential personal information including checking account number, credit card number, social security number, average account balance, and credit limit.

U.S. Bancorp, the holding company of U.S. Bank, denied the charges. Then, two days later, they ran full-page ads in the Minneapolis and St. Paul newspapers in which an open letter from the chairman stated that U.S. Bank was "ending our participation in this and all similar types of marketing programs for nonfinancial products."[4]

After the U.S. Comptroller of the Currency suggested banks stop selling customer data to unaffiliated telemarketers lest Congress legislate against it, Bank of America Corp announced it would not share any customer information with third-party marketers who offer their products and services to its customers, nor would the bank enable such marketers to offer its customers products unrelated to their financial needs.

In June 1999 The Financial Services Roundtable, a banking industry group, called for a "summit meeting" to address the issue of the privacy of financial records of banking customers.

We are at the point where privacy is, indeed, a marketing factor. Saul Klein, the privacy expert at Microsoft, says, "People will start spending time and money with companies based on their information policies."[5]

A 1998 study by Privacy and American Business reported that 81 percent of respondents believed that "consumers have lost all control over how personal information is circulated and used by companies." In addition, 78 percent believed that "business organizations generally ask for too much personal information from consumers"; only 39 percent believed that "my rights to privacy are adequately protected." But 70 percent believed that "companies' adopting good voluntary privacy policies is better than the government's enacting regulations."[6]

It won't be enough for us to require attorneys general, comptrollers of the currency, and the press to direct our privacy policies. We are even past the point where the DMA's widely accepted Guidelines for Ethical Business Practices was an adequate answer. We now must take stronger steps to ensure that the concerns of consumers and regulators are being met.

The DMA has recognized this and has taken action. To build consumer trust, protect industry information, demonstrate respect for consumer choice, and show support for self-regulation, the DMA board of directors approved a "Privacy Promise" to American consumers. Effective July 1, 1999, all DMA members had to sign on to the Privacy Promise and appoint a corporate privacy contact person or relinquish their DMA membership.

The Privacy Promise assures that:

1. Notice will be provided by all companies that market to consumers and rent, sell, or exchange names of their customers for marketing purposes. This will make customers aware of their ability to prevent their name and address from being exchanged.

2. Opt-out requests will be honored by all DMA members, giving consumers a choice as to how their information is used by companies.

3. In-house suppression lists will allow consumers to have their names removed from any list a company rents in the future.

4. The DMA's Mail Preference Service and Telephone Preference Service will allow consumers who do not wish to receive any unsolicited marketing offers by mail or telephone to make a single request for name removal.

By embracing the Privacy Promise, DMA members are taking an affirmative step in telling consumers that they care about the issues of consumer concern and in demonstrating to regulators that marketers can execute meaningful and effective self-regulation.

Privacy is a global issue. Every country in the world is addressing the issue of privacy regulation, but the spotlight has been on the EU's data protection directive that forbids companies in EU countries to export personal data to outside countries deemed not to have adequate privacy protection. It is generally assumed that the United States falls under that category.

As of spring 1999, U.S. and EU negotiators were discussing "safe harbor" measures, stating that the EU directive could be complied with if an EU company and a U.S. company (or any company outside the EU) sign contracts assuring that the data are secure and treated properly. At the annual conference of the Federation of European Direct Marketing in France in April 1999, it seemed the outcome of the talks was still uncertain. One commentator said, "The Americans put forward what seemed to be a compromise, but there are still major problems and disagreements."[7]

Like all EU directives, the data protection directive mandates the EU nations to make laws complying with it. As of May 1999, only 6 of the 15 member nations had passed privacy laws, and some of those are not up to compliance with the directive. Four countries seeking to become EU members—Poland, Hungary, Slovenia, and the Czech Republic—have passed such laws.[8]

The explosion of Web, e-mail, and e-commerce has magnified the privacy question in the uncharted land of the Internet, but there are encouraging signs.

In 1998 a Federal Trade Commission (FTC) survey found that only 14 percent of the 1400 Web sites checked informed customers of how they use personal information. In May 1999 the Georgetown Internet Private Policy Survey for the FTC had better news.[9]

The survey studied the top 100 sites on the Web and 364 commercial sites randomly chosen from the 7500 most visited. The survey showed that 94 percent of the top 100 sites had posted at least one type of privacy disclosure (a privacy policy notice or an information practice statement). Of the 364 randomly selected sites, 65.7 percent had at least one privacy notice.

Of the sampled sites, 92.9 percent collected some type of personal information such as e-mail address, phone number, or mailing address. Another 56.9 percent collected some type of demographic information such as gender, preferences, or zip code.

Of the sites that collected data, 87 percent posted some type of privacy notice, and 77 percent gave visitors instructions on how to opt out or bypass information collection.[10]

In June 1999 IBM announced that it would cease advertising on any Web site that does not post a privacy policy. As the number 2 Web advertiser (behind Microsoft), IBM's policy will certainly get attention.[11]

In July 1999 The Federal Trade Commission released a report to Congress stating that online companies are regulating themselves so well in the privacy arena that it felt no need at this time to step in. So, the FTC's conclusion was good news for CRM marketers, but the invasion of personal privacy on the Web still poses the greatest long-term threat to developing successful customer relationships.

There are many showing great respect for privacy online. Hickory Farms is a leader. Marco Pescara, Hickory Farms vice president of direct marketing, says, "In both the catalog and the online business we are very conscious of respecting people's privacy, so we approach the Internet very carefully in terms of how we use that data and how we build that relationship with the customer. Because there is more of an intimate relationship on the Internet, and people view their mailboxes as being very personal, we do not ask them to give personal details other than what is necessary to complete the transaction. We let that information come out only in the transaction.[12]

The Better Business Bureau (BBB) has launched a voluntary certification and assessment program that will evaluate and rate Internet merchants' privacy policies. At a cost of $150 for a small merchant and up to $3000 for a large national chain, BBB Online will review and assess the online retailer's consumer privacy plan. If the retailer meets all the bureau's criteria, BBB Online will issue a certification logo the retailer can display on his or her Internet site.[13]

Harold McGraw, president and CEO of the McGraw-Hill Companies, reaffirms our thoughts from the opening of this chapter:

> Internet users understand better than most people that information is knowledge and knowledge is power. Trust is the most precious asset any business has. It is the bedrock business is built on, and in this era of new media especially, trust becomes more critical than ever. . . .

> Privacy isn't just a U.S. issue or an EU issue, but a global issue, just as the Internet is a global network. Privacy is an issue that spans countries, continents, and cultures.[14]

McGraw reminds us that 80 bills regulating privacy were pending as the 105th Congress came to a close in October 1998. He believes most will be reintroduced, and new bills will be added. If we don't address the privacy issue—if we allow self-regulation to fail—we can count on the U.S. government and governments around the globe to tell us how it must be done.

For more information, or for a copy of the DMA's Privacy Promise, contact DMA's Jim Crowe at 212 861 2407, or *jcrowe@the-dma.org*. It's important.

CRM and Profits: Making the Case

Do you know where your profits are?

In *Circle of Innovation* (Knopf, 1997), author Tom Peters suggests that two components will drive the American economy in the new century: information and technology. Not only has the volume of information we receive grown exponentially, the changes in technology over the last decade have dramatically affected all aspects of how we rely on information to accomplish our business objectives.

More information has been produced in the last 30 years than in the previous 5000 and the information supply now doubles every 5 years,[1] and we have already talked about the dramatic growth of technology.

In Chapter 9 we talked about a computer software desktop query tool being right at the hands of the marketing team. That's what technology is all about. It takes minutes to do today what took us days or weeks to do only five years ago. Technology has enabled information to be delivered directly to the desktops of sales and marketing professionals.

But more information and more technology will not necessarily lead to increased values and return on investment in marketing. The only real values are the values you add for your customers and the values your customers deliver to your company. Real value is not in the data or the technology. It's in the customer knowledge and your use of that knowledge to manage customer relationships.

This distinction is the most important message in this book.

This is where so many points and discount loyalty programs miss the mark and fail to deliver added profit. They are all collecting information, and most are using the latest technology. Few are creating the kind of dialog to develop the active 1to1 Learning Relationship that can turn the information into the kind of *knowledge* that provides value in ways that are meaningful to the individual customer in his or her terms.

Don Tapscott, chairman of the Alliance for Converging Technologies, a think tank for how the Net changes business strategy, says:

> Although we live in the so-called information age, knowledge is the true asset. Information we have in abundance, piling up in databases and streaming onto desktops over broadband networks.
>
> Knowledge, on the other hand, is information that has been edited, put into context, and analyzed in a way that makes it meaningful—and therefore valuable to an organization.[2]

Remember what President Reagan said: "Information is the oxygen of the modern age." If information is the heart of modern commerce, knowledge is the soul of Customer Relationship Marketing.

In Chapter 4 we quoted the book *The Profit Zone: How Strategic Business Design Will Lead You to Tomorrow's Profits*, that made the case that market share is no longer the guaranteed profit producer, that what matters more than market share is "the design" of the business. The authors suggested that the best companies have started with the customer and worked back from there. They asked, do you know where your profits are?

For successful Customer Relationship Management, we must design the business to start with the customer and work back from there. We start with data capture and, as Don Tapscott said, move through the process of editing and analyzing to create meaningful knowledge. Finally, we use all this customer knowledge to build relationships that will create loyalty and build profits.

We must remember that loyalty is a journey, not a destination. Loyalty is never given in perpetuity. It is only loaned and cannot be bought.

Remember the quote from John Groman, executive vice president and cofounder of Epsilon:

> Loyalty marketing implies we can market to people and make them loyal to us. The truth is that loyalty is the result not the object of a successful relationship in business and in life. When we try to make another person loyal without providing a relationship that works for them, we waste time, money, and trust.[3]

Isn't it true, the bank that has loyal employees is the one in which you are the happiest as a customer? CRM requires more than just building relationships with customers. It requires nurturing relationships with the front-line people, who are the ones who can build successful relationships that work for customers.

That brings us back to something we have been saying throughout this book. Customer Relationship Management is a process of making it easier for the customer to do business with us. That's what builds loyalty and profit. This sounds so simple—why have so many companies failed in the attempt?

Robert McKim left the advertising industry in 1991 to found his own company, M\S Database Marketing, to address the deficiencies of mass marketing, and now he helps leading companies with CRM. After what he calls "three long, dry years of preaching the benefit of CRM to the somewhat deaf ears of corporate America," he concluded there were three main reasons corporate infrastructures did not allow CRM to prosper:

1. Companies tried to implement applications before the organization and its people were ready.

2. MIS and marketing departments focused on the latest technological tools before determining what business problem they were trying to solve for their customers.

3. Marketing departments implemented programs without getting a commitment from top management. Once problems occurred, the initiative would be put on hold, never again to see the light of day (and disappointing everyone, including their best customers).[4]

It's easy to agree with these reasons for the slow growth of CRM, but those three reasons do not represent the full story.

The number 1 reason why corporate infrastructures have not allowed CRM to prosper is the lack of understanding that relationship building must concentrate on customer benefits, not on what your company wants to sell, or more poignantly, the failure to understand that CRM means listening to the customer to learn instead of talking to the customer to sell.

Many companies talk as if they are now customer driven but walk as though still sales driven. They still have not learned to treat CRM as a business process, not a marketing program. It's not about the sales force. It's not about data mining and modeling lots of data. It's not about promotion marketing, and it's not about loyalty cards. It's about building relationships. Once real relationships have been established, marketing communications become anticipated, personal and relevant, and appreciative of the power of the customer.

The quote from Seth Godin in Chapter 29 supports this when he said, "The way to sell a consumer something in the future must be by engaging the consumer in a dialog—an interactive relationship, with both you and the customer participating."

Interactive dialog with both you and the customer participating is what CRM is all about, and Godin's point about the limits of customers' time makes the argument for CRM even more compelling.

Godin makes the point that the clutter of 2 million Web sites competing for the consumer's attention will *require* successful marketers to develop dialog and build customer relationships in order to be heard.

The clutter will get only worse as things marketers are now paying for—paper, printing, postage, mailing services, even telephone—become free on the Internet. People will have less time to pay attention to anything.

People are already looking for ways to cope with the information avalanche. A 1998 survey by ICONOCAST (http://www.iconocast.com), a leading Internet marketing newsletter, found that 17 percent of 510 respondents reported they scan articles to handle information overload.[5]

Many voices are saying the Internet is a personal medium. Lester Wunderman, founder of Wunderman, Cato, Johnson and now a member of the board of directors at MyPoints.com., has an even stronger view. In a 1999 interview with *Direct Marketing* magazine, when asked how the Internet would affect traditional media, he said:

> The Web is not a medium; it is a marketplace. It's a place where people can meet. It's a place where people can transact. It's a place where people can relate, and it's a place with an experience that is unmatched anywhere else, because you're in touch but you haven't lost your privacy, despite what people say.
>
> The Web is bringing us into a different dimension of buying and selling. It's the first medium in which the buyer and seller can say to each other, we have done well together because it is a relational transaction.[6]

For the buyer and seller to speak to each other, for people to meet and relate, the experience must be personalized—not just by adding a personal salutation but by customizing the experience your customers have as they visit your Web site. Anecdotal information is beginning to suggest that Web site personalization helps build customer loyalty; in fact, a 1998 research study by International Data Corp. and Relevant Knowledge, a company that measures Internet audiences, found that Internet users with personalized pages at Yahoo! and Excite tend to visit the sites three times as often as the average user.[7]

This brings us back to CRM and what Seth Godin calls "permission marketing." Godin makes a telling point that fits well here as we wrap up our case for moving from company-centric mass marketing to customer-centric CRM:

> Originally the Internet captured the attention of mass marketers. They rushed in, spent billions of dollars applying their interruption marketing techniques, and discovered almost total failure.
>
> Permission marketing [CRM] is the tool that unlocks the power of the Internet. The leverage it brings to this new medium, combined with the pervasive clutter that infects the Internet and virtually every other medium, makes permission marketing [CRM] the most powerful trend in marketing for the next decade.[8]

Customers *will* give permission. They will allow us to establish relationships. Customers now expect that companies can adapt to them. They want suppliers to understand their unique needs, but they must believe the relationship is worthwhile, and they must be assured that the time they spend to give us information will result in benefits they will value.

Relationships are built on trust and dialog. Customers will not be fooled into a relationship based solely on a points or discount loyalty program. People will not change from "strangers" into "friends" and from "friends" into "profitable customers" based on one more promotion or one more campaign, no matter how personal the communication sounds.

CRM cannot be another marketing campaign. It requires a change in the business process—creating ownership throughout the whole organization and convincing everyone that the CRM effort is a benefit to them and to their customers. A 1999 study by Cap Gemini/International Data Corporation found the obstacle that was most often encountered in CRM projects was the difficulty in changing business processes to align with CRM methodology. The study said this was named as the biggest challenge for companies in all the industries surveyed.[9]

Remember the importance of "the design of the business"—designing not just the CRM program but the business enterprise, based on where the profits are and remembering that profitability applies to customers rather than marketing campaigns.

CRM adds to profit by eliminating wasteful marketing expenditures and developing customer loyalty that grows customer lifetime value. With CRM each customer interaction becomes more efficient and more effective.

You can't buy customer loyalty with points and discounts and price. When I wrote an article in our monthly newsletter about a C-Span report saying discounts and low price were the things that mattered most to consumers, I received this thoughtful reply from Paul Higham, senior vice president of marketing and customer communications, Wal-Mart. It seems a fitting concluding argument:

> If there ever was a retailer who had built their reputation on the attribute of low pricing, it certainly is Wal-Mart. But, how well we know that low prices are only half the process. Only when it is counterbalanced by a commitment to the lives, needs, and wants of customers does it all make sense. Price deals with the fact of the matter. But the human factor, like customer care and service, leads us to another thing, every bit as important—the heart of the matter.

You can't buy customer loyalty by just collecting a lot of customer data and feeding them through the latest database technology to record customers' points. CRM requires the care and the commitment to take the time, invest the money, and have the patience to listen to the customer, to create a mutually beneficial dialog to learn what the customer really wants from your company, and finally, to deliver your promise of personalized caring consistently with every customer contact and communication.

Customer Relationship Management is the tool that unlocks your power including the power of the Internet where people can meet and relate. It is the tool that turns the call center from a nuisance to a customer benefit. It is the tool that makes the wonderful new printing technologies worthwhile, and in the final analysis it is the tool that contributes to profit. It will gain sharpness as we discover all the wonders and capacities of communication that lie ahead. Without CRM, a firm will have a difficult time existing profitably in the twenty-first century.

Committing to the lives, needs, and wants of customers is what makes CRM successful. Transforming your business process to enable you to excel at Customer Relationship Management is not an easy assignment, and the new era of the Internet will require a lot of learning. As you tackle the challenges, remember the words of that wise old philosopher, Anonymous: "Much of life is like skiing. If you're not falling down, you're not learning."

QUICK TIPS FROM PART FOUR

CHAPTER 27: The Missing Link: "Prodices"

- People don't want quarter-inch drill bits. They want quarter-inch holes.
- Self-service is not CRM.
- Some electronic services can help make loyal customers.
- Today's customer wants the service, not the stuff.

CHAPTER 28: It's a Matter of Degrees

- Don't lose sight of land.
- Communications planned over time can deliver vital information, recognition of customer importance, personalized attention, a sense of friendliness—all meaningful to customers.
- Have a communication plan for each customer.
- Be proactive; reach out to draw in former and potential customers.

- A good contact plan needs goals, a clear approach to achieving the goals, and measurements to determine how well the goals are achieved.

- When contacts are insufficient, profitable sales are lost.

- Emotions and promotions can't be measured in the same way.

- The new Y2K consumer wants to build relationships with companies that can show they care.

CHAPTER 29: Recognizing the Power of the Consumer

- *Dialog* is the most important word in the CRM lexicon.

- CRM is about selling solutions, not just products.

- Customer service is now about strengthening relationships. The goal is to create mutual benefits.

- Find your benchmarks by knowing your customers and their expectations.

- It takes time to prove yourself and build loyalty with customers.

CHAPTER 30: Information Is Knowledge, Knowledge Is Power, and Power Can Be Frightening

- The privacy issue taps into a powerful emotion: fear.

- People are afraid of what they don't understand, and generally they don't know much about database marketing.

- Relationships must be built on trust.

- Information about our customers and our potential customers is the fuel of our business, but great care is required to guard against information leaks.

- Privacy is, indeed, a marketing factor.

- It is important for all marketers to embrace the DMA Privacy Promise.
- The explosion of Web, e-mail, and e-commerce has magnified the privacy question.
- There is more intimacy in relationships on the Internet.
- Trust is the most precious asset any business has.

CHAPTER 31: CRM and Profits: Making the Case

- Information and technology will drive the American economy in the new century.
- More information and more technology will not necessarily lead to increased value and return on investment in marketing.
- Real value is in the customer knowledge and your use of that knowledge to manage customer relationships.
- Knowledge is information that has been edited, put into context, and analyzed in a way that makes it meaningful— and therefore valuable to an organization.
- Loyalty is a journey, not a destination.
- Loyalty is never given in perpetuity; it is only loaned, and cannot be bought.
- When we try to make another person loyal without providing a relationship that works for him or her, we waste time, money, and trust.
- Customer Relationship Management is a process of making it easier for the customer to do business with us.
- The number 1 reason why corporate infrastructures have not allowed CRM to prosper is the lack of understanding that relationship building must concentrate on customer benefits, not on what the company wants to sell.

- CRM is not about modeling lots of data, and it's not about loyalty cards. It's about building relationships.

- The way to sell a consumer something in the future must be by engaging the consumer in a dialog—an interactive relationship.

- The clutter of 2 million Web sites competing for the consumer's attention will *require* successful marketers to develop dialog and build customer relationships in order to be heard.

- The Web is not a medium, it is a marketplace. It's a place where people can meet, transact, and relate.

- CRM is the tool that unlocks the power of the Internet.

- Relationships are built on trust and dialog. Customers will not be fooled into a relationship based solely on points or discount loyalty programs.

- CRM requires a change in the business process, creating ownership throughout the whole organization.

- Profitability applies to customers rather than marketing campaigns.

- Committing to the lives, needs, and wants of customers is what makes CRM successful.

Endnotes

Chapter 1

[1]Arthur M. Hughes, "Why Databases Fail," DMA 81st Annual Conference, San Francisco, October 14, 1998.

Chapter 2

[1]Denise Duclaux, "Banks: Big Money in Data Warehouses," *DM News*, June 15, 1998, p. 3.

[2]Richard H. Levey, "What's Your Database IQ?" *Direct*, February 1998, p. 1.

[3]Michael P. Burwen, Data Solutions White Paper, Palo Alto Management Group, July 1998.

[4]Stacey Riordan and Mike Barlow, "Customer Clubs Weave Ties That Bind," *INSIDE 1to1*, June 4, 1998, p. 2–3.

[5]Susan Fournier, Susan Dobscha, and David Glen Mick, "Preventing the Premature Death of Relationship Marketing," *Harvard Business Review*, January/February 1998.

[6]"Divided Loyalties," *Retail Week*, November 14, 1998, p. 18.

[7]Levey, "What's Your Database IQ?" p. 31.

Chapter 3

[1]"Selling Database to Your Management," *Case-in-POINT*, vol. 2, Issue 5 Report, 1996, www.acxiom.com/caseinpoint/cip-rpt-s.asp.

[2]"Viking Personalizes Marketing," *Case-in-POINT*, Case Study vol. 4, Issue 1, 1998.

[3]Bruce Kasanoff, "Great Plains Software Embraces 1to1," *INSIDE 1to1*, September 16, 1998, p. 2.

[4]Jon Lowder, "Stop Selling Solo," *Marketnow*, December 9, 1998, p. 1.

[5]Douglas R. Pruden, "If We Are Concerned about Customer Retention, Why Do We Want to Keep Making Contact through Customer Satisfaction RESEARCH?" *Direct Marketing*, November 1997, p. 30.

[6]Ibid., pp. 30–31.

[7]Martha Rogers, "Attention to MVCs Pays off for Hickory Farms," *INSIDE 1to1*, September 11, 1997, p. 1.

[8]"Selling Database to Your Management."

Chapter 4

[1]Jonathan Boorstein, "Premium Blend," *Direct*, September 1, 1998, pp. 1, 35–36.

Chapter 5

[1]Arthur Middleton Hughes, "Why Customers Leave, and What You Can Do About It," *Relationship Marketing Report*, July 1998, pp. 1, 5.

[2]Don Peppers, "FedEx Focuses on Profitable Customers," *INSIDE 1to1*, November 20, 1997, p. 1.

[3]Martha Rogers, "Pontiac-GMC's Customized Drive," *INSIDE 1to1*, December 16, 1998, p. 1.

[4]Murray Raphel, "Marketing Strategies," *Direct Marketing*, August 1998, p. 52.

Chapter 6

[1]Alan Rosenspan, "Airline Soars to New Heights," *Direct Marketing*, December 1998, p. 21.

[2]Arthur M. Hughes, "Measuring the Loyalty Effect," *Direct*, September 15, 1998, pp. 44–45.

[3]Martin Baier, *Elements of Direct Marketing*, McGraw-Hill, New York, 1983, pp. 59–61.

Chapter 7

[1]Adrian Slywotsky and David Morrison, *The Profit Zone: How Strategic Business Design Will Lead You to Tomorrow's Profits*, Times Books, 1998.

[2]Arthur M. Hughes, *Strategic Database Marketing*, McGraw-Hill, New York, 1994, p. 16.

[3]Carol Krol, "Databases Not Being Used to Best Advantage," Advertising Age, October 19, 1998, p. 58.

[4]P. Kotler and G. Armstrong, *Principles of Marketing*, 7th ed. Prentice-Hall, Englewood Cliffs, N.J., 1996.

[5]Mark Voboril, "Steering Clear of Failure in Corporate Database Marketing Programs," NCDM Integrated Database Marketing Conference, Orlando, Fla., December 13, 1998.

Chapter 8

[1]Bob McKim, "Summit Report," *Relationship Marketing Report*, September 1998, p. 11.

[2]Jay L. Johnson, "Face to Face with Faith B. Popcorn," *Discount Merchandiser*, September 1998, pp. 9–10.

[3]Terril Yue Jones, "Gender Motors," *Forbes*, May 17, 1999, pp. 50–51.

[4]Del Jones, "What Glass Ceiling?" *USA Today*, July 20, 1999, p. B1.

[5]Mary Lou Quinlan, "Women: We've Come a Long Way Maybe," *Advertising Age,* February 23, 1999, p. 46.

[6]Ibid.

[7]"Changing the Face of Distribution," *Retail Technology Directions*, May 1999, p. 38.

[8]Tom Post, "The Convergence Gamble," *Forbes*, February 22, 1999, pp. 112–117.

[9]Michael Bush, "Service Gets Message to Customers," *DM News*, September 14, 1998, p. 31.

[10]Don Peppers and Martha Rogers, "NatWest Addresses Information Overload," *INSIDE 1to1*, September 3, 1998, p. 2.

[11]"French Catalogers Discover a Robust 50+ Market," *DM News*, May 10, 1999, p. 13.

[12]"Six Myths That Undermine DM Campaigns to 50-Plus Consumers," *DM News*, September 14, 1998, p. 12.

Chapter 9

[1]"Database Technology—A 21st Century View," *Anchor Computer Line*, Spring 1998, p. 1.

[2]Don Hinman, "Measuring Data's Incremental Value: A Primer on Data ROI," *Case-in-POINT*, vol. 4, Issue 2, 1998, pp. 3–7, www.acxiom.com/casein-point/cip-rpt-ak.asp.

[3]"State of the Industry," *Chain Store Age*, August 1998, sec. 2, p. 21A.

Chapter 10

[1]David Cameron, "Do You Really Need a Data Warehouse?" *Direct Marketing*, June 98, pp. 43–44.

[2]Natalie Engler, "The New Business Technologists," *Computerworld*, November 16, 1998, p. 106.

Chapter 11

[1]Michael Krantz, "Click Till You Drop, The Internet Has Become a Shopper's Paradise, Stocked with Everything from Wine to Cars. Business Will Never Be the Same," *Time*, July 20, 1998, p. 34.

[2]Richard H. Levey, "You've Got Sales," *Direct*, January 1999, p. 37.

[3]"Internet Shopping, An Ernst & Young Special Report," *Stores,* January 1998, sec. 2.

[4]"Web Grows by 1.5 Million Pages Daily, Study Estimates," *Friday Report*, Hoke Communications, September 1998, pp. 4–5.

[5]Greenfield Online, "August Digital Consumer Shopping Index," August 1998.

[6]"Top e-Commerce Sites Predicted to Process 60,000 Transactions a Day This Holiday Season," *TM Tipline*, September 27, 1999, p. 3.

[7]Dan Keating, "The Amish Meet Y2K," *The Herald*, May 22, 1999, p. C1.

[8]Web Grows by 1.5 Million Pages Daily," *Friday Report*.

[9]Michael Krantz, "Virtual Shopping. Is It Better Than the Real Thing?" *Time*, July 20, 1998, p. 36.

[10]"Internet Shopping," p. 4.

[11]Jared Sandberg, "Net Gain," *Newsweek*, December 7, 1998, p. 48.

[12]Patricia B. Seybold with Ronnie T. Marshak, *customer.com*, "How to Create a Profitable Business Strategy for the Internet and Beyond," Times Business Random House, New York, 1998, p. 33

[13]Ibid., p. 34

[14]Ibid.

[15]"Jupiter Finds Many Web Sites Fail at Customer Service," *DIRECT Newsline*, November 10, 1998, pp. 6–7.

[16]"Pushing at the Next Frontier, Multichannel Marketer Beefs up Data Integration Abilities," *Case-in-POINT* Case Study, vol. 4, Issue 3–4, 1998 (out of print).

[17]"Internet Shopping."

[18]Bruce Kasanoff, "First-ever Review of World's Best 1to1 Web Sites," *INSIDE 1to1*, April 29, 1999, pp. 1–2.

[19]Joan Magtretta, "The Power of Vertical Integration: An Interview with Dell Computer's Michael Dell," *Harvard Business Review*, March/April 1998, p. 74.

[20]Eugene Marlow, "Does the Net Level the Playing Field?" *Retail Marketer*, The DMA Retail Marketing Council, fall 1998, p. 4.

[21]Ray Jutkins, *Power Direct Marketing: A Direct Marketing & Sales Letter*, Rockingham*Jutkins*Marketing, November/December 1998, p. 1.

[22]Ken Magill, "Retention Strategy May Signal Start of Online's Second Wave," *DM News*, June 22, 1998, p. 21.

[23]Don Peppers and Martha Rogers, "The Mass Customized Catalog," *INSIDE 1to1*, October 21, 1998, p. 2.

[24]Leslie Walker, "Looking Beyond Books," *The Washington Post*, November 8, 1998, p. 1.

[25]David Bohnett, "Building an Online Community," *The DMA Insider*, spring 99, p. 10.

[26]Ibid., p. 11.

[27]Ibid.

[28]Don Peppers, "E-Commerce: Your Worst Nightmare or Your Greatest Opportunity," *INSIDE 1to1*, March 31, 1999, p. 1.

Chapter 12

[1]Don Rappaport, "The Next Big Thing Really Is Big," *DM News*, October 12, 1998, p. 12.

[2]Deena Flammang and Harvey John Morris, "INDUSTRY UPDATE Using Permission Email to Power Up Your Online Direct Marketing," a study released by yes.mail.com, August 1999.

[3]Kelly J. Andrews, "Warming up to E-mail Marketing," *Target*, May 1999, p. 67.

[4]Sean Donahue, "Outsourced and Out of Mind," *Business 2.0*, April 1999, p. 96.

[5]Michelle V. Rafter, "Customer Disservice," *The Industry Standard*, May 17–24, 1999, p. 92.

[6]Don Peppers and Martha Rogers, "Hello, I Want You, Won't You Tell Me Your Name," *INSIDE 1to1*, January 14, 1999, pp. 1–2.

Chapter 13

[1]Renee Wijnen, "Fledgling Telemarketing Unit Delivers Strong Sales," *TeleServices News*, May 3, 1999, p. 6.

[2]"American Telemarketing Association Announces New Name," *Friday Report*, Hoke Communications, November 20, 1998, pp. 5–6. And Sean Sexton/Renee Wijnen, "ATA Changes Name, Prepares for '99," *DM News*, November 23, 1998, p. 1.

[3]Evelyn Schlaphoff, "How Telemarketing and Database Marketing Work Together," *Relationship Marketing Report*, October 1998, p. 5.

[4]Jacques Werth, "Profound Relationships of Mutual Trust and Respect in Twenty Minutes," *Relationship Marketing Report*, November 1998, pp. 2–3.

[5]Susan Fournier, Susan Dobscha, and David Glen Mick, "Preventing the Premature Death of Relationship Marketing," *Harvard Business Review*, January/February 1998.

[6]Kim Girard, "Call Center Reorg Unites Travel Info," *Computerworld*, July 13, 1998, pp. 1, 85.

[7]Al Subbloie, "Technology Can Help to Create a Customer-Friendly Interaction Center," *TeleServices News*, July 6, 1998, p. 18.

[8]Ibid.

[9]Sandra Herman, "Ease of Data Access Increases Customer Satisfaction," *TeleServices News*, July 6, 1998, p. 16.

[10]Steven Dresner, "The Web-Enabled Call Center, Using the Internet to Reach Out and Touch the Online Community," *TeleProfessional*, March 1998, pp. 50, 52.

[11]Ibid.

[12]"Inbound Gets High-Tech Boost," *Target Marketing*, December 1998, p. 63.

[13]Kim Girard, "Call Center Reorg Unites Travel Info," p. 1.

[14]"Mercedes to use Genesys Telecom Product in Call Center," *Direct Newsline*, October 23, 1998, p. 3.

[15]Nadine J. Kjellberg, "Lexus Drives Sales with New Focus on Call Center," *TeleServices News*, October 6, 1998, p. 1.

[16]Theresa Howard, "Sears Chooses the Human Touch Over IVR," *TeleServices News*, July 6, 1998, p. 6

[17]Ibid.

[18]Renee Wijnen, "Wachovia Bank Changes to Phone-Based Customer Service," *TeleServices News*, September 7, 1998, pp. 1, 18.

[19]Mark McLaughlin, "Study: Inbound Cross-Selling for Banks Can Outdo Outbound," *TeleServices News*, July 6, 1998, p. 8.

[20]Peter G. W. Keen, "IT Is Wired to 'Outward' Thinking," *Computerworld*, January 11, 1999, p. 49.

[21]"Call Centers to Remain Key to Business Strategy Despite Growth in Web," *TM Tipline/Target Marketing*, April 25, 1999, p. 2.

Chapter 14

[1]James Morris-Lee, "Digital Drives Direct Mail," *Target Marketing*, May 1999, pp. 39–44, 109.

[2]Rachel McLaughlin, "Making It Personal," *Target Marketing*, January 1999, pp. 51, 54.

[3]Charles A. Pesko, Jr., "Convergence: The State of the Industry 1998," *Print on Demand Business*, May 1998, p. 21.

[4]Hallie Mummert, "Stepping up to the Plate," *Target Marketing*, September 1998, p. 76.

[5]Pesko, "Convergence," p. 23.

[6]Richard H. Levey, "No Two Alike," *Direct*, September 15, 1998, p. 29.

[7]Ibid.

[8]Ibid.

[9]Ibid.

[10] Pesko, "Convergence," p. 19.

[11]Ibid., p. 20.

Chapter 15

[1]Herb Edelstein, "Data Mining: Exploiting the Hidden Trends in Your Data," *DB2online magazine*, spring 1996, p. 1.

[2]Information Discovery, Inc., "OLAP and DataMining: Bridging the Gap," http://www.datamining.com/datamine/bridge.htm, p. 13.

[3]Ibid.

[4]K. Van der Heijden, *Scenarios: The Art of Strategic Conversation*, Wiley, New York, 1996.

[5]Charles Berger, "Data Mining to Reduce Churn," *Target Marketing*, August 1999, pp. 26, 28.

[6]Edelstein, "Data Mining," p. 2.

Chapter 16

[1]Brian Amaral, "Retailing's New Paradigm," *Microsoft Technology News for Retailers*, vol. 1. no. 2.

[2]Don Peppers, "New Epiphany for CRM Applications," *INSIDE 1to1*, January 27, 1999, p. 2.

[3]Ibid.

[4]David M. Raab, "System Offers Solutions for Data Access," *DM News*, January 18, 1999, p. 28.

[5]"Business Intelligence Gives Complete View of Customers," *DM News*, January 18, 1999, p. 34.

[6]Carleen Hawn, "Cell Phones for the Masses," *Forbes*, February 8, 1999, pp. 50–51.

[7]"Alternative Access Methods Are Becoming a Factor on the Internet," *INSIDE 1to1*, May 25, 1999, pp. 3–4.

[8]Stephen Manes, "Gutenberg Need Not Worry—Yet," *Forbes*, February 8, 1999, pp. 106–107.

[9]Leslie Walker, "Looking Beyond Books," *The Washington Post*, November 8, 1998, p. 1.

CHAPTER 17

[1]Kate Maddox, "Study: Broad Band Ads More Effective Than Narrow Band," *Advertising Age*, March 1, 1999, p. S8.

[2]Dana Blakenhorn, "MatchLogic Arms Advertisers, Agencies," *Advertising Age*, March 1, 1999, p. S16.

[3]Anu Shukla, "The Missing Link," *The Industry Standard*, February 22–March 1, 1999, p. 74.

[4]Mark McLaughlin, "BTB Marketers Gain Tools to Empower the Customer," *DM News*, February 15, 1999, pp. 1, 58.

[5]"Profiting from Customer Dissatisfaction," Hepworth Company Ltd. (Hepworthco.com), March 31, 1999.

[6]Ibid.

[7]Nadine M. Kjellberg, "Jewelry Telemarketing Campaign a Real Gem," *TeleServices News*, June 8, 1998, p. 13.

[8]Angela Karr, "The Growth of the Multimedia Call Center," *TeleProfessional*, March 1998, p. 10.

[9]*Call Center Benchmark Report*, Purdue University Center for Customer-Driven Quality, 1998.

[10]Jack Neff, "Dawn of the Online Icebox," *Advertising Age,* March 15, 1999, p. 17.

Chapter 18

[1]Murray Raphel, "Meet the Millennium Customer," *Direct Marketing*, December 1998, p. 48.

[2]Robert L. Tillman, "A Retail Career—The Path to Success," *Arthur Anderson Retailing Issues Letter*, November 1998, p. 2.

[3]Donna Harris, "AutoNation Expects to Hit $500 Mil in Net Revenues," *Advertising Age,* May 17, 1999, p. 52.

[4]Ibid.

[5]Ibid.

[6]Jacob Ward and Mickey Butts, "Small Shops Battle Back Using BookSense," *The Industry Standard*, May 17–24, 1999, p. 38.

[7]Ibid, p. 40.

[8]Kelly Baron, "Theme Players," *Forbes*, March 22, 1999, p. 53.

[9]Frank F. Britt, "Building a Lifestyle Solution Brand—The Unfolding Story of Streamline, Inc.," *Arthur Andersen Retailing Issues Newsletter*, July 1998, p. 1.

[10]Tillman, "A Retail Career," p. 4.

[11]Britt, "Building a Lifestyle Solutions Brand," p. 5.

Chapter 19

[1]Lisa Singhania, Associated Press, "Cereal Business Is Losing Its Snap," *San Diego Union-Tribune*, November 22, 1998, p. I–2.

[2]Garth Hallberg, *All Customers Are Not Created Equal*, Wiley, New York, 1995, p. 7.

[3]Jack Neff, "Shelf-Space Wars Raging at Major Retailers," *Advertising Age*, November 9, 1998, p. 32.

[4]The *Friday Report*, Hoke Communications, September 11, 1998, p. 2.

[5]Denise Duclaux, "Kraft, TCI Take the Narrow View," *DM News*, March 16, 1998, p. 6.

[6]"SEATTLE DRTV FIRM IS THE FASTEST GROWING COMPANY IN WASHINGTON," *DIRECT Newsline*, November 9, 1998, p. 2.

[7]Charlie Breen, "Why 'Infomercial' Is Such a Dirty Word," *DM News*, DRTV News Section, August 17, 1998, p. 10.

[8]Patricia Odell, "Off the Shelf, Packaged Goods Firms Get Out of the Stores and Onto the Web," *Direct*, October 1, 1998, pp. 1, 46–47.

[9]Ken Magill, "Kroger's Small Step May Be E-Coupon's Big Leap," *DM News*, September 14, 1998, p. 1.

[10]Kate Maddox, "P&G's Plan: Jump-Start Web as Viable Ad Medium," *Advertising Age*, August 17, 1998, pp. 1, 16–17.

[11]Richard H. Levey, "The New Mix at Kraft," *Direct*, May 15, 1998, pp. 1, 33–34.

Chapter 20

[1]"Bankers Develop New Skills in Data Integration—The Customer Loyalty Report," Centaur Publications, London, England, as cited in *Case-in-POINT*, vol. 4, Issue 5 Report, 1998, p. 2, www.acxiom.com/caseinpoint/cip-rpt-an.asp.

[2]Jackie Cohen, "Everybody's a Banker," *The Industry Standard*, March 15, 1999, p. 38.

[3]Mercedes M. Cardona, "Diverse Players Build Banks Online," *Advertising Age*, August 2, 1999, p. 32.

[4]Thomas Hoffman, "Banks Turn to IT to Reclaim Most Profitable Customers," *Computerworld*, December 7, 1998, p. 14.

[5]Melissa Campenelli, "Fleet Bank Launches Campaign Based on New Data Warehouse," *DM News*, September 21, 1998, p. 29.

[6]Denise Duclaux, "Banks: Big Money in Data Warehouses," *DM News*, June 15, 1998, p. 3.

[7]Sharon Machlis, "Banks Eye Online Billing," *Computerworld*, January 11, 1999, p. 41.

[8]Don Tapscott, "Death-Spiral Fears for Traditional Banks," *Computerworld*, October 26, 1998, p. 36.

[9]Ibid.

[10]"In-Store Banking: A Profitable Two-Way Relationship," *Retail Technology Directions*, May 1999, p. 48.

[11] Renee Wijnen, "Citigroup Restructures Call Centers," *TeleServices News*, January 4, 1999, p. 3.

[12]Mark McLaughlin, "Chase Building Data Warehouse—Merges Database Divisions to Gain Insight on Customer Transactions, Prospecting," *DM News*, June 22, 1998, p. 10.

[13]Ann B. Graham and John W. Geyer, "All for One and One for All—How KeyCorp Reacquainted Itself with Its Customers," *Executive Edge*, September 1998, pp. 24–28.

[14]Ibid.

[15]Ibid.

[16]"Fidelity's Future—Stephen Cone Brings the Financial Giant Closer to Its Customers," *Direct*, January 1999, p. 13.

[17]Richard Homby, "Offering a Different Version," *INSIDE 1to1*, July 29, 1999, p. 2.

[18]Mark McLaughlin, "Survey: Banks Have Yet to Leverage Data," *DM News*, December 21, 1998, p. 12.

[19]Elizabeth Rech, *INSIDE 1to1*, May 12, 1999, pp. 2–3.

[20]"Right Customer, Right Channel, Right Product," *Case-in-POINT*, Case Study, vol. 4, Issue 5, 1998, www.acxiom.com/caseinpoint/cip-cs-au.asp, p. 1.

[21]Ibid.

Chapter 21

[1]Melinda Nykamp, "Relationships—Keep in Touch . . . ," *Direct*, winter 1999, p. 3.

[2]Maysel R. McGowen, "BTB: The All Powerful Database," *DM News*, October 19, 1998, p. 24.

[3]Ernan Roman, "How to Achieve Double-Digit Response in the New Year," *Relationship Marketing Report*, December 1998, p. 3.

[4]Ibid, p. 2.

[5]Bradley Johnson, "Tech Commerce Sites Enjoy Boom in Online Sales," *Advertising Age*, October 26, 1998, p. 24.

[6]Arthur Middleton Hughes, "Building Profits with Relationship Marketing," *Direct*, January 1999, pp. 49, 52.

[7]Richard G. Barlow, "Use Your Data to Upgrade B-to-B Frequency," *Direct*, October 15, 1998, p. 144.

Chapter 22

[1]"Radio's Intimacy, Accessibility in Workplace Make it Perfect Medium for Web Advertisers," New York Market Radio Update, May/June 1999, p. 1.

[2]Laurie Freeman, "Inter-Act Helps Retailers Save on Ads," *DM News*, February 23, 1998, p. 4.

[3]Denise Duclaux, "Radio Station Tests Web Relationship," *DM News*, p. 22.

[4]"A Natural Combination: Radio Listening and Surfing the Web," *New York Market Radio Update*, September/October 1998, p. 1.

Chapter 26

[1]Thom Weidlich, "A Customer in the Palm Is Worth . . . ," *Direct*, August 1998, p. 16.

[2]Ibid.

[3]"Keeping Up With Technology Has Its Price," *Frequent Flyer,* October 1998, p. 14.

[4]"Etc.," *Meetings and Conventions*, August 1998, p. 19.

[5]"Store Loyalty Cards: Meeting Customer's Expectations," *Retail Technology Directions*, Issue 1, 1999, pp. 14–16.

Chapter 27

[1]Josh Stailey, "Customer Loyalty Zoots Them," *INSIDE 1to1*, May 19, 1999, pp. 2–3.

[2]Jane Sutton, Reuters, "Concierges Want to Serve Someone Right," *San Diego Union-Tribune*, June 11, 1999, p. E-2.

[3]Elizabeth Weise, "It's about Time, and Tech," *USA Today*, May 26, 1999, pp. D1–2.

Chapter 28

[1]Dava Sobel, *Longitude: The True Story of a Lone Genius Who Solved the Greatest Scientific Problem of His Time*, Penguin Books, 1995.

[2]"Building a Longitudinal Contact Strategy," *Journal of Interactive Marketing*, vol. 12, no. 1, winter 1998, pp. 56–59.

[3]Don Peppers and Martha Rogers, "Big Blue Inks a Personal Deal," *Relationship Marketing Report*, March 1999, p. 11.

Chapter 29

[1] Suzanne Bidlake, "Nestlé CEO Strives for Dialogue That Individualizes Consumers," *Ad Age International,* January 1998, p. 33.

[2] Ibid.

[3] Ibid., p. 34.

[4] Ibid., p. 33.

[5] Rance Crain, "Convenience of Marketers Drives Brand Consolidation," *Advertising Age*, August 17, 1998, p. 26.

[6] Mary Ann Falzone, "Productivity vs. Profitability," *Direct*, June 1999, p. 51.

[7] Steven H. Krein, "DM As We Know It Is Dead Thanks to the Net," *DM News*, December 7, 1998, p. 25.

[8] Ibid.

[9] Ibid.

Chapter 30

[1] Renee Wijnen, "Privacy's the Talk of DMA Conference," *TeleServices News*, July 5, 1999, p. 1.

[2] Garry C. Meyers III, "Peeking in on Privacy," *The DMA*, winter 1999, p. 19.

[3] Ibid., p 21.

[4] Larry Riggs, "U.S. Bank Ends Phone Program, Launches Newspaper Effort," *Direct Newsline,* June 11, 1999, p. 1.

[5] Alex Lash, "Does Big Brother Live in Redmond?" *The Industry Standard*, May, 17–14, 1999, p. 35.

[6] Patricia Fraley, "Privacy—Who's Minding the Database Storehouse?" Editors Briefing, 1999, Supermarket Industry Convention, May 3, 1999.

[7] "Live from Strasbourg: Outcome of Privacy Talks Still Uncertain," *Direct Newsline*, April 27, 1999, p. 1.

[8] Thom Weidlich, "Up in the Air in Europe," *Direct*, May 15, 1999, p. 13.

[9] Internet Privacy Policy Survey Reveals That Strides Have Been Made, But Gaps Remain," *Target News*, May 17, 1999, p. 2.

[10] Ibid.

[11] John Groman, "Loyalty Marketing Is an Oxymoron," Presentation at DMB Direct Marketing to Business 10th Annual Conference, Orlando, Fla., February 8, 1999.

[12] Robert McKim, "One Step at a Time," *The DMA Insider,* winter 1999, p. 26.

[13] "Certifying the Public's Right to Privacy," *Internet Retailer*, March–April 1999, p. 7.

[14] Harold McGraw III, "Manage the Privacy Revolution," *Direct Marketing*, April 1999, p. 37.

Chapter 31

[1]Rachel McLaughlin, "Desktop Tools for Marketing to Businesses," *Target Marketing*, December 1998, p. 17.

[2]Don Tapscott, "Make Knowledge an Asset for the Whole Company," *Computerworld*, December 1998, p. 32.

[3]John Groman, "Loyalty Marketing Is an Oxymoron," Presentation at DMB Direct Marketing to Business 10th Annual Conference, Orlando, Fla., February 8, 1999.

[4]Robert McKim, "One Step at a Time," *The DMA Insider*, winter 1999, p.26.

[5]"Iconocast Survey Reveals Defenses Against Information Overload," *Relationship Marketing Report*, September 1998, p. 10.

[6]"Don't Just Transact—How to Relate on the Web," *Direct Marketing*, May 1999, pp. 78–79.

[7]John Gantz, "The Web Gets Personal," *Computerworld*, October 26, 1998, p. 33.

[8]Seth Godin, "Permission Marketing: The Way to Make Advertising Work Again," *Direct Marketing*, May 1999, p. 43.

[9]"Companies Take Phased Approach to Customer Relationship Management Projects with Average Investment of $3.1 Million," Company Press Release, Cap Gemini/International Data Corporation, June 16, 1999, p. 2.

Index